A Theory of
Cognitive Dissonance

A Theory of

Cognitive Dissonance

LEON FESTINGER

Professor of Psychology, Stanford University

STANFORD UNIVERSITY PRESS
STANFORD, CALIFORNIA

Stanford University Press
Stanford, California

© 1957 by Leon Festinger

All rights reserved

Liberty of Congress Catalog Card Number: 57-11351

Printed in the United States of America

First published 1957 by Row, Peterson and Company

REISSUED 1962 BY STANFORD UNIVERSITY PRESS
Third printing, 1965

24397

Foreword

This Foreword contains primarily a bit of the history of how the ideas which form the core of this book arose. This chronological form is the best way to acknowledge properly the assistance received from others—assistance which was considerable and crucial—and at the same time to explain how this book relates to the purposes which originally motivated it.

In the late fall of 1951 the writer was asked by Bernard Berelson, the Director of the Behavioral Sciences Division of the Ford Foundation, whether he would be interested in undertaking a "propositional inventory" of the substantive area of "communication and social influence." A large body of research literature exists in this area that has never been integrated at a theoretical level. It ranges all the way from studies on the effects of the mass media to studies on interpersonal communication. If a set of conceptual propositions could be adduced that tied together many of the known facts in the area, and from which additional derivations could be made, this would be of obvious value.

The notion of attempting such a theoretical integration

is always intellectually attractive and challenging, although it seemed clear to everyone concerned at the time that even if successfully accomplished, it could not hope to cover the whole of the designated area. A plan that seemed to promise some useful results was to start out with some narrowly defined problem within the general area of "communication and social influence" and attempt to formulate a specific set of hypotheses or propositions that would adequately account for the data. If this worked out, then another narrowly defined problem could be considered, and the theory extended and modified. Admittedly, one would be confronted again and again with bodies of data with which no progress could be made theoretically. It was to be hoped that one would quickly recognize the dead end and move on to other data.

Funds provided by the Behavioral Sciences Division of the Ford Foundation made possible the collaboration of May Brodbeck, Don Martindale, Jack Brehm, and Alvin Boderman. Together we began the job by selecting the spreading of rumors as our first narrowly defined problem to work on.

The chores of collecting an exhaustive bibliography of research literature on rumor spreading, of reading the material, and of sifting fact from supposition and conjecture were comparatively easy. More difficult were the problems of integrating the material and of getting some theoretical hunches that would begin to handle the data in a satisfactory way. It was easy enough to restate empirical findings in a slightly more general form, but this kind of intellectual exercise does not lead to much progress.

The first hunch that generated any amount of enthusiasm among us came from trying to understand some data, reported by Prasad, concerning rumors subsequent to the Indian earthquake of 1934. This study is described in detail in Chapter Ten. The fact reported by Prasad which puzzled us was that following the earthquake, the vast majority of the rumors that were widely circulated predicted even worse disasters to come in the very near future. Certainly the belief that horrible disasters were about to occur is not a very pleasant belief, and we may ask why rumors that were "anxiety provoking" arose and were so widely accepted. Finally a possible answer to this question occurred to us— an answer that held promise of having rather general application: perhaps these rumors predicting even worse disasters to come were not "anxiety provoking" at all but were rather "anxiety justifying." That is, as a result of the earthquake these people were already frightened, and the rumors served the function of giving them something to be frightened about. Perhaps these rumors provided people with information that fit with the way they already felt.

From this start, and with the help of many discussions in which we attempted to pin the idea down and to formalize it somewhat, we arrived at the concept of dissonance and the hypotheses concerning dissonance reduction. Once the formulation in terms of dissonance and the reduction of dissonance was made, numerous implications became obvious. Following these implications through soon became the major activity of the project. For a while we continued to pursue the original notion of the "propositional inventory" and to explore the implications of the notion of dissonance; but the extraordinary difficulty of the former, together with our excitement concerning the latter, served more and more to focus our efforts.

The development of the theory did not, of course, proceed in the order in which it is presented in this book. Here the material is arranged so that the first chapters deal with relatively simple situations and later chapters become more and more concerned with complicated problems. Actually, the first implications of the theory of dissonance that we explored were those involving problems of voluntary and involuntary exposure to information. These occurred to us first, of course, because they were related to the area of communication with which we were basically concerned. These implications also were suggested by the rumor study itself. If people sought information that would fit with how they were already reacting, certainly this process would not be confined to rumors but would also extend generally to information-seeking processes. The implications from the theory that suggested themselves, however, soon extended beyond the bounds of "communication and social influence." Nevertheless, we felt it was more fruitful to follow the leads of what now seemed to be a promising theory than to adhere rigidly to a prior plan and a designated content area.

Fortunately for the development of the theory of dissonance, we were not restricted to finding relevant data in the existing research literature, but were able to conduct our own studies specifically designed to test derivations from the theory. With funds and assistance provided by the Laboratory for Research in Social Relations of the University of Minnesota, and with some funds available from a personal grant-in-aid from the Ford Foundation, we were able to collect our own data. All the people who assisted in these studies will not be named here, since they are acknowledged in the pages of the book itself where these studies are described.

According to some points of view, the writer should have waited another four or five years before writing this book. By that time many more studies of relevance to the theory would have been made and many unclarities would have been eliminated. But piecemeal journal publication seemed a poor way to present the theory and the variety of data relevant to it. One of the important aspects of the theory of dissonance is its ability to integrate data from seemingly different areas, and this aspect would be largely lost if it were not published in one unitary volume. Also, the writer feels that there are sufficient data now relevant to the theory to warrant communicating it to others, and sufficient corroboration of the theory to hope that others will also pursue it.

One final word of thanks is due those who in various ways helped in writing and rewriting the chapters of this book, notably, Judson Mills, Robert R. Sears, Ernest R. Hilgard, Herbert McClosky, Daniel Miller, James Coleman, Martin Lipset, Raymond Bauer, Jack Brehm, and May Brodbeck. Assistance from many of these people was possible because they and I were resident fellows at the Center for Advanced Study in the Behavioral Sciences while most of the writing on this book was done.

LEON FESTINGER

Palo Alto, California
March, 1956

Table of Contents

ONE

An Introduction to the Theory of Dissonance

It has frequently been implied, and sometimes even pointed out, that the individual strives toward consistency within himself. His opinions and attitudes, for example, tend to exist in clusters that are internally consistent. Certainly one may find exceptions. A person may think Negroes are just as good as whites but would not want any living in his neighborhood; or someone may think little children should be quiet and unobtrusive and yet may be quite proud when his child aggressively captures the attention of his adult guests. When such inconsistencies are found to exist, they may be quite dramatic, but they capture our interest primarily because they stand out in sharp contrast against a background of consistency. It is still overwhelmingly true that related opinions or attitudes are consistent with one another. Study after study reports such consistency among one person's political attitudes, social attitudes, and many others.

There is the same kind of consistency between what a person knows or believes and what he does. A person who believes a college education is a good thing will very likely encourage his children to go to college; a child who knows he will be severely punished for some misdemeanor will not commit it or at least will try not to be caught doing it. This is not surprising, of course; it is so much the rule that we take it for granted. Again what captures our attention are the exceptions to otherwise consistent behavior. A person may know that smoking is bad for him and yet continue to smoke; many persons commit crimes even though they know the high probability of being caught and the punishment that awaits them.

Granting that consistency is the usual thing, perhaps overwhelmingly so, what about these exceptions which come to mind so readily? Only rarely, if ever, are they accepted psychologically *as inconsistencies* by the person involved. Usually more or less successful attempts are made to rationalize them. Thus, the person who continues to smoke, knowing that it is bad for his health, may also feel (*a*) he enjoys smoking so much it is worth it; (*b*) the chances of his health suffering are not as serious as some would make out; (*c*) he can't always avoid every possible dangerous contingency and still live; and (*d*) perhaps even if he stopped smoking he would put on weight which is equally bad for his health. So, continuing to smoke is, after all, consistent with his ideas about smoking.

But persons are not always successful in explaining away or in rationalizing inconsistencies to themselves. For one reason or another, attempts to achieve consistency may fail. The inconsistency then simply continues to exist. Under such circumstances—that is, in the presence of an inconsistency—there is psychological discomfort.

The basic hypotheses, the ramifications and implications of which will be explored in the remainder of this book, can now be stated. First, I will replace the word "inconsistency" with a term which has less of a logical connotation, namely, *dissonance*. I will likewise replace the word "consistency" with a more neutral term, namely, *consonance*. A more formal definition of these terms will be given shortly; for the moment, let us try to get along with the implicit meaning they have acquired as a result of the preceding discussion.

The basic hypotheses I wish to state are as follows:

1. The existence of dissonance, being psychologically uncomfortable, will motivate the person' to try to reduce the dissonance and achieve consonance.

2. When dissonance is present, in addition to trying to reduce it, the person will actively avoid situations and information which would likely increase the dissonance.

Before proceeding to develop this theory of dissonance and the pressures to reduce it, it would be well to clarify the nature of dissonance, what kind of a concept it is, and where the theory concerning it will lead. The two hypotheses stated above provide a good starting point for this clarification. While they refer here specifically to dissonance, they are in fact very general hypotheses. In place of "dissonance" one can substitute other notions similar in nature, such as "hunger," "frustration," or "disequilibrium," and the hypotheses would still make perfectly good sense.

In short, I am proposing that dissonance, that is, the existence of nonfitting relations among cognitions, is a motivating factor in its own right. By the term *cognition,* here and in the remainder of the book, I mean any knowledge, opinion, or belief about the environment, about oneself, or about one's behavior. Cognitive dissonance can be seen as an antecedent condition which leads to activity oriented toward dissonance reduction just as hunger leads to activity oriented toward hunger reduction. It is a very different motivation from what psychologists are used to dealing with but, as we shall see, nonetheless powerful.

And now a word about the remainder of the book. It explores, in a wide variety of contexts, the consequences of the existence of cognitive dissonance and the attempts on the part of humans to reduce it. If someone cared to write a certain kind of book about the hunger drive in human beings, it would turn out to be similar in nature to the present volume. There might be chapters exploring the consequences of attempts to reduce hunger in a variety of contexts, ranging from a child in a highchair to an adult group at a formal banquet. In a similar way, this book explores contexts ranging from individual decision situations to mass phenomena. Since reduction of dissonance is a basic process in humans, it is not surprising that its manifestations may be observed in such a wide variety of contexts.

The Occurrence and Persistence of Dissonance

Why and how does dissonance ever arise? How does it happen that persons sometimes find themselves doing things that do not fit with what they know, or having opinions that do not fit with other opinions they hold? An answer to this question may be found in discussing two of the more common situations in which dissonance may occur.

1. New events may happen or new information may become known to a person, creating at least a momentary dissonance with existing knowledge, opinion, or cognition concerning behavior. Since a person does not have complete and perfect control over the information that reaches him and over events that can happen in his environment, such dissonances may easily arise. Thus, for example, a person may plan to go on a picnic with complete confidence that the weather will be warm and sunny. Nevertheless, just before he is due to start, it may begin to rain. The knowledge that it is now raining is dissonant with his confidence in a sunny day and with his planning to go to a picnic. Or, as another

example, a person who is quite certain in his knowledge that automatic transmissions on automobiles are inefficient may accidentally come across an article praising automatic transmissions. Again, at least a momentary dissonance is created.

2. Even in the absence of new, unforeseen events or information, the existence of dissonance is undoubtedly an everyday condition. Very few things are all black or all white; very few situations are clear-cut enough so that opinions or behaviors are not to some extent a mixture of contradictions. Thus, a midwestern farmer who is a Republican may be opposed to his party's position on farm price supports; a person buying a new car may prefer the economy of one model but the design of another; a person deciding on how to invest his money may know that the outcome of his investment depends upon economic conditions beyond his control. Where an opinion must be formed or a decision taken, some dissonance is almost unavoidably created between the cognition of the action taken and those opinions or knowledges which tend to point to a different action.

There is, then, a fairly wide variety of situations in which dissonance is nearly unavoidable. But it remains for us to examine the circumstances under which dissonance, once arisen, persists. That is, under what conditions is dissonance not simply a momentary affair? If the hypotheses stated above are correct, then as soon as dissonance occurs there will be pressures to reduce it. To answer this question it is necessary first to have a brief look at the possible ways in which dissonance may be reduced.

Since there will be a more formal discussion of this point later on in this chapter, let us now examine how dissonance may be reduced, using as an illustration the example of the habitual cigarette smoker who has learned that smoking is bad for his health. He may have acquired this information from a newspaper or magazine, from friends, or even from some physician. This knowledge is certainly dissonant with cognition that he continues to smoke. If the hypothesis that there will be pressures to reduce this dissonance is correct, what would the person involved be expected to do?

1. He might simply change his cognition about his behavior by changing his actions; that is, he might stop smoking. If he no longer smokes, then his cognition of what he does will be consonant with the knowledge that smoking is bad for his health.

2. He might change his "knowledge" about the effects of smoking. This sounds like a peculiar way to put it, but it expresses well what must happen. He might simply end up believing that smoking does not have any deleterious effects, or he might acquire so much "knowledge" pointing to the good effects it has that the harmful aspects become negligible. If he can manage to change his knowledge in either of these ways, he will have reduced, or even eliminated, the dissonance between what he does and what he knows.

But in the above illustration it seems clear that the person may encounter difficulties in trying to change either his behavior or his knowledge. And this, of course, is precisely the reason that dissonance, once created, may persist. There is no guarantee that the person will be able to reduce or remove the dissonance. The hypothetical smoker may find that the process of giving up smoking is too painful for him to endure. He might try to find facts and opinions of others to support the view that smoking is not harmful, but these attempts might fail. He might then remain in the situation where he continues to smoke and continues to know that smoking is harmful. If this turns out to be the case, however, his efforts to reduce the dissonance will not cease.

Indeed, there are some areas of cognition where the existence of major dissonance is customary. This may occur when two or more established beliefs or values, all relevant to the area of cognition in question, are inconsistent. That is, no opinion can be held, and no behavior engaged in, that will not be dissonant with at least one of these established beliefs. Myrdal (41), in the appendix to his classic book, states this quite well in connection with attitudes and behavior toward Negroes. In discussing the simultaneous existence of opinions and values concerning human beings in general, Negroes in general, specific groups of Negroes, and so on, Myrdal states:

A need will be felt by the person or group, whose inconsistencies in valuations are publicly exposed, to find a means of reconciling the inconsistencies. . . . The feeling of need for logical consistency within the hierarchy of moral valuations . . . is, in its modern intensity, a rather new phenomenon. With less mobility, less intellectual communication, and less public discussion, there was in previous generations less exposure of one another's valuation conflicts [pp. 1029, 1030].

While I find myself in disagreement with Myrdal in the importance he places on the public exposure of the dissonance, I feel it is a good statement of some of the reasons why strong dissonance exists in this area.

The notions introduced thus far are not entirely new; many similar ones have been suggested. It may be of value to mention two whose formulation is closest to my own. Heider (25), in an as yet unpublished manuscript, discusses the relationships among people and among sentiments. He states:

Summarizing this preliminary discussion of balanced, or harmonious, states, we can say that they are states characterized by two or more relations which fit together. If no balanced state exists, then forces toward the [balanced] state will arise. Either there will be a tendency to change the sentiments involved, or the unit relations will be changed through action or cognitive reorganization. If a change is not possible, the state of imbalance will produce tension, and the balanced states will be preferred over the states of imbalance [Part II].

If one replaces the word "balanced" with "consonant" and "imbalance" with "dissonance," this statement by Heider can be seen to indicate the same process with which our discussion up to now has dealt.

Osgood and Tannenbaum (43) recently published a paper in which they also formulated and documented a similar idea with respect to changes in opinions and attitudes. In discussing the "principle of congruity," as they call it, they state: "Changes in evaluation are always in the direction of increased congruity with the existing frame of reference [p. 43]." The particular kind of "incongruity" or cognitive dissonance with which they deal in their study is produced by the knowledge that a person or other source of information which a subject regards positively (or negatively) supports an opinion which the subject regards negatively (or positively). They proceed to show that under such circumstances there is a marked tendency to change either the evaluation of the opinion involved or the evaluation of the source in a direction which would reduce the dissonance. Thus, if the source were positively evaluated and the opinion negatively evaluated, the person might end up reacting less positively to the source or more positively to the issue. It is also clear from their data that the particular outcome depends on whether the evaluation of the source or of the issue is initially more firmly rooted in the person's cognition. If his attitude toward the source is highly "polarized," then the opinion is more likely to change, and vice versa. Indeed, by careful initial measurement of the attitudes toward the sources and toward the opinions before the dissonance is introduced, and by careful measurement of how resistant each of these is to change, the authors are able to predict quite nicely the direction, and in some instances the amount, of change in evaluation.

The important point to remember is that there is pressure to produce consonant relations among cognitions and to avoid and reduce dissonance. Many other writers have recognized this, although few have stated it as concretely and as succinctly as the authors we have mentioned. The task which we are attempting in this book is to formulate the theory of dissonance in a precise yet generally applicable form, to draw out its implications to a variety of contexts, and to present data relevant to the theory.

Definitions of Dissonance and Consonance

Most of the remainder of this chapter will deal with a more formal exposition of the theory of dissonance. I will attempt to state the theory in as precise and unambiguous terms as possible. But since the ideas which constitute this theory are by no means yet in a completely precise form, some vagueness is unavoidable.

The terms "dissonance" and "consonance" refer to relations which exist between pairs of "elements." It is consequently necessary, before proceeding to define these relations, to define the elements themselves as well as we can.

These elements refer to what has been called cognition, that is, the things a person knows about himself, about his behavior, and about his surroundings. These elements, then, are "knowledges," if I may coin the plural form of the word. Some of these elements represent knowledge about oneself: what one does, what one feels, what one wants or desires, what one is, and the like. Other elements of knowledge concern the world in which one lives: what is where, what leads to what, what things are satisfying or painful or inconsequential or important, etc.

It is clear that the term "knowledge" has been used to include things to which the word does not ordinarily refer—for example, opinions. A person does not hold an opinion unless he thinks it is correct, and so, psychologically, it is not different from a "knowledge." The same is true of beliefs, values, or attitudes, which function as "knowledges" for our purposes. This is not to imply that there are no important distinctions to be made among these various terms. Indeed, some such distinctions will be made later on. But for the definitions here, these are all "elements of cognition," and relations of consonance and dissonance can hold between pairs of these elements.

There are further questions of definition one would like to be able to answer. For example, when is an "element of cognition" *one* element, or a group of elements? Is the knowledge, "the winter in Minneapolis is very cold" an element, or should this be considered a cluster of elements made up of more specific knowledge? This is, at present, an unanswerable question. Indeed, it may be a question which does not need answering. As will be seen in those chapters where data are presented and discussed, this unanswered question does not present a problem in connection with measurement.

Another important question concerning these elements is, how are they formed and what determines their content? At this point we want to emphasize the single most important determinant of the content of these elements, namely, *reality*. These elements of cognition are responsive to reality. By and large they mirror, or map, reality. This reality may be physical or social or psychological, but in any case the cognition more or less maps it. This is, of course, not surprising. It would be unlikely that an organism could live and survive if the elements of cognition were not to a large extent a veridical map of reality. Indeed, when someone is "out of touch with reality," it becomes very noticeable.

In other words, elements of cognition correspond for the most part with what the person actually does or feels or with what actually exists in the environment. In the case of opinions, beliefs, and values, the reality may be what others think or do; in other instances the reality may be what is encountered experientially or what others have told him.

But let us here object and say that persons frequently have cognitive elements which deviate markedly from reality, at least as we see it. Consequently, the major point to be made is that *the reality which impinges on a person will exert pressures in the direction of bringing the appropriate cognitive elements into correspondence with that reality*. This does not mean that the existing cognitive elements will *always* correspond. Indeed, one of the important consequences of the theory of dissonance is that it will help us understand some circumstances where the cognitive elements do not correspond with reality. But it does mean that if the cognitive elements do not correspond with a certain reality which impinges, certain pressures must exist. We should therefore be able to observe some manifestations of these pressures. This hypothesized relation between the cognitive elements and reality is important in enabling measurement of dissonance, and we will refer to it again in considering data.

It is now possible to proceed to a discussion of the relations which may exist between pairs of elements. There are three such relations, namely, irrelevance, dissonance, and consonance. They will be discussed in that order.

IRRELEVANT RELATIONS

Two elements may simply have nothing to do with one another. That is, under such circumstances where one cognitive element implies nothing at all concerning some other element, these two elements are irrelevant to one another. For example, let us imagine a person who knows that it sometimes takes as long as two weeks for a letter to go from New York to Paris by regular boat mail and who also knows that a dry, hot July is good for the corn crop in Iowa. These two elements of cognition have nothing to do with one another; they exist in an irrelevant relation to each other. There is not, of course, much to say about such irrelevant relations except to point to their existence. Of primary concern will be those pairs of elements between which relations of consonance or dissonance can exist.

In many instances, however, it becomes quite a problem to decide a priori whether or not two elements are irrelevant. It is often impossible to decide this without reference to other cognitions of the person involved. Sometimes situations will exist where, because of the behavior of the person involved, previously irrelevant elements become relevant to one another. This could even be the case in the example of irrelevant cognitive elements which we gave above. If a person living in Paris was speculating on the corn crop in the United States, he would want information concerning weather predictions for Iowa but would not depend upon boat mail for getting his information.

Before proceeding to the definitions and discussion of the relations of consonance and dissonance which exist if the elements are relevant, it may be well to stress again the special nature certain cognitive elements have—usually those cognitive elements which correspond to behavior. Such a "behavioral" element, by being relevant to each of two irrelevant cognitive elements, may make them in fact relevant to each other.

RELEVANT RELATIONS: DISSONANCE AND CONSONANCE

We have already acquired some intuitive notion of the meaning of dissonance. Two elements are dissonant if, for one reason or another, they do not fit together. They may be inconsistent or contradictory, culture or group standards may dictate that they do not fit, and so on. It is appropriate now to attempt a more formal conceptual definition.

Let us consider two elements which exist in a person's cognition and which are relevant to one another. The definition of dissonance will disregard the existence of all the other cognitive elements that are relevant to either or both of the two under consideration and simply deal with these two alone. *These two elements are in a dissonant relation if, considering these two alone, the obverse of one element would follow from the other.* To state it a bit more formally, x and y are dissonant if not-x follows from y. Thus, for example, if a person knew there were only friends in his vicinity and also felt afraid, there would be a dissonant relation between these two cognitive elements. Or, for another example, if a person were already in debt and also purchased a new car, the corresponding cognitive elements would be dissonant with one another. The dissonance might exist because of what the person has learned or come to expect, because of what is considered appropriate or usual, or for any of a number of other reasons.

Motivations and desired consequences may also be factors in determining whether or not two elements are dissonant. For example, a person in a card game might continue playing and losing money while knowing that the others in the game are professional gamblers. This latter knowledge would be dissonant with his cognition about his behavior, namely, continuing to play. But it should be clear that to specify the relation as dissonant is to assume (plausibly enough) that the person involved wants to win. If for some strange reason this person wants to lose, this relation would be consonant.

It may be helpful to give a series of examples where dissonance between two cognitive elements stems from different sources, that is, where the two elements are dissonant because of different meanings of the phrase "follow from" in the definition of dissonance given above.

1. Dissonance could arise from logical inconsistency. If a person believed that man will reach the moon in the near future and also believed that man will not be able to build a device that can leave the atmosphere of the earth, these two cognitions are dissonant with one another. The obverse of one follows from the other on logical grounds in the person's own thinking processes.

2. Dissonance could arise because of cultural mores. If a person at a formal dinner uses his hands to pick up a recalcitrant chicken bone, the knowledge of what he is doing is dissonant with the knowledge of formal dinner etiquette. The dissonance exists simply because the culture defines what is consonant and what is not. In some other culture these two cognitions might not be dissonant at all.

3. Dissonance may arise because one specific opinion is sometimes included, by definition, in a more general opinion. Thus, if a person is a Democrat but in a given election prefers the Republican candidate, the cognitive elements corresponding to these two sets of opinions are dissonant with each other because "being a Democrat" includes, as part of the concept, favoring Democratic candidates.

4. Dissonance may arise because of past experience. If a person were standing in the rain and yet could see no evidence that he was getting wet, these two cognitions would be dissonant with one another because he knows from experience that getting wet follows from being out in the rain. If one can imagine a person who had never had any experience with rain, these two cognitions would probably not be dissonant.

These various examples are probably sufficient to illustrate how the conceptual definition of dissonance, together with some specific meaning of the phrase "follow from," would be used empirically to decide whether two cognitive elements are dissonant or consonant. It is clear, of course, that in any of these situations, there might exist many other elements of cognition that are consonant with either of the two elements under consideration. Nevertheless, the relation between the two elements is dissonant if, disregarding the others, the one does not, or would not be expected to, follow from the other.

While we have been defining and discussing dissonance, the relations of consonance and irrelevance have, of course, also been defined by implication. If, considering a pair of elements, either one *does* follow from the other, then the relation between them is consonant. If neither the existing element nor its obverse follows from the other element of the pair, then the relation between them is irrelevant.

The conceptual definitions of dissonance and consonance present some serious measurement difficulties. If the theory of dissonance is to have relevance for empirical data, one must be able to identify dissonances and consonances unequivocally. But it is clearly hopeless to attempt to obtain a complete listing of cognitive elements, and even were such a listing available, in some cases it would be difficult or impossible to say, a priori, which of the three relationships holds. In many cases, however, the a priori determination of dissonance is clear and easy. (Remember also that two cognitive elements may be dissonant for a person living in one culture and not for a person living in another, or for a person with one set of experiences and not for a person with another.) Needless to say, it will be necessary to cope with this problem of measurement in detail in those chapters where empirical data are presented and discussed.

The Magnitude of Dissonance

All dissonant relations, of course, are not of equal magnitude. It is necessary to distinguish degrees of dissonance and to specify what determines how strong a given dissonant relation is. We will briefly discuss some determinants of the magnitude of dissonance between two elements and then turn to a consideration of the total amount of dissonance which may exist between two clusters of elements.

One obvious determinant of the magnitude of dissonance lies in the characteristics of the elements between which the relation of dissonance holds. *If two elements are dissonant with one another, the magnitude of the dissonance will be a function of the importance of the elements.* The more these elements are important to, or valued by, the person, the greater will be the magnitude of a dissonant relation between them. Thus, for example, if a person gives ten cents to a beggar, knowing full well that the beggar is not really in need, the dissonance which exists between these two elements is rather weak. Neither of the two cognitive elements involved is very important or very consequential to the person. A much greater dissonance is involved, for example, if a student does not study for a very important examination, knowing that his present fund of information is probably inadequate for the examination. In this case the elements that are dissonant with each other are more important to the person, and the magnitude of dissonance will be correspondingly greater.

It is probably safe to assume that it is rare for no dissonance at all to exist within any cluster of cognitive elements. For almost any action a person might take, for almost any feeling he might have, there will most likely be at least one cognitive element dissonant with this "behavioral" element. Even perfectly trivial cognitions like knowing one is taking a walk on a Sunday afternoon would likely have some elements dissonant with it. The person who is out for a walk might also know that there are things around the house requiring his attention, or he might know that rain was likely, and so on. In short, there are generally so many other cognitive elements relevant to any given element that some dissonance is the usual state of affairs.

Let us consider now the total context of dissonances and consonances in relation to one particular element. Assuming momentarily, for the sake of definition, that all the elements relevant to the one in question are equally important, *the total amount of dissonance between this element and the remainder of the person's cognition will depend on the proportion of relevant elements that are dissonant with the one in question.* Thus, if the overwhelming majority of relevant elements are consonant with, say, a behavioral element, then the dissonance with this behavioral element is slight. If in relation to the number of elements consonant with the behavioral element the number of dissonant elements is large, the total dissonance will be of appreciable magnitude. Of course, the magnitude of the total dissonance will also depend on the importance or value of those relevant elements which exist in consonant or dissonant relations with the one being considered.

The above statement can of course be easily generalized to deal with the magnitude of dissonance which exists between two clusters of cognitive elements. This magnitude would depend on the proportion of the relevant relations between elements in the two clusters that were dissonant and, of course, on the importance of the elements.

Since the magnitude of dissonance is an important variable in determining the pressure to reduce dissonance, and since we will deal with measures of the magnitude of dissonance repeatedly in considering data, it may be well to summarize our discussion concerning the magnitude of dissonance.

1. If two cognitive elements are relevant, the relation between them is either dissonant or consonant.

2. The magnitude of the dissonance (or consonance) increases as the importance or value of the elements increases.

3. The total amount of dissonance that exists between two clusters of cognitive elements is a function of the weighted proportion of all relevant relations between the two clusters that are dissonant. The term "weighted proportion" is used because each relevant relation would be weighted according to the importance of the elements involved in that relation.

The Reduction of Dissonance

The presence of dissonance gives rise to pressures to reduce or eliminate the dissonance. The strength of the pressures to reduce the dissonance is a function of the magnitude of the dissonance. In other words, dissonance acts in the same way as a state of drive or need or tension. The presence of dissonance leads to action to reduce it just as, for example, the presence of hunger leads to action to reduce the hunger. Also, similar to the action of a drive, the greater the dissonance, the greater will be the intensity of the action to reduce the dissonance and the greater the avoidance of situations that would increase the dissonance.

In order to be specific about how the pressure to reduce dissonance would manifest itself, it is necessary to examine the possible ways in which existing dissonance can be reduced or eliminated. In general, if dissonance exists between two elements, this dissonance can be eliminated by changing one of those elements. The important thing is how these changes may be brought about. There are various possible ways in which this can be accomplished, depending upon the type of cognitive elements involved and upon the total cognitive context.

CHANGING A BEHAVIORAL COGNITIVE ELEMENT

When the dissonance under consideration is between an element corresponding to some knowledge concerning environment (environmental element) and a behavioral element, the dissonance can, of course, be eliminated by changing the behavioral cognitive element in such a way that it is consonant with the environmental element. The simplest and easiest way in which this may be accomplished is to change the action or feeling which the behavioral element represents. Given that a cognition is responsive to "reality" (as we have seen), if the behavior of the organism changes, the cognitive element or elements corresponding to this behavior will likewise change. This method of reducing or eliminating dissonance is a very frequent occurrence. Our behavior and feelings are frequently modified in accordance with new information. If a person starts out on a picnic and notices that it has begun to rain, he may very well turn around and go home. There are many persons who do stop smoking if and when they discover it is bad for their health.

It may not always be possible, however, to eliminate dissonance or even to reduce it materially by changing one's action or feeling. The difficulty of changing the behavior may be too great, or the change, while eliminating some dissonances, may create a whole host of new ones. These questions will be discussed in more detail below.

CHANGING AN ENVIRONMENTAL COGNITIVE ELEMENT

Just as it is possible to change a behavioral cognitive element by changing the behavior which this element mirrors, it is sometimes possible to change an *environmental* cognitive element by changing the situation to which that element corresponds. This, of course, is much more difficult than changing one's behavior, for one must have a sufficient degree of control over one's environment—a relatively rare occurrence.

Changing the environment itself in order to reduce dissonance is more feasible when the social environment is in question than when the physical environment is involved. In order to illustrate rather dramatically the kind of thing that would be involved, I will give a rather facetious hypothetical example. Let us imagine a person who is given to pacing up and down in his living room at home. Let us further imagine that for some unknown reason he always jumps over one particular spot on the floor. The cognitive element corresponding to his jumping over that spot is undoubtedly dissonant with his knowledge that the floor at that spot is level, strong, and in no way different from any other part of the floor. If, some evening when his wife is away from home, he breaks a hole in the floor at that exact spot, he would completely eliminate the dissonance. The cognition that there is a hole in the floor would be quite consonant with the knowledge that he jumps over the place where the hole exists. In short, he would have changed a cognitive element by actually changing the environment, thus eliminating a dissonance.

Whenever there is sufficient control over the environment, this method of reducing dissonance may be employed. For example, a person who is habitually very hostile toward other people may surround himself with persons who provoke hostility. His cognitions about the persons with whom he associates are then consonant with the cognitions corresponding to his hostile behavior. The possibilities of manipulating the environment are limited, however, and most endeavors to change a cognitive element will follow other lines.

If a cognitive element that is responsive to reality is to be changed without changing the corresponding reality, some means of ignoring or counteracting the real situation must be used. This is sometimes well-nigh impossible, except in extreme cases which might be called psychotic. If a person is standing in the rain and rapidly getting soaked, he will almost certainly continue to have the cognition that it is raining no matter how strong the psychological pressures are to eliminate that cognition. In other instances it is relatively easy to change a cognitive element although the reality remains the same. For example, a person might be able to change his opinion about a political officeholder even though the behavior of that officeholder, and the political situation generally, remain unchanged. Usually, for this to occur, the person would have to be able to find others who would agree with and support his new opinion. In general, establishing a social reality by gaining the agreement and support of other people is one of the major ways in which a cognition can be changed when the pressures to change it are present. It can readily be seen that where such social support is necessary, the presence of dissonance and the consequent pressures to change some cognitive element will lead to a variety of social processes. This will be developed in detail in Chapters Eight, Nine, and Ten, which consider the social manifestations of pressures to reduce dissonance.

ADDING NEW COGNITIVE ELEMENTS

It is clear that in order to eliminate a dissonance completely, some cognitive element must be changed. It is also clear that this is not always possible. But even if it is impossible to eliminate a dissonance, it is possible to reduce the total magnitude of dissonance by adding new cognitive elements. Thus, for example, if dissonance existed between some cognitive elements concerning the effects of smoking and cognition concerning the behavior of continuing to smoke, the total dissonance could be reduced by adding new cognitive elements that are consonant with the fact of smoking. In the presence of such dissonance, then, a person might be expected to actively seek new information that would reduce the total dissonance and, at the same time, to avoid new information that might increase the existing dissonance. Thus, to pursue the example, the person might seek out and avidly read any material critical of the research which purported to show that smoking was bad for one's health. At the same time he would avoid reading material that praised this research. (If he unavoidably came in contact with the latter type of material, his reading would be critical indeed.)

Actually, the possibilities for adding new elements which would reduce the existing dissonances are broad. Our smoker, for example, could find out all about accidents and death rates in automobiles. Having then added the cognition that the danger from smoking is negligible compared to the danger he runs driving a car, his dissonance would also have been somewhat reduced. Here the total dissonance is reduced by reducing the *importance* of the existing dissonance.

The above discussion has pointed to the possibility of reducing the total dissonance with some element by reducing the proportion of dissonant as compared with consonant relations involving that element. It is also possible to add a new cognitive element which, in a sense, "reconciles" two elements that are dissonant. Let us consider an example from the literature to illustrate this. Spiro (51) gives an account of certain aspects of the belief system of the Ifaluk, a nonliterate society. The relevant points for our purposes here are as follows:

1. In this culture there is a firm belief that people are *good*. This belief is not only that they should be good but that they *are* good.

2. For one reason or another, young children in this culture go through a period of particularly strong overt aggression, hostility, and destructiveness.

It seems clear that the belief about the nature of people is dissonant with the knowledge of the behavior of the children in this culture. It would have been possible to reduce this dissonance in any number of ways. They might have changed their belief about the nature of people or have modified it so that people are wholly good only at maturity. Or they might have changed their ideas about what is and what is not "good" so that overt aggression in young children would be considered good. Actually, the manner of reducing the dissonance was different. A third belief was added which effectively reduced the dissonance by "reconciliation." Specifically, they also believe in the existence of malevolent ghosts which enter into persons and cause them to do bad things.

As a result of this third belief, the knowledge of the aggressive behavior of children is no longer dissonant with the belief that people are good. It is not the children who behave aggressively—it's the malevolent ghosts. Psychologically, this is a highly satisfactory means of reducing the dissonance, as one might expect when such beliefs are institutionalized at a cultural level. Unsatisfactory solutions would not be as successful in becoming widely accepted.

Before moving on, it is worth while to emphasize again that the presence of pressures to reduce dissonance, or even activity directed toward such reduction, does not guarantee that the dissonance will be reduced. A person may not be able to find the social support needed to change a cognitive element, or he may not be able to find new elements which reduce the total dissonance. In fact, it is quite conceivable that in the process of trying to reduce dissonance, it might even be increased. This will depend upon what the person encounters while attempting to reduce the dissonance. The important point to be made so far is that in the presence of a dissonance, one will be able to observe the *attempts* to reduce it. If attempts to reduce dissonance fail, one should be able to observe symptoms of psychological discomfort, provided the dissonance is appreciable enough so that the discomfort is clearly and overtly manifested.

Resistance to Reduction of Dissonance

If dissonance is to be reduced or eliminated by changing one or more cognitive elements, it is necessary to consider how resistant these cognitive elements are to change. Whether or not any of them change, and if so, which ones, will certainly be determined in part by the magnitude of resistance to change which they possess. It is, of course, clear that if the various cognitive elements involved had no resistance to change whatsoever, there would never be any lasting dissonances. Momentary dissonance might occur, but if the cognitive elements involved had no resistance to change, the dissonance would immediately be eliminated. Let us, then, look at the major sources of resistance to change of a cognitive element.

Just as the reduction of dissonance presented somewhat different problems depending upon whether the element to be changed was a behavioral or an environmental one, so the major sources of resistance to change are different for these two classes of cognitive elements.

RESISTANCE TO CHANGE OF BEHAVIORAL COGNITIVE ELEMENTS

The first and foremost source of resistance to change for *any* cognitive element is the responsiveness of such elements to reality. If one sees that the grass is green, it is very difficult to think it is not so. If a person is walking down the street, it is difficult for his cognition not to contain an element corresponding to this. Given this strong and sometimes overwhelming responsiveness to reality, the problem of changing a behavioral cognitive element becomes the problem of changing the behavior which is being mapped by the element. Consequently, the resistance to change of the cognitive element is identical with the resistance to change of the behavior reflected by that element, assuming that the person maintains contact with reality.

Certainly much behavior has little or no resistance to change. We continually modify many of our actions and feelings in accordance with changes in the situation. If a street which we ordinarily use when we drive to work is being repaired, there is usually little difficulty in altering our behavior and using a different route. What, then, are the circumstances that make it difficult for the person to change his actions?

1. The change may be painful or involve loss. A person may, for example, have spent a lot of money to purchase a house. If for any reason he now wants to change, that is, live in a different house or different neighborhood, he must endure the discomforts of moving and the possible financial loss involved in selling the house. A person who might desire to give up smoking must endure the discomfort and pain of the cessation in order to accomplish the change. Clearly, in such circumstances there will be a certain resistance to change. The magnitude of this resistance to change will be determined by the extent of pain or loss which must be endured.

2. The present behavior may be otherwise satisfying. A person might continue to have lunch at a certain restaurant even though they served poor food if, for example, his friends always ate there. Or a person who is very domineer-

ing and harsh toward his children might not easily be able to give up the satisfactions of being able to boss someone, even if on various grounds he desired to change. In such instances, of course, the resistance to change would be a function of the satisfaction obtained from the present behavior.

3. Making the change may simply not be possible. It would be a mistake to imagine that a person could consummate any change in his behavior if he wanted to badly enough. It may not be possible to change for a variety of reasons. Some behavior, especially emotional reactions, may not be under the voluntary control of the person. For example, a person might have a strong reaction of fear which he can do nothing about. Also, it might not be possible to consummate a change simply because the new behavior may not be in the behavior repertory of the person. A father might not be able to change the way he behaves toward his children simply because he doesn't know any other way to behave. A third circumstance which could make it impossible to change is the irrevocable nature of certain actions. If, for example, a person has sold his house and then decides he wants it back, there is nothing that can be done if the new owner refuses to sell it. The action has been taken and is not reversible. But under circumstances where the behavior simply cannot change at all, it is not correct to say that the resistance to change of the corresponding cognitive element is infinite. The resistance to change which the cognitive element possesses can, of course, not be greater than the pressure to respond to reality.

RESISTANCE TO CHANGE OF ENVIRONMENTAL
COGNITIVE ELEMENTS

Here again, as with behavioral cognitive elements, the major source of resistance to change lies in the responsiveness of these elements to reality. The result of this, as far as behavioral elements go, is to tie the resistance to change of the cognitive element to the resistance to change of the reality, namely, the behavior itself. The situation is somewhat different with regard to environmental elements. When there is a clear and unequivocal reality corresponding to some cognitive element, the possibilities of change are almost nil. If one desired, for example, to change one's cognition about the location of some building which one saw every day, this would indeed be difficult to accomplish.

In many instances, however, the reality corresponding to the cognitive element is by no means so clear and unambiguous. When the reality is basically a social one, that is, when it is established by agreement with other people, the resistance to change would be determined by the difficulty of finding persons to support the new cognition.

There is another source of resistance to change of both behavioral and environmental cognitive elements. We have postponed discussion of it until now, however, because it is a more important source of resistance to change for environmental elements than for others. This source of resistance to change lies in the fact that an element is in relationship with a number of other elements. To the extent that the element is consonant with a large number of other elements and to the extent that changing it would replace these consonances by dissonances, the element will be resistant to change.

The above discussion is not meant to be an exhaustive analysis of resistance to change or a listing of conceptually different sources. Rather, it is a discussion which attempts to make distinctions that will help operationally rather than conceptually. In considering any dissonance and the resistance to change of the elements involved, the important factor in the attempt to eliminate the dissonance by changing an element is the total amount of resistance to change; the source of the resistance is immaterial.

Limits of the Magnitude of Dissonance

The maximum dissonance that can possibly exist between any two elements is equal to the total resistance to change of the less resistant element. The magnitude of dissonance cannot exceed this amount because, at this point of maximum possible dissonance, the less resistant element would change, thus eliminating the dissonance.

This does not mean that the magnitude of dissonance will frequently even approach this maximum possible value. When there exists a strong dissonance that is less than the resistance to change of any of the elements involved, this dissonance can perhaps still be reduced for the total cognitive system by adding new cognitive elements. In this way, even in the presence of very strong resistances to change, the total dissonance in the system could be kept at rather low levels.

Let us consider an example of a person who spends what for him is a very large sum of money for a new car of an expensive type. Let us also imagine that after purchasing it he finds that some things go wrong with it and that repairs are very expensive. It is also more expensive to operate than other cars, and what is more, he finds that his friends think the car is ugly. If the dissonance becomes great enough, that is, equal to the resistance to change of the less resistant element, which in this situation would probably be the behavioral element, he might sell the car and suffer whatever inconvenience and financial loss is involved. Thus the dissonance could not exceed the resistance the person has to changing his behavior, that is, selling the car.

Now let us consider the situation where the dissonance

for the person who bought a new car was appreciable but less than the maximum possible dissonance, that is, less than the resistance to change of the less resistant cognitive element. None of the existing cognitive elements would then be changed, but he could keep the total dissonance low by adding more and more cognitions that are consonant with his ownership of the car. He begins to feel that power and riding qualities are more important than economy and looks. He begins to drive faster than he used to and becomes quite convinced that it is important for a car to be able to travel at high speed. With these cognitions and others, he might succeed in rendering the dissonance negligible.

It is also possible, however, that his attempts to add new consonant cognitive elements would prove unsuccessful and that his financial situation is such that he could not sell the car. It would still be possible to reduce the dissonance by what also amounts to adding a new cognitive element, but of a different kind. He can admit to himself, and to others, that he was wrong to purchase the car and that if he had it to do over again, he would buy a different kind. This process of divorcing himself psychologically from the action can and does materially reduce the dissonance. Sometimes, however, the resistances against this are quite strong. The maximum dissonance which could exist would, in such circumstances, be determined by the resistance to admitting that he had been wrong or foolish.

Avoidance of Dissonance

The discussion thus far has focused on the tendencies to reduce or eliminate dissonance and the problems involved in achieving such reduction. Under certain circumstances there are also strong and important tendencies to avoid increases of dissonance or to avoid the occurrence of dissonance altogether. Let us now turn our attention to a consideration of these circumstances and the manifestations of the avoidance tendencies which we might expect to observe.

The avoidance of an increase in dissonance comes about, of course, as a result of the existence of dissonance. This avoidance is especially important where, in the process of attempting to reduce dissonance, support is sought for a new cognitive element to replace an existing one or where new cognitive elements are to be added. In both these circumstances, the seeking of support and the seeking of new information must be done in a highly selective manner. A person would initiate discussion with someone he thought would agree with the new cognitive element but would avoid discussion with someone who might agree with the element that he was trying to change. A person would expose himself to sources of information which he expected would add new elements which would increase consonance but would certainly avoid sources which would increase dissonance.

If there is little or no dissonance existing, we would not expect the same kind of selectivity in exposure to sources of support or sources of information. In fact, where no dissonance exists there should be a relative absence of motivation to seek support or new information at all. This will be true in general, but there are important exceptions. Past experience may lead a person to fear, and hence to avoid, the initial occurrence of dissonance. Where this is true, one might expect circumspect behavior with regard to new information even when little or no dissonance is present to start with.

The operation of a fear of dissonance may also lead to a reluctance to commit oneself behaviorally. There is a large class of actions that, once taken, are difficult to change. Hence, it is possible for dissonances to arise and to mount in intensity. A fear of dissonance would lead to a reluctance to take action—a reluctance to commit oneself. Where decision and action cannot be indefinitely delayed, the taking of action may be accompanied by a cognitive negation of the action. Thus, for example, a person who buys a new car and is very afraid of dissonance may, immediately following the purchase, announce his conviction that he did the wrong thing. Such strong fear of dissonance is probably relatively rare, but it does occur. Personality differences with respect to fear of dissonance and the effectiveness with which one is able to reduce dissonance are undoubtedly important in determining whether or not such avoidance of dissonance is likely to happen. The operational problem would be to independently identify situations and persons where this kind of a priori self-protective behavior occurs.

Summary

The core of the theory of dissonance which we have stated is rather simple. It holds that:

1. There may exist dissonant or "nonfitting" relations among cognitive elements.

2. The existence of dissonance gives rise to pressures to reduce the dissonance and to avoid increases in dissonance.

3. Manifestations of the operation of these pressures include behavior changes, changes of cognition, and circumspect exposure to new information and new opinions.

Although the core of the theory is simple, it has rather wide implications and applications to a variety of situations which on the surface look very different. The remainder of the book will spell out these specific implications of the theory and will examine data relevant to them.

TWO

The Consequences of Decisions:
Theory

Although psychologists have paid a great deal of attention to the decision-making process, there has only been occasional recognition of the problems that ensue when a decision has been made. One of the major consequences of having made a decision is the existence of dissonance. But before going into this in detail, let us take a look at some of the statements that have recognized the problems of postdecision processes.

Discussing the problem of deciding between two mutually exclusive alternatives, both of which are attractive, Adams (1) states:

But mere decision is not the whole story. The unsatisfied appetite, the undischarged tension of the rejected alternative is still there unless a further process, which may be called "conflict resolution," takes place [p. 554].

In other words, Adams points out that after a decision is made, something must still be done to handle the unpleasantness of having rejected something which is, after all, attractive. He also suggests that this requires some "restructuring" or "revaluation" of the alternatives which were involved in the decision.

That this is not always easy or even possible, and that these discomforts or dissonances can build up and accumulate, is also recognized by Adams:

It can be said, however, that the person is fortunate in whom these revaluations or restructurings or insights occur as the conflicts arise rather than letting the latter accumulate until they precipitate a more or less violent, wholesale, and uncritical revaluation of valued objects [p. 555].

When Adams speaks of "conflict resolution" and the "accumulation of conflict," he is talking about "dissonance reduction" and "accumulation of dissonance." The broadness with which the term "conflict" has come to be used seems to me to include dissonance within it. I will later suggest a more restricted use of the term "conflict."

The fact that a decision, once having been made, gives rise to processes that tend to stabilize the decision has also been recognized, particularly by Kurt Lewin. For example, Lewin (36), in discussing the results of experiments on the effectiveness of group decisions, states:

In the experiment on hand we are dealing with a group decision after discussion. The decision itself takes but a minute or two. (It was done through raising of hands as an answer to the question: Who would like to serve kidneys, sweetbreads, beef hearts next week?) The act of decision, however, should be viewed as a very important process of giving dominance to one of the alternatives, serving or not serving. It has an effect of freezing this motivational constellation for action [p. 465].

And again in another article discussing similar material, Lewin (35) states:

This seems to be, at least in part, the explanation for the otherwise paradoxical fact that a process like decision which takes only a few minutes is able to affect conduct for many months to come. The decision links motivation to action and, at the same time, seems to have a "freezing" effect which is partly due to the individual's tendency to "stick to his decision". . . [p. 233].

This so-called "freezing effect" of decision would indeed result from the process of establishing cognitive elements consonant with the decision and eliminating dissonant elements. The end result would be that having made the decision, and having taken the consequent action, one would begin to alter the cognition so that alternatives which had previously been nearly equally attractive ceased to be so. The alternative which had been chosen would seem much more attractive, and the alternative which had been rejected would begin to seem less attractive than it had been. The result of the process would be to stabilize or "freeze" the decision.

Decisions Resulting in Dissonance

To understand why and when dissonance follows from a decision, let us first attempt to analyze one type of decision situation, namely, one where a choice is to be made between two positive alternatives. This discussion can easily be generalized to include other decision situations. Imagine a person having to choose between two alternatives, each of which is quite attractive to him. Before the decision is made he considers the features of each of the alternatives and, in some manner, compares them. Thus, for example, a person might have to make a choice between two very desirable jobs. Before the decision is made he would probably acquaint himself thoroughly with the details of each offer. We would then have a situation where, in his cognition, there were a number of elements that, *considered alone,* would lead him to choose job A and also a number of elements that, *considered by themselves,* would lead him to choose job B.

Eventually the person makes a decision—he chooses one of the two alternatives and, simultaneously, rejects the other. Let us examine the relations which then exist between the cognitive elements corresponding to this action and the cognitive elements that accumulated during the process of coming to a decision. Let us proceed as if the person in question chose job A and rejected job B. All of those cognitive elements that, considered alone, would lead him to choose job A are now consonant with the cognitive elements corresponding to the action he took. But there also exist a number of elements that, considered by themselves, would lead him to choose job B. All of these elements are now dissonant with the cognition about the action he took. The existence of this dissonance follows from the definitions in the previous chapter. Dissonance then will be a result of the simple act of having made a decision. Consequently, one may expect to see manifestations of pressures to reduce dissonance after a choice has been made.

Before proceeding to a discussion of the specific determinants of the magnitude of the dissonance which follows a decision and of the specific manifestations of the pressure to reduce it, a brief discussion expanding this analysis to include other types of decision situations is in order.

There have already been stated some excellent analyses of decision or conflict situations by Lewin (34) and by Hovland and Sears (27). I will not attempt to repeat them here, but will briefly summarize only what is pertinent to our purpose.

1. Decision between completely negative alternatives. While this is a theoretically possible condition, it probably rarely occurs. The mere presence of two negative alternatives does not put the person in a decision situation unless there are some other factors that force him to choose between them. If this occurs, the same consequences concerning dissonance will exist after the choice has been made. There will be some cognitive elements favoring the choice of one alternative and some cognitive elements favoring the choice of the other alternative. No matter which is chosen, there will then be a number of cognitive elements dissonant with the cognition about this action.

2. *Decision between two alternatives, each having both positive and negative aspects.* This is probably the most usual type of decision situation. It is certainly clear from our previous discussion that, here too, dissonance will result when action is taken. There will be some cognitive elements corresponding to the positive aspects of the unchosen alternative and some elements corresponding to the negative aspects of the chosen alternative which will be dissonant with the cognition of having chosen one particular alternative.

3. *Decision involving more than two alternatives.* Certainly many, if not most, decisions involve more than two alternatives. Many possibilities may be present initially, or the person in the decision situation may invent compromises, new modes of action, and the like. This added complexity makes the analysis of the decision process difficult but, happily, adds very little complexity to the analysis of the dissonances which exist after the decision is made. Once more, *all those elements that, considered alone, would lead to action other than the one taken are dissonant with the cognitive elements corresponding to the action taken.*

One may, then, offer the generalization that dissonance is an almost inevitable consequence of a decision, and proceed to an examination of the factors that affect the magnitude of this dissonance.

The Magnitude of Dissonance Following Decisions

How strong the dissonance is will depend, of course, upon the general determinants which we have stated in the previous chapter. The task here is to spell out the specific nature of these determinants as they exist in postdecision situations.

The *importance* of the decision will affect the magnitude of the dissonance that exists after the decision has been made. Other things being equal, the more important the decision, the stronger will be the dissonance. Thus, a decision to buy one automobile rather than another will result in more dissonance than a decision to buy one brand of soap rather than another; a decision to take one job rather than another will produce a greater magnitude of dissonance than a decision to go to a movie rather than a concert. In future chapters we shall refer to the variable of importance again and again since it is a general determinant of the magnitude of dissonance. Let us now move on to those considerations which are peculiar to postdecision situations.

Another major determinant of the magnitude of postdecision dissonance is the *relative attractiveness of the unchosen alternative*. This, of course, follows directly from our analysis of the postdecision situation and the reasons that dissonance exists at all. The dissonance exists because, following the decision, the person continues to have in his cognition elements that, if considered alone, would lead to an action other than the one he has taken or is engaged in. These elements reflect the desirable characteristics of the unchosen alternatives and the undesirable characteristics of the chosen alternatives. Consequently, the greater the relative attractiveness of the unchosen alternatives to the chosen alternative, the greater will be the proportion of relevant elements that are dissonant with the cognition corresponding to the action.

Figure 1 shows the relations we would expect between the magnitude of postdecision dissonance and the relative attractiveness of the unchosen alternative, holding constant the importance and the attractiveness of the chosen alternative. For any given relative attractiveness of the unchosen alternative, the more important the decision or the greater the attractiveness of the chosen alternative, the greater would be the resulting dissonance. As the relative attractiveness of

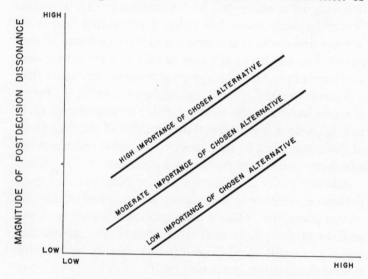

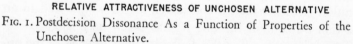

RELATIVE ATTRACTIVENESS OF UNCHOSEN ALTERNATIVE

Fig. 1. Postdecision Dissonance As a Function of Properties of the Unchosen Alternative.

the unchosen alternative decreases, the resulting dissonance also decreases. The pressure to reduce dissonance, it will be recalled, varies directly with the magnitude of dissonance. The discussion later on will focus on how the pressure to reduce dissonance will show itself in such situations.

First, however, it would be well to clarify a few points. Figure 1 is certainly not meant to imply that these relationships are linear. The exact form which these relationships would exhibit would, of course, depend upon the exact nature of the metric by means of which dissonance, importance, and relative attractiveness were measured. Since as of now there is no precise metric, it is not meaningful to talk about the exact form of the relationship. What can be stated, however, and all the figure is intended to convey, is the existence of steadily increasing functions.

It is best, before going on, to also discuss the distinction between conflict and dissonance, because they are dynamically different in their effects. The person is in a conflict situation before making the decision. After having made the decision he is no longer in conflict; he has made his choice; he has, so to speak, resolved the conflict. He is no longer being pushed in two or more directions simultaneously. He is now committed to the chosen course of action. It is only here that dissonance exists, and the pressure to reduce this dissonance is *not* pushing the person in two directions simultaneously.

Making this distinction necessitates specific usage of both terms. The term "conflict" has, unfortunately, come to be used very broadly by many persons. For example, in a recent article by Smock (50) on intolerance of ambiguity, one finds this statement:

Incongruity, by definition, indicates a stimulus configuration composed of elements that *conflict with the "expectancies" of the individual in the sense he seldom, if ever, is presented with such a stimulus configuration in a "real-life" situation* [p. 354, italics ours].

This statement has been chosen because it tries to specify the sense in which the word "conflict" is used. When persons speak of conflict between opinions or values, it is frequently difficult to know just what is meant. In Smock's use of the term, there is perhaps little distinction between it and dissonance. But the sense is clearly different from that use of the term that means an opposition of forces acting on the person.

Let us examine a predecision and postdecision situation to clarify the distinction. Imagine a person who has two job offers. All the cognitive elements corresponding to favorable characteristics of job A and unfavorable characteristics of job B (call this cognitive cluster A) steer him in the direction of taking job A. Cognitive cluster B, elements corresponding to favorable characteristics of job B and unfavorable characteristics of job A, steer him in the direction of taking job B. Since job A and job B are mutually exclusive, he cannot have both; he is in conflict.

But it is necessary to specify further where the conflict lies. It is not between cognitive cluster A and cognitive cluster B. That is, there is no conflict between knowing that job A is good and also knowing that job B is good. On a cognitive level this could simply add up to a nice, rosy picture of the world. There is no opposition between liking one thing and also liking another thing. The conflict arises because one must choose between the two possible courses of action. The person is pushed in two opposite directions at once.

Sooner or later the person makes the decision and chooses job A. Now he is no longer pushed in two opposite directions; he has chosen one of the alternatives and is no longer in conflict. But now cognitive cluster B is dissonant with his knowledge of the direction in which he is moving. This dissonance exists on a cognitive level. There is still no necessary relation between the two cognitive clusters; but while cognitive cluster A is consonant with the decision, cluster B is dissonant with it. The person now moves in one direction and attempts to reduce the cognitive dissonance.

A third variable affecting the magnitude of postdecision dissonance may be termed the degree of *cognitive overlap* of the alternatives which are involved in the decision. The degree of overlap is high if many of the elements in the cluster corresponding to one alternative are identical with elements of the cluster corresponding to the other alternative. High cognitive overlap is generally loosely implied when we speak of two things being "similar." Low degree of cognitive overlap is generally implied when we speak of two things being "qualitatively different." There is no overlap between the clusters of cognitive elements corresponding to two alternatives if none of the cognitive elements in one cluster is identical with any of the elements in the other cluster.

How, then, does the degree of cognitive overlap affect the magnitude of dissonance which results from a decision? It seems clear that the greater the cognitive overlap between the two alternatives, that is, the less the qualitative distinction between them, the smaller the dissonance that exists after the choice has been made. This follows from consideration of the reasons for the existence of dissonance. The dissonance, it will be recalled, exists between the cognitive elements corresponding to the action that has been taken and those cognitive elements that correspond to desirable features of the unchosen alternative and to undesirable features of the chosen alternative. But let us consider that subset of the elements that identically correspond to desirable features of both the unchosen and the chosen alternatives. Clearly, these elements are not dissonant with cognition about the action which has been taken since, considered alone, they would lead to the action taken just as cogently as they would lead to the rejected action. Exactly the same state of affairs exists with respect to those elements that correspond to identical undesirable aspects of both the chosen and the unchosen alternatives. Therefore, if the cognitive overlap is complete, that is, if *every* element in the cluster corresponding to one alternative also exists identically in the cognitive cluster corresponding to the other alternative, no dissonance at all will result as a mere consequence of the decision.

For example, if a person were offered a choice between $5.00 and $4.99, he would undoubtedly choose the first alternative. There would be no dissonance resulting from this decision even though the attractiveness of the unchosen alternative is very high relative to the attractiveness of the chosen alternative. The same absence of dissonance following the decision would hold irrespective of the absolute magnitude of the attractiveness of the alternatives. There is, of course, complete cognitive overlap. Every element corresponding to desirable properties of the unchosen alternative is identical with some element in the cluster corresponding to desirable properties of the chosen alternative. Similarly, we would expect the dissonance resulting from a choice between, say, two books to be less than the dissonance resulting from the choice between a book and a ticket to a concert. In the former instance, the cognitive overlap is undoubtedly greater.

Manifestations of Pressure to Reduce Postdecision Dissonance

As has been stated many times, the existence of dissonance will give rise to pressures to reduce it. Let us, consequently, examine the ways in which postdecision dissonance can be reduced. There are three main ways in which this might be accomplished, namely, (a) changing or revoking the decision, (b) changing the attractiveness of the alternatives involved in the choice, and (*c*) establishing cognitive overlap among the alternatives involved in the choice. The discussion will deal with them in that order.

CHANGING OR REVOKING THE DECISION

It should be emphasized that this analysis concerns itself with the state of affairs that exists immediately after the decision has been made and before further experience accumulates concerning the results and consequences of the action which has been taken. It must be recognized that at this point the existing dissonance cannot be overwhelming. Indeed, assuming that the individual chose the most favorable alternative, the weighted sum of the dissonances (each dissonant relation somehow weighted for its importance) would not exceed the weighted sum of the consonances. Consequently, reversing the decision, assuming this is possible for the moment, is not an adequate way of reducing dissonance since it would simply reverse which cognitive elements were dissonant or consonant with the cognition about the action. There may exist occasional temptations to reverse the decision since the person may be more troubled by the dissonance which exists than comforted by the consonances. But it would not constitute a reduction in dissonance. It would actually, in most cases, increase the dissonance and hence will not usually occur. It may happen that after additional information and experience has been acquired, the dissonance may have increased to a point where the person would desire to reverse the decision. It is probably correct, though, that the dissonance would have to become nearly overwhelming, that is, more than half of the cognitive elements would have to be dissonant with the cognition about the action taken, before reversal of the action would be a feasible means of coping with dissonance. This will be dealt with in later chapters.

It is possible, however, to reduce or even eliminate the

dissonance by revoking the decision psychologically. This would consist of admitting to having made the wrong choice or insisting that really no choice had been made for which the person had any responsibility. Thus, a person who has just accepted a new job might immediately feel he had done the wrong thing and, if he had it to do over again, might do something different. Or he might persuade himself that the choice had not been his; circumstances and his boss conspired to force the action on him. These are probably not usual types of solutions to the existence of dissonance. In essence they put the person back in conflict, that is, in the choice-making situation, although the choice need not, or perhaps cannot, be remade; or else it puts the person in a situation where he does not accept responsibility for what he does. These last two factors probably account in large measure for the rarity of this mode of eliminating dissonance.

CHANGING COGNITION ABOUT THE ALTERNATIVES

This is the most direct and probably most usual manner of reducing postdecision dissonance. Since the dissonance exists in the first place because there were cognitive elements corresponding to favorable characteristics of the unchosen alternative and also cognitive elements corresponding to unfavorable characteristics of the chosen alternative, it can be materially reduced by eliminating some of these elements or by adding new ones that are consonant with the knowledge of the action taken. The net effect of this would be to increase the proportion of relevant cognitive elements that are consonant with the action taken and hence to lessen the total dissonance that exists.

Whether or not a person is successful in reducing dissonance in this manner will depend in part on his mental agility and in part on the availability of support of one kind or another for the changes he wishes to make in his cognition. He may now be able to magnify the importance of the good points associated with the chosen alternative and to think of new advantages that he hadn't thought of before. He may be able to discover new information that favors the decision he took or to get others to agree with his action. Let us consider a hypothetical example to elucidate the process.

Imagine a person who has had to make a choice between going to a concert and accepting a friend's invitation to dinner, both being desirable activities for him. Further imagine that he accepts the dinner invitation, thus giving up the possibility of hearing the concert. He may now attempt to think of every bad thing he can about the concert. He may be very familiar with the works to be played which lessens the advantage of going to the concert. Or he may not be at all familiar with some of the things to be played, and he knows well from past experience that he doesn't get much out of hearing something for the first time. He might even reread a review of the last performance which happens to have been highly critical. In like manner he may try to think of attractive things about the evening he will spend in good social company.

Of course, the attempt to reduce dissonance might not be successful. The concert program might give no scope to his ingenious mind. The review he recalled as critical and reread might re-emphasize for him many favorable factors. And when he gets to his dinner party he might get into a conversation with someone else who wishes he had been able to go to the concert. Whether or not he gets support will determine, in part, the efficacy of these attempts.

Establishing Cognitive Overlap

As may be recalled from our previous discussion, the more the cognitive elements corresponding to the different alternatives involved in a decision are alike, the less is the resulting dissonance. Postdecision dissonance can consequently be reduced by establishing or inventing cognitive overlap. This type of reduction of dissonance is also stressed by Adams (1) in the previously cited article. In discussing a boy who has made a decision between playing ball and going to the circus, for example, he states:

> . . . our boy restructures the situation (and hence the sentiments involved) and experiences an insight such that the conflicting consummatory values are seen as alternative instruments or means to a single one. . . . Thus our boy may perceive for the first time that ball game and circus are both means to recreation in general . . . [p. 554].

In other words, one way of establishing cognitive overlap is to take elements corresponding to each of the alternatives and to put them in a context where they lead to the same end result. If this is accomplished, some cognitive elements are identical in this larger context, and dissonance is reduced.

It is also possible to establish cognitive overlap in a more direct fashion. Let us briefly revert to our example of the person who accepted the dinner party invitation. Following the decision, he may remind himself that his friend has a very good collection of records. Indeed, once there he might even suggest that some music be played. Or if he had alternatively chosen to go to the concert, he might consider that he would probably meet many of his friends at the concert and that afterward they would undoubtedly spend some time together socially. In other words, cognitive overlap may be established by discovering or creating elements corresponding to the chosen alternative that are identical with favorable elements that already exist for the corresponding unchosen alternative.

Detailed discussion of the possible reduction of dissonance by lowering the importance of the whole matter has been omitted, but it must be remembered that it can and does occur. Our hunch is that it is not a major manifestation of the pressure to reduce postdecision dissonance.

Summary

Dissonance has been shown to be an inevitable consequence of a decision. The magnitude of the postdecision dissonance has been hypothesized to depend upon the following factors:

1. The importance of the decision.
2. The relative attractiveness of the unchosen alternative to the chosen one.
3. The degree of overlap of cognitive elements corresponding to the alternatives.

Once dissonance exists following a decision, the pressure to reduce it will manifest itself in attempts to increase the relative attractiveness of the chosen alternative, to decrease the relative attractiveness of the unchosen alternative, to establish cognitive overlap, or possibly to revoke the decision psychologically.

The operational problems of testing this theory will be dealt with in the next chapter where data relevant to postdecision dissonance will be considered.

THREE

The Consequences of Decisions: Data

This chapter will be concerned with processes that arise from a decision and, consequently, will deal with situations where it is possible to observe what a person does following a decision. To corroborate the implications discussed in the previous chapter, it is necessary to show the theoretically anticipated differences in the person's behavior before and after making the decision. If one cannot manage to observe some evidence of the cognitive process itself, one must at least be able to measure some change in cognition. But all this is still not enough. It is also necessary to show that the magnitude of the effects dependent on the existence of postdecision dissonance does vary with changes in the variables that theoretically affect the magnitude of this dissonance, namely, importance of decision, relative attractiveness of unchosen alternative, and degree of cognitive overlap. Let us consider some data relevant to these questions.

Data on Advertising Readership

Since one manifestation of the pressure to reduce post-decision dissonance is the seeking of information which the person expects will supply cognition consonant with the action taken, readership of advertising is one possible source of data. Let us examine this a bit more closely. Ignoring for present purposes the objectives of advertising and the variety of more or less ingenious ways which advertisers use to capture people's attention, there is at least one thing common to all advertising which everyone knows from experience: it always boosts the product which is being advertised. It may state in general or specific ways why this product is good, it may recount how it is better than any number of unspecified competitive products, and the like. Clearly, then, advertising material is a potential source of cognition which would be consonant with having purchased the particular product being advertised. It would be a source to which persons who are trying to reduce dissonance might go.

Persons who have recently purchased a product usually have gone through a decision-making process and have made their choice. A person who has just purchased a new automobile most likely shopped around, examined various models, and finally made a decision to purchase one particular make of car. A person who goes to buy a suit will do likewise. He frequently will not purchase one before having shopped around sufficiently. Even a housewife who goes to a grocery store will probably look over the various brands of canned soup on display before making her selection. One could, consequently, regard a new purchaser of a product as a person who has recently made a decision. Pursuant to the discussion, such a person would be expected to have some cognitive elements dissonant with the decision which was made, and one would expect to observe some manifestations of the pressure to reduce dissonance. Reading advertisements about the product he bought would provide information that would be consonant with the cognition about having made the purchase, thus reducing the dissonance. Reading advertisements of competing products would probably increase the dissonance.

If the theory is correct, then, we would expect to find that recent purchasers of some product should, provided the purchase is an important one, read advertisements of the company whose product they bought and avoid reading the advertisements of competing companies. To test this implication of the theory of dissonance, Ehrlich, Guttman, Schönbach, and Mills (13) designed and conducted a study which involved interviewing purchasers of new automobiles concerning their reading of automobile advertising in the period immediately subsequent to the purchase. Specifically, they state:

The purchase of a new automobile, for example, is usually a rather important decision for a person. Considerable dissonance should exist for a new car owner immediately after he has bought his car; all "good" features of the makes he considered, but did not buy, and "bad" features of the one he bought are now dissonant with his ownership of the car. He should also attempt to reduce this dissonance [p. 98].

Certainly, there would be many ways in which this attempted reduction of postdecision dissonance could proceed. The study deals with only one of those possibilities, namely, the reduction of dissonance through acquiring more cognitive elements consonant with the cognition about the action taken and avoiding the acquisition of cognitive elements which would be dissonant with that action. The authors state that since automobile advertising contains material which praises only the make of car being advertised, the following results would be expected:

1. New car owners would read many more ads about the car they just bought than about other cars.

2. New car owners would tend to avoid reading ads about cars they considered but did not purchase.

3. Comparable owners of old cars should show little or no discrimination in their advertising reading since their dissonance would largely have been eliminated or at least stabilized. Furthermore, new car ads which emphasize all the attractive features of the latest model would hardly reduce the dissonance which may still exist in the owner of a car which is two years old.

The procedure employed was as follows: Sixty-five adult males in the Minneapolis area were interviewed four to six weeks after they had purchased a new automobile. Another sixty adult males who were roughly comparable to the new car purchasers in terms of neighborhood in which they lived, and who owned cars three or more years old, were also interviewed. Each respondent was contacted by phone to arrange a time for the interview. He was told that the interview would be part of a survey on readership of magazines and newspapers and was asked what magazines and newspapers he read regularly. When the interviewer visited him, he brought along the previous four weeks' copies of the magazines which the respondent had said he read regularly. This time interval was chosen so that the magazine issues would all have appeared subsequent to the purchase of the new car. The time interval was, of course, kept identical for the old car owners. The interviewer also brought with him the previous seven days' copies of those Minneapolis newspapers which the respondent read.

The main body of the interview was taken up largely with showing the respondent each automobile ad which appeared in the above-mentioned newspapers and magazines, asking whether the respondent had or had not noticed that ad, and if he had noticed it, whether he had gone farther and read all or some of it. At the conclusion of the interview the respondent was also asked to name those makes of cars that he had seriously considered before actually making his final purchase.

The results of the study, in terms of the average per cent of advertisements that the respondents noticed and the average per cent that they read *of those they had noticed,* are presented in Table 1.

Let us first examine the data for the new car owners. It is clear that they noticed a high proportion (70 per cent) of ads that dealt with the car they just bought. It is also clear that they went on to read an extraordinarily high proportion of those "own car" ads which they had noticed. On the average, a new car owner read 65 per cent of the

TABLE 1

Readership of "Own Car" and "Other Car" Ads

Ads Dealing with	Mean Per Cent of Ads Noticed by		Mean Per Cent of Ads Read by	
	New Car Owners	Old Car Owners	New Car Owners	Old Car Owners
Own car	70	66	65	41
Considered cars	66	—	40	—
Other cars	46	—	34	—
Considered plus other cars	48	41	35	30

ads he noticed which concerned his recently purchased automobile. The comparable percentages for the readership of ads dealing with other cars, that is, cars not at all involved in the decision, were, respectively, 46 and 34. Clearly, the prediction from dissonance theory is borne out so far. In the presence of dissonance following a decision, new car owners attempt to reduce their dissonance by reading material advertising the car they just bought.

The theory, however, also has something to say about the reading of ads dealing with cars they considered but did not buy. Specifically, it would be expected, from the theory, that they would avoid reading these ads since such material would increase their dissonance. The obtained data are not in line with this expectation. While it is true that "considered car" ads were read significantly less frequently than "own car" ads, they were read as much as (or perhaps slightly more than) "other car" ads; hence we can hardly speak of avoidance of these "considered car" ads. This inconsistency with the theoretical prediction can perhaps be understood if we realize that recent new car purchasers were still rather sensitive to car ads and were used to reading them. Undoubtedly, during the period of decision they had noticed and read ads of all the cars they were considering. This sensitivity continued, and they still noticed the ads of the cars they had considered. "Considered car" ads were noticed by new car owners almost as frequently as "own car" ads were noticed. However, they did not read them as much as they used to. There was, very likely, an attempt to avoid reading these ads which, until recently, they had perused very carefully. The existence of dissonance is, after all, only one among many determinants of behavior such as reading ads. It is not surprising that once in a while these other factors override the effects of pressure to reduce dissonance.

The higher sensitivity to car advertising among new car owners is also seen in the comparison with old car owners. New car owners noticed and read more car ads of all types than did old car owners. The big difference between the two groups lies, however, in the frequency with which they read ads of their own car. As expected, new car owners read "own car" ads much more than did old car owners, 65 per cent as compared with 41 per cent. For old car owners the data have not been presented separately for considered cars and other cars because the great majority of the old car owners did not mention any other makes they had considered before making their purchase. It is interesting to note that over a period of time, old car owners tended to forget or deny that they even seriously considered other makes.

One other incidental result emerged from this study which is interesting theoretically. Some of the new car owners, when asked which cars they had seriously considered before making their purchases, named two or more cars in addition to the one they bought. Others named only one car as having been seriously considered, and a few stated that they had not considered any other cars seriously. What is the implication of this difference for the magnitude of dissonance which would ensue following the purchase of the chosen car? Since all the cognitive elements corresponding to desirable features of rejected alternatives are dissonant with the action taken, the more alternatives that are involved in a decision (other factors held constant), the greater will be the dissonance following the decision. One would then expect, on theoretical grounds, that those new car purchasers who named two or more cars as ones they had considered and rejected would have greater dissonance following the decision and should, hence, show greater activity oriented toward reducing this dissonance. This turns out to be the case although the difference is not very marked. The excess of reading "own car" ads over reading "considered car" plus "other car" ads is 36 per cent for those who considered many cars and 26 per cent for those who considered only one or none. The difference, however, does not reach a statistically acceptable level of significance.

An Experiment on Confidence in Decisions

Another effect of the pressure to reduce postdecision dissonance which may be examined is the end result of the dissonance-reduction process. In order to do this, one would need data on the magnitude of the dissonance that exists immediately after having ·made a particular decision and also on the magnitude of dissonance that remains and persists. If there is pressure to reduce dissonance, then to the extent that the person's efforts in this direction are successful, the latter magnitude should be smaller than the former.

There are, of course, certain measurement problems here which must be solved before such data can be obtained. It is clearly impossible to measure the dissonance or consonance between each of the cognitive elements corresponding to the action taken and every other relevant cognitive element. Consequently, we must look for some overall measure that will reflect the total magnitude of dissonance which exists. In the experiment which we conducted, the results of which will be presented shortly, the actual measure employed was the subject's rating of how confident he was that his decision was the correct one. This measure was used on the assumption that the greater the dissonance, that is, the greater the number of cognitive elements corresponding to favorable characteristics of the unchosen alternative, the lower would be the confidence expressed by the subject. If this is true, one would then expect a reduction in dissonance to be reflected by an increase in confidence in the decision.

Another problem of design had to be solved before the data could be collected. How could one obtain two measures of confidence in rather close succession, one before the dissonance-reducing process starts and the second later on? Repeating such measurements presents problems of practice and memory. And how could one be certain that the initial measure came before any dissonance-reduction process had gotten under way? This problem was solved by having each subject make a pair of matched decisions, although the subject was not aware that they were closely matched. One of these decisions was a final, definite decision while the other was a purely tentative guess. One can then take the confidence expressed in the tentative guess as indicative of the magnitude of dissonance that would have existed had a final decision been made. If the theory is correct, the confidence expressed following the final decision should be greater than the confidence expressed in connection with the tentative one. The specific procedure employed in collecting the data is described below.[1]

Seven sets of numbers, ten in each set, were typed on index cards, each set of ten numbers on a separate card. The numbers varied from -50 to $+50$. Two of these sets were matched so that, for each, the average of the ten numbers was 4 points away from zero, one average being $+4$ and the other -4. These two sets were also matched so that they contained virtually the same numbers with opposite signs. Very slight differences in the actual numbers were allowed so that the subject would not perceive that the two sets were matched. These are the important sets for us. The other five sets had averages ranging from 2 to 7 points away from zero. One of these was used as a practice set, the other four being used as follows.

Each subject, when he came to the laboratory, was told

[1] The suggestion for this experiment was made to me by Dr. Francis W. Irwin in an informal conversation. I am deeply grateful to him. I would also like to acknowledge the help of Miss Danuta Ehrlich and Mr. Judson Mills in collecting the actual data.

by the experimenter that he was doing research on how people made decisions on the basis of partial information. The subject was told that each set of numbers typed on each index card had been drawn at random—each set from a different group of 250 numbers. The task for the subject was to examine each set of numbers and then to make the best decision he could as to whether the average of all 250 numbers from which that random sample was drawn was positive or negative. He was also told that in some instances he would see a sample of only ten numbers while in other instances he would see twenty numbers before being asked for his decision. (For each of sets A, B, D, and F, that is, those given first, second, fourth, and sixth in order, there was prepared an additional card containing another set of ten numbers, presumably drawn from the same 250 as the set on the first card. The purpose of this will be explained shortly.) After he had made his decision he was also to state how confident he was that his decision was correct. He was asked to do this using a scale from zero to one hundred, where zero meant it was only a guess and one hundred meant that he was completely and absolutely certain that his decision was correct.

For each of sets A and B, the first two given, the experimenter said, "On this set we have a sample of twenty numbers drawn at random from a larger group of numbers. After you have seen all twenty numbers, you are to make a decision as to whether the average of the larger group is positive or negative. However, it makes a difference whether a person is asked to look at twenty numbers all at once or only ten at a time. Consequently, I am going to show you these numbers ten at a time. I will give you the first card and after you have finished looking at that I will take it away and give you the second card. You will have to look very carefully at the first card because you will have to make your final decision based on all twenty numbers and so will have to remember what you learn from the first card."

On these sets (A and B) where the subject was to make his final decision after seeing twenty numbers, he was given the first card and as he was handing this card back to get the second, the experimenter said, "What would you say about the average so far?" and then, "About how confident would you say you are so far?" The subject was then given the second card and asked for his final decision and confidence based on all twenty numbers.

For sets C and E, the ones given third and fifth in order, the subject was given only one card and was told, "On this set I have a sample of only ten numbers. On the basis of just these ten numbers you are to make your decision as to whether the average of the larger group from which these ten were drawn at random is positive or negative."

The critical matched sets, D and F, were given fourth and sixth in the order of presentation. For half of the subjects, set D was presented as a sample of ten numbers, thus yielding a final decision after seeing the first card, and set F was presented as a sample of twenty numbers but again only ten numbers (i.e., one card) at a time, thus yielding only a tentative judgment after seeing the first card. For the other half of the subjects this was reversed, set D yielding the tentative judgment and set F yielding the final decision. The second ten numbers, when given, were designed, of course, to emphasize the fact that the final decision was on the basis of all twenty numbers so that the subject's response after seeing the first card would be only a tentative judgment. The only data of concern to us, however, are the subjects' responses to the first ten numbers alone.

In order to control for any possible effects which the experience on the early sets of numbers would have, half of the subjects, on those sets where they received a second card to look at before making their final decision, were shown a second card that strongly supported the conclusion that would have been reached on the basis of the first card. The other half of the subjects received second cards which strongly contradicted the conclusion they would have reached on the first card. Data were collected from a total of 137 subjects.

The data to be presented concern the confidence the subjects expressed after seeing only the first card on the two matched sets, D and F. Each subject made two statements. One of these statements was an expression of confidence in a tentative judgment where the final decision was still to come; the other was an expression of confidence following a final decision. The information the subjects had was in both cases virtually identical—the cards were closely matched. Since the order of presentation was also balanced, that is, the final decision came before the tentative decision half the time and afterward the other half, any difference between the confidence in these two decisions is attributable to the fact that one was final and the other tentative. One may be reasonably sure that the subjects paid the same amount of attention to the card in both cases because when it was part of a sample of twenty numbers, he had to remember the first ten in order to make his final decision later.

If the confidence the subject expressed in his tentative judgment was an adequate, overall measure of the relative amount of information he had which did not support the judgment he inclined to at the moment (the lower the confidence, the greater the amount of contrary information), then it can also be regarded as a measure of the amount of dissonance which would have existed if a final decision had been made. One would expect the confidence the subject expressed in his final decision to be greater than in his tentative judgment if, indeed, following the decision there was pressure to reduce the dissonance which existed. Table 2 presents the obtained data in terms of the number of subjects for whom the confidence expressed in the final decision was greater than, equal to, or less than, the confidence expressed in connection with their tentative judgment. The data are presented separately for those subjects for whom "second cards" supported, and those for whom "second cards" contradicted, their tentative decisions.

Altogether, seventy subjects showed higher confidence in their final decision than in their tentative judgment.

TABLE 2

COMPARISON OF CONFIDENCE IN CORRECTNESS
OF FINAL AND TENTATIVE DECISIONS

Number of Subjects for Whom

	Final Greater than Tentative	Final Equals Tentative	Final Less than Tentative
Supporting condition	37	10	20
Contradicting condition	33	15	22
Total	70	25	42

Forty-two subjects showed the opposite trend. It is clear from Table 2 that there is a significant tendency for the subjects to state a higher confidence in connection with a final decision than in connection with a tentative judgment based on the same information (ten numbers). Furthermore, whether the second card, when there was one, supported or contradicted the tentative judgment made on the first card did not materially affect the tendency to express higher confidence in the final decision. One might, if seeking an alternative explanation for the result, imagine that perhaps the difference between final and tentative confidence was a result of previous experience with the way the tentative judgments seemed to stand up. From this type of notion one would expect that perhaps in the contradicting condition where the second card always contradicted the impression gained from the first card, the confidence in later tentative judgments would have been depressed and, hence, the final confidence might have turned out to be higher. This sort of explanation would then imply that the effect would be considerably stronger in the contradicting condition than in the supporting condition. The data, however, show no such difference. If anything, the effect seems to be somewhat weaker in the contradicting than in the supporting condition. For both conditions combined, the proportion of subjects whose final confidence is higher is significantly greater (1 per cent level of confidence) than the proportion whose final confidence is lower.

On the other hand, it should also be emphasized that the effect of postdecision dissonance in this experiment was small. Seventy subjects showed a difference in the theoretically predicted direction while forty-two subjects showed a difference between final and tentative confidence in the opposite direction. While the results are statistically different from chance, they are not otherwise significant. It must be borne in mind, however, that we were dealing with a decision that was rather unimportant to the subjects. The dissonance which existed was not very great in magnitude.

An Experiment on Change in Attractiveness of Alternatives

It will be recalled that one of the major ways in which postdecision dissonance can be reduced is by changing the attractiveness of the alternatives so that the discrepancy between the chosen and rejected alternatives is increased. It is certainly possible to measure this kind of change directly, at least in relatively simple situations. An experiment was designed and conducted by Brehm (7) to test the theory using this type of measurement. The objective of this experiment was simple, namely, to give persons a choice between two objects and to measure change in attractiveness of the objects from before to after the decision was made. The exact procedure employed was as follows.

Each subject was told by the experimenter that he was engaged in market research for a number of manufacturers of various kinds of products. These manufacturers were planning new sales campaigns to expand their markets and wanted to discover whatever they could about how people reacted to their products. Each subject (they were all female college students taking the introductory psychology course) was told that college students were one among many kinds of groups that were being studied. The experimenter then apologized for asking the student to spend some of her time in this manner; participation in experiments should be educational, and this was mere market research. Because of this the experimenter felt the student should be recompensed somehow for the time she spent, and he would give her a rather valuable gift from one of the manufacturers in return for helping out in the study.

The experimenter then took eight products out of their cartons and arranged them in front of the subject, briefly explaining something about each. Each of the objects was worth about twenty dollars. Specifically, they were an automatic toaster, an electric coffee maker, a small portable radio, a desk lamp, a silk screen print of a painting, a stop watch, an art book, and a sandwich grill. The subject was told these were the products being studied, and she was invited to inspect each one carefully.

After she had inspected and was familiar with each, the student was handed a sheet of paper on which she was asked to rate each of the products in terms of how attractive it was to her, considering all aspects of the product as she reacted to it. These ratings were made on an eight-point scale ranging from (1) *definitely not at all desirable* to (8) *extremely desirable.*

The subject was then reminded of the fact that she was to be given a gift for participating in the study. It was explained that each manufacturer had contributed a number of his products to be given away in this manner, and she would be given one of the eight products which she had just finished evaluating. In order to be sure that the experimenter didn't run out of one product in case everyone wanted the same thing and, on the other hand, in order to be sure that each subject had some choice so that she didn't end up with something she didn't want, a scheme had been worked out whereby each subject, it was explained, was given her choice between two of the products. The subject was then told which two products she could choose between. After she made her choice, the chosen product was wrapped up and given to her, and the other products were returned to their cartons.

Each subject was then asked to read research reports concerning four of the products. These reports had presumably been made by an independent research organization. Each of the reports mentioned a number of both good and bad characteristics of the product under consideration. After reading the reports, the subject was asked to tell the experimenter what she felt was the salient feature of each report. This step was included in the experiment to allow some time to elapse before another rating of the eight products was requested and also to obtain some data concerning which parts of the reports the subject paid most attention to.

After this step was concluded, the subject was asked to rate each product again on the same scale she had used before. The experimenter explained to her that the original rating might be considered a first impression of the products and, now that she had had more time to consider them, he would like her to rate them again. After these ratings were completed, the experimenter explained the experiment and what he was actually investigating. Unfortunately, each subject could not be allowed to take a valuable gift home with her since the experimenter was only a poor graduate student at the time. All subjects, he reports, took this in good grace. They did, incidentally, get credit in their introductory psychology course for their participation.

Within this procedure it was possible to vary a number of the factors which, theoretically, should affect the magnitude of dissonance. The two products between which the subject was to choose were selected by the experimenter after having seen her initial ratings of the products. For each subject, one of the products involved in the choice had been rated as quite desirable, point 5, 6, or 7 on the scale. For about one-half of the subjects, the other object had been rated one point below on the scale, that is, 4, 5, or 6, respectively. For the remaining subjects, the second product involved in the choice had been rated, on the average, two and one-half scale points below the other product. Thus, following the decision the first condition should, theoretically, result in high dissonance, and the second, in moderate or low dissonance. For half of the subjects in each of these conditions, two of the four research reports they read dealt with the two products involved in the choice. For the other half of the subjects all the research reports dealt with products that had not been involved in the decision. This was done to discover how the availability of information about the products affected the degree to which, and the manner in which, the dissonance was reduced. This made four conditions in all, data being collected from about thirty subjects in each condition.

A fifth experimental condition was also conducted in the same manner as described above except that no choice at all was presented to the subject. Instead, at the point where the subject was given a choice in the other conditions, the experimenter simply selected one product, told the subject that this was her gift, wrapped it up, and gave it to her. The gift chosen by the experimenter was always one that had been rated at point 5, 6, or 7 by the subject.

The results, analyzed in terms of changes in the attractiveness rating of the objects from before to after having made a decision, are presented in Table 3 (p. 66).

Let us examine the data from Table 3 in relation to the predictions from the theory of dissonance. The pressure to reduce dissonance following the decision, if effective, should be reflected in an increase in the attractiveness of the chosen object and a decrease in the attractiveness of the rejected object. In all conditions where dissonance was created by a decision (this does not include the gift condition), there was some reduction of dissonance. The magnitude of dissonance reduction was significant for both of the high dissonance conditions and for the low dissonance condition where the subject did not see a research report dealing with the objects involved in the choice.

The theory states that the more cognitive elements there are corresponding to desirable features of the rejected alternative, the greater would be the dissonance following the decision and, hence, the greater the pressure to reduce dissonance. One would, hence, expect that in the high dissonance conditions, where the rejected alternative was initially closer in attractiveness to the chosen alternative, the pressure to reduce dissonance would be stronger than in the low dissonance conditions. To the extent, then, that this pressure was effective, one would expect to observe greater reduction of dissonance in the high than in the low

TABLE 3

REDUCTION OF POSTDECISION DISSONANCE BY CHANGING THE ATTRACTIVENESS OF CHOSEN AND REJECTED ALTERNATIVES

	Net Change from First to Second Rating for		
	---	---	---
Condition	Chosen Object	Rejected Object	Total Reduction of Dissonance
Without research reports			
Low dissonance (N * = 33)	+.38 †	+.24	+.62
High dissonance (N = 27)	+.26	+.66	+.92
With research reports			
Low dissonance (N = 30)	+.11	.00	+.11
High dissonance (N = 27)	+.38	+.41	+.79
Gift (N = 30)	.00	—	—

* N is the number of cases.

† In all instances a positive sign means a change in the direction of dissonance reduction. Changes toward increased attractiveness of the chosen alternative and decreased attractiveness of the unchosen alternative are in the direction of reducing dissonance.

conditions. This holds for both comparisons, with and without research reports. When the subjects read research reports dealing with the objects involved in the choice, the total reduction in dissonance for the low condition was only .11, while the comparable figure for the high condition was .79, a statistically significant difference. When the subjects did not see research reports dealing with the alternatives involved in the decision, the comparable figures were .62 and .92, a difference which is not statistically significant but is in the same direction. In short, the greater the experimentally created dissonance, the greater the ensuing reduction of dissonance.

The effect on the reduction of dissonance of the introduction of research reports dealing with the objects which had been involved in the choice is less clear. It had been anticipated that these research reports, by giving the subject an opportunity to acquire new cognitive elements, would facilitate the effective reduction of dissonance. If this were true, one would expect the total reduction of dissonance, as well as the difference between the high and low dissonance conditions, to have been greater in the condition where the subjects saw research reports concerning the chosen and rejected objects than in the conditions where they did not. The latter of these two expectations was indeed borne out by the data. The difference in total reduction of dissonance between high and low conditions was large and significant for those subjects who saw research reports concerning the chosen and rejected alternatives. For the other subjects the difference was smaller and not significant.

But altogether, there is less total reduction of dissonance with research reports than without research reports. The explanation for this probably lies in the nature of the research reports themselves. These reports were written to contain a mixture of good and bad statements about the object. For example, the research report on the electric grill read as follows:

This grill is versatile, grills toast, sandwiches, hot dogs, frozen waffles, etc. Waffle plates may be easily attached (cord and optional waffle plates are not supplied, these require additional purchases). The grill plates may be damaged if kept heated too long (7 or 8 min.) in closed position. The heat indicator dial fluctuates, usually underestimating amount of heat. The outer surface is durable, easy to clean, won't rust [Brehm, p. 62].

It may be that the negative characteristics mentioned in these research reports were so strong that for many subjects the reduction of dissonance was made more difficult. Thus, under high dissonance conditions the subjects' total reduction of dissonance was lessened somewhat while under low dissonance conditions the effect of these negative attributes in the research reports was to make the attempted reduction of dissonance completely unsuccessful.

Let us now turn to a discussion of the gift condition which up to now has been ignored. This condition was introduced as a control because there is at least one other, not implausible, explanation of some of the results we anticipated. According to the analysis in the last chapter, the dissonance in the Brehm experiment exists as a result of having made a decision. The cognitive elements corresponding to favorable characteristics of the rejected alternative were dissonant with the cognition about action taken. If there is no rejected alternative, then there should be little or no dissonance. In the absence of a control condition, however, it would be possible to maintain that the increase in attractiveness of the chosen alternative comes about solely as an effect of ownership. Indeed, people have maintained that ownership does have this kind of effect. Thus Heider (25) states, for example, "The situation is balanced if we like what we own and own what we like [Part II]." Heider further states that if the situation is not balanced, processes will ensue in an attempt to create balance and harmony. Thus, he would expect an increase in the attractiveness of an object simply as a result of ownership.

And there are, indeed, studies which show precisely this kind of effect, that is, increased preference resulting from mere ownership. Irwin and Gebhard (28), for example, conducted a series of experiments in which a person was shown two objects, was arbitrarily given one to keep as his own, and was told the other object was for someone else. The subject was then asked to state which of the two objects he liked better. In one experiment, using residents of an orphan home ranging in age from fourteen to nineteen years, 25 out of 38 subjects indicated a preference for the object they were given. In another experiment with children from five to eight years of age, 28 out of 36 subjects preferred the object they now owned. The effect of mere ownership is not terribly strong, however. For example, in another experiment in which the recipient of the other object was to be a friend of theirs, only 16 out of 30 subjects indicated a preference for the object they owned.

Another experiment by Filer (21) indicates the same type of effect. Using children ranging from six to nine years of age as subjects, he had them play a game after which they either won or did not win a predesignated object. The results show that the children increased their liking of the object if they won it and decreased their liking of it if they did not win it. The effect again seemed to be one of mere ownership since it was not affected by whether the object was won through merit or chance, or whether they expected to win it.

Whatever the reason for this effect of ownership, it is necessary to demonstrate that the change in attractiveness of the objects in the Brehm experiment is not attributable to simple ownership. In Table 3 (p. 66) it is clear that, at least in this experiment, the effect of ownership itself is zero. There was no change at all in the attractiveness of the object received as a gift. The change obtained in the other conditions is unequivocally attributable, then, to the reduction of dissonance. It is interesting to speculate for a moment on the reasons why Brehm found no effect of a gift while Filer (21) and Irwin and Gebhard (28) did.

There are at least two possible explanations for this. In the Brehm experiment the gift condition was conducted only with research reports concerning the object given to the subject. The negative impact of these research reports, which we have already discussed, may have counteracted any increase in attractiveness due to ownership. Another possible explanation may lie in the fact that Brehm used college students as subjects while the other investigators dealt mainly with children. It is conceivable that mere ownership is a more potent thing for children than for adults. For children there may be some dissonance between owning an object and cognitions corresponding to undesirable features of that object.

Before leaving the Brehm experiment, there is one additional set of results which will be discussed. Some subjects in the experiment were given a choice between two objects which had many elements of similarity and where, consequently, there would result considerable cognitive overlap of the elements corresponding to the two objects. It will be recalled from the discussion in the previous chapter that where there is cognitive overlap between the alternatives involved in a decision, the resulting dissonance will be weaker. If the cognitive elements corresponding to desirable characteristics of the rejected alternative are identical with elements corresponding to desirable characteristics of the chosen alternative, then these elements are not dissonant with cognition about the action taken.

Consequently, the data were analyzed separately for those subjects who had been given a choice between any two among the coffee maker, the toaster, or the grill (all kitchen objects connected with eating) or who had been given a choice between the art book and the silk screen reproduction (both art objects). For the subjects who had these objects to choose between, the decision should produce less dissonance; one would, hence, not expect to see as much evidence of pressure to reduce dissonance. The results for these subjects were quite unequivocal. When there was cognitive overlap, regardless of the experimental condition, there was no evidence of any reduction of dissonance. Altogether, for a total of thirty subjects the total reduction of dissonance measure was —.28, a negligible amount which is actually in the direction of increasing rather than reducing dissonance.[2]

The Difficulty of Reversing Decisions

If there is a change in attractiveness of alternatives following a decision such that the chosen alternative becomes more desirable or the unchosen alternative becomes less desirable, or both, then there are additional consequences of this reduction in dissonance which must be examined. In the Brehm experiment, for example, where changes in attractiveness of the alternatives occurred as predicted from the theory of dissonance, one would expect that if in some way the subjects had to make the decision over again, the second decision would be easier for them to make since the two alternatives are now more different in attractiveness than they had been. Likewise, if for some reason they had to reverse their decision, one would expect this to be a very difficult thing for them to do even though the initial decision may have been a close one.

A study reported by Martin (38) is pertinent to this

[2] The measure of total reduction of dissonance used here and in the previous results (Table 3, p. 66) gives the amount of change in the attractiveness of the alternatives involved in the choice compared with a baseline of changes in initially similarly rated objects not involved in the choice. In this way any effects of repeated ratings or regression are dealt with.

question. The subjects in this study, eight of them in all, were each given a series of decisions to make. Twenty-six of these decisions were of a hypothetical character. A situation was described, two alternative courses of action were offered, and the subject was asked to decide which he would follow. A typical example is: "You have made a true but damaging statement about an individual who is pronouncedly hostile to you: Would you rather apologize to your enemy, or make a public defense before an unsympathetic audience?" [P. 17.] The other decisions involved a series of choices as to which of two odors the subject would prefer to smell. After each decision he actually was required to smell the one he had chosen.

Following each decision, the subject was asked to give an introspective account of the process of making the decision and also to rate the degree of confidence he had in his choice and the degree of difficulty he had in making it. For half of the decisions the subject was then given a slip of paper which read: "Now endeavor to reconsider your decision and make a reversal of your choice [p. 21]." For half of the decisions, then, data exist on the process of making the decision and also on the process of attempting to reverse the decision after it had been made.

Before we proceed, it may be well to say a word about the validity and trustworthiness of the kind of data which this study yields. The study used trained subjects (professional psychologists or students trained in introspection) and depended almost exclusively on introspective reports for its data. For many years now this type of data has been in disrepute, perhaps justifiably so. One may not want to trust a person's introspections as giving an adequate description of psychological processes, nor may conscious processes be of central importance. But for present purposes one can treat these data just as one would treat data collected from interviews.

Present-day research workers would also feel consider-able uneasiness about the use of hypothetical examples which are, perhaps, farfetched in relation to the experience of the subject. The subjects were, of course, instructed to try to make the decision a personal matter and to deliberate carefully about it. The question, however, is, did they? As far as one can make out from the detailed reports of the subjects' introspection, surprisingly they did—at least such trained subjects did. The evidence for this was the real conflict they reported while making the decision, the evident discomfort they felt when contemplating some of the alternatives, and the great difficulty they had in trying to reverse their decision when asked to. Surely this last would have been an easy matter if the decisions had been made on an impersonal and hypothetical basis. At any rate, let us take the data for what they are worth and see what they show.

On the basis of the verbal reports describing the process of making the decision, Martin distinguished three types of decisions.

1. Preference. These decisions were characterized by a clear preference for one of the alternatives over the other. The decisions were important, but usually there was not very great conflict. The preferred alternative was suffi-ciently preferred so that the choice was made rather easily. Of incidental interest to us here in relation to dissonance theory and the Brehm experiment is Martin's description of what frequently happened in this type of decision after the decision was made.

. . . there was a tendency to justify the alternative chosen, by specific reasons, which often arrived with a "rush," thus en-hancing the satisfaction of the choice. This process may well be classed as one of "rationalization" in the commonly accepted psychological sense, i.e., a process of justification for the choice after its completion to satisfy oneself rather than of affording

logical presentation of reasons to influence the process before-
hand [pp. 40–41].

2. *Conflict.* These decisions were characterized by considerable difficulty because the alternatives were so nearly
equal in attractiveness. The alternatives were apparently so
nearly equal that

> The decision comes slowly and with effort. . . . The choice may
> be attended with doubt and a disagreeable feeling tone as op-
> posed to assurance and satisfaction: there may even sometimes
> occur a tendency to wish afterwards that the other had been
> chosen [p. 46].

3. *Indifference.* These decisions were characterized by
lack of clear preference for one alternative over the other
and also by indifference about the whole matter. The decision was highly unimportant for the subject here.

All of the decisions made by each subject were classi-
fied in one of these three categories. Since this categorization is important, let us consider some of the more objective evidence for its validity. If the characterization of the
three types is accurate, one would then expect the actual
time it takes to make the decision to differ markedly
among them. The preference type should have a relatively
low decision time simply because one alternative is so
much more attractive than the other. The indifference type
should also have a rather low decision time since, although
the alternatives are not too different in attractiveness, the
decision is not important. The conflict type, on the other
hand, should show a rather long time of decision. Table 4
presents these average decision times. It is clear that these
data support the validity of the categorization of decision
types. In both the hypothetical situations and the choices
between odors, the conflict type had markedly higher decision time than the others.

One would also expect, of course, that the reported degree of difficulty in making the decision would parallel differences in decision times, and indeed they do. The subjects were asked after each decision to rate the difficulty of

TABLE 4

AVERAGE DECISION TIME
(In Seconds)

	Decisions Characterized by		
	Preference	Conflict	Indifference
Hypothetical choice	23.3	51.0	37.2
Choice between odors	4.1	14.1	6.2

making the decision. We will not take the space to reproduce these figures since they show precisely the same thing that the decision time shows.

After each decision the subjects were also asked to rate how confident they were that the decision was a good one. These confidence ratings were made on a four-point scale. If the categorization of the decision types is valid, we would *not* expect these confidence ratings to correspond to the decision time measures. On the contrary, the preference type which showed a very low time of decision should yield the highest confidence rating. Table 5 shows these

TABLE 5

AVERAGE DEGREE OF CONFIDENCE FOR EACH TYPE OF DECISION
(Measured on a Four-Point Scale)

	Decisions Characterized by		
	Preference	Conflict	Indifference
Hypothetical choice	3.7	2.4	2.0
Choice between odors	3.9	2.8	1.9

data, and we may notice that this was the case. For both varieties of decision, the confidence was highest for the preference type and lowest for the indifference type—lowest here, undoubtedly, because the decision regarded as of little importance was made hastily and without too much thought. All these data lead us to accept the validity of the categorization.

Now let us consider the data on reversals, that is, on what happened when the subject was instructed to try to reverse his decision. For the preference type of decision, one would expect there to have been great difficulty reversing the decision. These were decisions that were made quickly, easily, and confidently because the preference of one alternative over the other was clear. Reversing the decision would have meant reversing this clear preference. It is not surprising then that in Table 6, which presents the

TABLE 6

Per Cent of Decisions That Subjects Could Not Reverse

Decisions Characterized by

	Preference	Conflict	Indifference
Hypothetical choice	90.3	75.8	40.0
Choice between odors	84.2	50.0	10.0

data, it is found that 90 per cent of the decisions of the preference type could not be reversed for the hypothetical choices and 84 per cent for the choices between odors. After trying to reverse these decisions, the subjects reported that it was impossible.

But what would one expect concerning the conflict and indifference decisions? In both of these types there was no clear preference for one alternative over the other. Thus, if nothing had changed as a result of having made the decision, it should have been easy to reverse that decision. But if, as a result of dissonance consequent upon the decision, there was some effective reduction of dissonance by changing the attractiveness of the alternatives, then some difficulty of reversal might have been encountered. From the stated theory concerning dissonance, one would expect that for unimportant decisions the magnitude of dissonance following the decision would be rather small and consequently there would be little if any change in attractiveness of the alternatives. In other words, in the indifference type of decision one would expect little dissonance, little pressure to reduce dissonance, and little difficulty in reversing the decision.

In the conflict type of decision, however, one would expect that following the decision there would be considerable dissonance. The pressure to reduce this dissonance would lead to increasing the attractiveness of the chosen alternative or decreasing the attractiveness of the rejected alternative, or both. If, following such a successful process of reducing dissonance, the subject were asked to reverse the decision, one would expect to find that he had considerable difficulty in doing this. Table 6 indeed shows this to have been the case. For the hypothetical choices, only 40 per cent of the indifference type could not be reversed while 76 per cent of the conflict type showed no reversal. For the choices between odors, these percentages were 10 and 50, respectively.

In short, the data revealed what we were led to expect theoretically. With the creation of dissonance following a decision, the pressures to reduce this dissonance lead to stabilizing the decision. Following the decision, provided appreciable dissonance is present, the alternatives are more different than during the decision, as we saw in the Brehm experiment. One consequence of this is the difficulty or impossibility of reversing the decision once it is made.

The Effect of Decision on Future Action

A number of studies have been reported in the literature in which lectures or individual instruction are compared with group decision in terms of their effectiveness in producing some change in behavior. These studies are summarized by Lewin (36). They generally show that after a group decision there is more change of behavior than after a persuasive lecture.

Although these studies are rather well known, it is worth while to review one of them briefly to show the details of the procedure commonly employed in these studies and to illustrate the effects which are involved. In one study, which was part of a program of research on changing food habits during the last war, an attempt was made to persuade housewives to increase their use of glandular meats. Six women's groups were used in the study. In three of them an informative and persuasive lecture on the matter was given, accompanied by the distribution of recipes. A follow-up (made a week later) determined that only 3 per cent of the women from these groups had gone ahead and served a glandular meat which they had never before served.

Instead of a lecture, approximately the same information was imparted to the other three groups during a group discussion of the matter. In addition, at the end of the meeting the women were asked to indicate, by raising their hands, who would serve their family one of the meats they had never served before. The follow-up indicated that from these groups, 32 per cent of the women actually did serve a new glandular meat. The obtained difference between the conditions is rather striking. Other studies using different types of groups and different kinds of "action to be taken" have produced comparable results.

Let us examine these results from the point of view of the

theory of dissonance. In those groups where no decision was asked for, some persons may have been sufficiently persuaded by the lecture to go ahead and do whatever had been recommended. In the study reviewed briefly, the action was serving glandular meats, and about 3 per cent of the women were persuaded by the lecture to go ahead and serve them. However, in the groups that were induced to make a decision, dissonance may have been created by that decision. The knowledge that they or their husbands wouldn't like the glandular meats, for example, would have been dissonant with the action they took in deciding to serve such meat. Pressures to reduce this dissonance would then arise, and to the extent that they were successful in reducing it, one might expect them to convince themselves, and each other, that perhaps their husbands would like it after all. Once the cognition was changed in this manner, the fact that so many went ahead and actually served the glandular meats is not surprising. In other words, the effect on action would be a consequence of the successful reduction of dissonance following the decision.

Although it is possible to explain the results of these group-decision studies in terms of the reduction of post-decision dissonance, it must be kept in mind that many other explanations are possible. The studies on group decision are largely uncontrolled, with many factors varying simultaneously. Because of this they cannot be regarded as providing good evidence in support of the theory of dissonance. The important thing to be pointed out, however, is that the results are consistent with the implications of the theory of dissonance; and what is more, if these results are a consequence of dissonance reduction, other implications also follow. For example, dissonance theory would imply that the same type of effect would occur whether the decision was made publicly in a group or by an isolated individual, whether it was made following a discussion or following a lecture. The important thing is that a decision was made and that dissonance resulted from this decision, and not whether there had or had not been group discussion preceding the decision or whether the decision itself was public or private. The group-decision studies, by simultaneously manipulating all these variables, make it impossible to pinpoint the interpretation more closely.

A study by Bennett (4), however, makes an attempt to separate these various factors and to examine their separate effects. The subjects used in this experiment were students in the introductory psychology class at the University of Michigan. The study was concerned with getting students to volunteer to serve as subjects in psychological experiments. The attempt to sort out the possible contributing effects of the variables that were generally grouped together in the group-decision studies involved using twelve conditions. Approximately one-third of the subjects heard a lecture which attempted to persuade them to volunteer. Another third of the subjects (in groups of about thirteen persons) had a group discussion about it, during which the experimenter imparted the same information contained in the persuasive lecture. The remainder of the subjects were not persuaded at all; they were simply and briefly reminded of the fact that requests would be made for volunteers.

Within each of these conditions there were four variations of requested decision. For approximately one-fourth of the subjects no decision was requested at all. For another fourth, individual anonymous decisions were requested by asking each student to write down an anonymous statement expressing whether or not he was willing to volunteer. Another fourth of the subjects were asked to raise their hands if they were willing to volunteer, although no attempt was made to record openly who did and who did not raise their hands.

The remainder of the subjects were asked to raise their hands if they were willing to volunteer, and the experimenter openly recorded the names of those who raised their hands. Thus altogether there were twelve conditions in which "no persuasion," "lecture," and "group discussion" were combined with "no decision," "private decision," and two varieties of "public or group decision." The experiment was conducted with small class sections so that the subjects in the twelve conditions could be approximately matched on the basis of their responses to a questionnaire concerning their attitudes toward volunteering for psychological experiments. One may, then, regard the subjects in each of the twelve conditions as initially the same in terms of willingness to volunteer.

Soon after the experimental manipulations discussed above had taken place, all subjects were sent letters telling them to come to a certain place at a certain time if they wanted to volunteer. The important data for us to examine are the proportions of subjects in the various conditions who actually showed up at the designated time and place. The data show no difference at all between the "lecture," "discussion," and "no persuasion" conditions. The percentages of subjects who showed up at the designated time and place are, respectively, 22, 21, and 19. In other words, neither the persuasive lecture nor the group discussion was more effective than a simple reminder in persuading people to volunteer. It is certainly possible that more persuasive lectures or more effectively conducted group discussions might have had a significant effect, but in this experiment, we may ignore this variable for present purposes and see if the type of decision made any difference in how many actually did show up to volunteer. Table 7 (p. 82) presents these data.

An examination of Table 7 shows a rather slight tendency for the "no decision" condition to have fewer persons actually coming to the designated place to volunteer. The difference between the "no decision" condition (15 per cent) and the "private anonymous decision" condition (29 per cent) is significant at the 1 per cent level of confidence. If all the decision conditions are combined (22 per cent), the difference as compared with the "no decision" condition is significant at the 7 per cent level of confidence. There seems to be some effect of decision per se, although in this experiment the effect is rather small and does not compare in magnitude to the effects reported in the less well-controlled group-decision experiments.

It is clear from the Bennett experiment, however, that the effect is not attributable to "public decision" as compared with "private decision." In this experiment the largest

TABLE 7

Effect on Action of Different Conditions of Decision

Condition	Total Number of Subjects	Number of Subjects Who Showed Up	Per Cent of Subjects Who Showed Up
No decision	135	20	15
Private anonymous decision	112	32	29
Public anonymous decision	113	22	19
Public identified decision	113	22	19

effect was obtained when the decision was a private and anonymous one.

The Bennett study provides some additional data relevant to the implications of the theory of dissonance. If the dissonance interpretation is correct, and the difference in action was a consequence of the reduction of postdecision dissonance, one would expect there to have been some cognitive change. That is, after having made the decision, the pressure to reduce dissonance would have led to a generally more favorable attitude toward volunteering than the subject had before. It will be remembered that the conditions were initially equated on just exactly this attitude toward volunteering. A few weeks after the experiment the subjects were given another questionnaire asking their attitude toward volunteering. The percentage expressing positive attitudes was 45 for the "no decision" condition and 54 for the three decision conditions grouped together. The difference is again small and does not reach an adequate level of statistical significance (13 per cent level of confidence), but it is in the direction one would expect and, perhaps, of a magnitude comparable to the small difference obtained on the actual action of volunteering.

Summary

This chapter has reviewed a number of studies which in one way or another deal with events that occur after a decision has been made. The data show:

1. Following a decision there is active seeking out of information which produces cognition consonant with the action taken.

2. Following a decision there is an increase in the confidence in the decision or an increase in the discrepancy in attractiveness between the alternatives involved in the choice, or both. Each reflects successful reduction of dissonance.

3. The successful reduction of postdecision dissonance is further shown in the difficulty of reversing a decision once it is made and in the implication which changed cognition has for future relevant action.

4. The effects listed above vary directly with the magnitude of dissonance created by the decision.

FOUR

The Effects of Forced
Compliance: Theory

There are circumstances in which persons will behave in a manner counter to their convictions or will publicly make statements which they do not really believe. As will be shown later, such a state of affairs is accompanied by dissonance and by various manifestations of pressure to reduce the dissonance. Before examining why dissonance exists in such situations and how the pressures to reduce dissonance manifest themselves, it is necessary to discuss the circumstances in which this type of discrepancy between public behavior and private belief occurs. Only if the conditions that produce such a situation are clearly understood is it possible to analyze when and why dissonance occurs.

Let us imagine that influence or pressure is exerted on a person to change his opinions or beliefs or actions. Sometimes such influence will not be successful in that no change is brought about. Sometimes it will be successful in the sense that the person will actually change his opinions or beliefs. Other times such influence may be successful in that the person changes his overt behavior or overt verbal expression of his opinions while *privately* he still holds to his original beliefs. The type of successful influence that actually changes the opinion or belief will be discussed in detail in Chapter Eight which deals with the role of social support in reducing dissonance. The present discussion will concern itself mainly with overt or public compliance *without* accompanying change of private opinion. A few years ago I published an article (16) in which I attempted to state the theoretical conditions under which public compliance without private acceptance occurs. I will briefly summarize that discussion here.

Public compliance without an accompanying change in private opinion or belief will occur when the following conditions exist:

1. The compliance is brought about mainly through the exertion of a threat of punishment for noncompliance, the individual against whom the threat is directed being sufficiently restrained from leaving the situation. Under such circumstances the person is faced with the alternatives of complying or of suffering the threatened punishment. If the threatened punishment is stronger than whatever resistance he has to showing compliance, he will overtly change his behavior or statements. In this case, however, his private opinion will not be affected. If no other factors enter the situation, he will continue to believe privately what he has held to previously.

2. The compliance is brought about mainly through the offer of a special reward for complying. Under these circumstances, if the reward is sufficiently attractive to overcome the existing resistance, the individual may comply overtly in order to obtain the promised reward. Once more, if compliance is obtained in this manner on an overt or public level, the private opinion will remain essentially unchanged for the moment and hence will be at variance with the public behavior or expression.

The empirical question, of course, arises as to how one can identify and distinguish public compliance without private change from instances where private opinion is also altered. Clearly, this must be done by somehow identifying the discrepancy between overt behavior or statement and private opinion. There are two general ways in which this may be done.

1. The first is by removing the source of influence or pressure. Assume that a person exhibits a certain changed behavior in the presence of others who have exerted pressure on him to behave in that manner. One may then attempt to observe the behavior of this person when he is *not* in the presence of those people. If private change has occurred, the behavior should persist under these circumstances. If the change has been only on the level of public compliance, the behavior should revert to what it had been previously.

Coch and French (10) cite an example which illustrates this type of measurement. They report a study of a factory in which slight job changes had been causing considerable difficulty. Workers who had been operating at satisfactory speeds frequently showed marked drops in production following such a change. In instances where the workers never recovered their previous level of production, the authors feel that group standards to restrict production were largely responsible. They give a striking example of a presser who, together with a number of others, had her job changed slightly. The average production of these pressers dropped from 60 to about 50 units per hour. After ten days or so, this particular presser started to increase her production above the level of the others with whom she worked. The authors state, "Starting on the thirteenth day when she reached standard production (60 units per hour) and exceeded the production of the other members, she became a scapegoat of the group. During this time her production decreased toward the level of the remaining members of the group [p. 520]." In other words, in the face of threats and punishment, this presser, who perhaps wanted to work faster, complied with the pressure exerted on her by the others in the group.

Twenty days after the change, the other pressers were transferred to other jobs leaving the one with whom we are concerned alone at this particular work. Her production immediately increased markedly. During the first four days alone she averaged 83 units per hour and thereafter worked steadily at the rate of 92 units per hour. In other words, when the source of the pressure had been removed, her behavior did not stay the same. It is clear that she had been complying publicly without private acceptance; that is, her private opinions were not in favor of production restriction.

2. The second way to identify the discrepancy between overt behavior and private opinion is by direct measurement of private opinion. In the above example there was never any direct measurement of the private opinions of the presser. These were simply inferred from her change of behavior after the removal of the other girls. In addition to observing the public behavior, it is also possible to identify a discrepancy between public and private opinion by eliciting a statement under circumstances where the person is assured of anonymity. The latter may be regarded as reflecting private opinion. If the anonymous and public statements differ, there is evidence that public compliance without accompanying private change of opinion has occurred.

Before proceeding to a discussion of the circumstances under which dissonance results from *forced compliance* (we shall use this term as shorthand for public compliance without private acceptance), let us digress momentarily to the empirical world to see whether forced compliance is indeed produced by threat of punishment and by offer of special reward. Once we have satisfied ourselves on this point we will be able to pursue our theoretical discussion with more assurance.

McBride (39) and Burdick (9) conducted two experiments specifically designed to test whether or not public compliance resulted from threatened punishment or offered reward. The two experiments were jointly designed so that all groups were run identically except that in the experiment by McBride there was an offer of reward for compliance, in the experiment by Burdick there was a threat of punishment for noncompliance, and in the control groups there was neither offer of reward nor threat of punishment.

The results were as follows:

1. Reward condition. Of 135 subjects in 32 different groups, 19 (14 per cent) showed forced compliance. That is, they changed their overt opinion when a reward was offered for compliance but then reverted to their initial opinion on an anonymous questionnaire.

2. Threat condition. Out of 124 subjects in 32 different groups, 15 (12 per cent) showed forced compliance.

3. Control condition. Out of 116 subjects in 31 different groups, only 3 (3 per cent) showed evidence of forced compliance. The difference between the control condition and either of the other conditions is highly significant statistically.

In short, the evidence does show that forced compliance does occur when the pressure to comply is accompanied by threat of punishment or offer of reward. In the absence of threatened punishment or offered reward, forced compliance does not occur frequently. More data from these studies will be considered in the next chapter which discusses the dissonance that results from forced compliance.

The details of the procedure of these experiments will be described then. For now, suffice it to say that threat of punishment or offer of special reward does produce some degree of forced compliance, and consequently, we can use these a priori conditions to infer the existence of such compliance as well as the dissonance resulting from it. Now let us proceed to a discussion of how and why dissonance results from such situations.

Dissonance Resulting from Forced Compliance

From the point of view of the purpose here, the most obvious aspect of a situation in which compliance has been forced by either the offer of reward or the threat of punishment is that once compliance is exhibited, there is a non-correspondence between the overt behavior and the private opinion. On the one hand, there are cognitive elements corresponding to the opinion or belief in question, and on the other hand, there are cognitive elements corresponding to the overt behavior or statement. These two sets of elements are clearly dissonant with one another.

The statement that there is a dissonant relation between these two sets of elements follows immediately from the definition of dissonance in Chapter One. It was stated there that two elements would be considered in a dissonant relation if, considering those two alone, the obverse of one would follow from the other. It is clear that in considering forced compliance, the overt expression or behavior would certainly not follow from the private opinion considered alone. One may assert, then, that dissonance is to some degree an inevitable consequence of forced compliance. When relevant data are considered in the next chapter, it will frequently be assumed that if reward was promised for compliance, or if punishment was threatened for non-compliance, at least some persons would exhibit forced compliance and, hence, suffer dissonance.

The Magnitude of Dissonance Resulting from Forced Compliance

As was stated in Chapter One, the magnitude of the dissonance that exists between two clusters of cognitive elements is in part determined by the proportion of the relations between relevant elements that are dissonant. The greater the proportion of dissonant relations, the greater is the magnitude of the total dissonance which exists between the clusters. Let us, then, examine what cognitive elements exist which are consonant, and what elements exist which are dissonant, with cognition about the overt behavior in a situation of forced compliance. It should be possible to identify factors that would affect the relative proportion of dissonant to consonant relations. Each relation, you will recall, is somehow weighted by the importance of the elements involved.

In a forced compliance situation one can unequivocally identify a set of cognitive elements that are clearly consonant with the overt behavior. These elements correspond to the knowledge that a reward has been obtained or that a punishment has been avoided. To determine the magnitude of dissonance which exists, it is crucial to determine the number and importance of the cognitive elements which are dissonant with the cognition about the overt behavior and to know something about the weighted proportion of dissonance which exists. It is clear, just as was true in the case of dissonance resulting from decision, that the weighted proportion of dissonant elements cannot be greater than 50 per cent. Presumably the expected reward or punishment had to be sufficient, in relation to the resistance to change, to produce the compliant behavior in the first place. Consequently, it is a reasonable inference to suppose that the sum of consonant relations is greater than the sum of dissonant relations.

It also becomes apparent from the preceding discussion that the magnitude of the reward or punishment, that is, the attractiveness and desirability of the offered reward or the unpleasantness and undesirability of the threatened punishment, is an important determinant of the magnitude of dissonance which exists once compliance is exhibited. Too great a reward or punishment will result in only little dissonance. Consider, for example, a situation where a man came up to you and said he would give you a million dollars if you publicly stated that you liked reading comic books. Let us assume, for the sake of the example, that you believe him and that you do not like reading comic books. Very likely you would publicly announce your preference for comic books, pocket the million dollars, and be quite content. There is some slight dissonance, to be sure. You said you liked comic books and you really do not. But there are some very important elements that are consonant with having uttered this public statement, namely, the knowledge of the money now in your pocket. Relative to this, the dissonance is negligible. Essentially the same situation would ensue if a person threatened to shoot you unless you publicly declared you liked comic books. As the promised reward, or threatened punishment, becomes smaller in importance, the dissonance resulting from compliance increases. The maximum possible dissonance would be created if the reward, or punishment, was just barely enough to elicit the desired overt behavior or expression.

But also of interest to us here is the situation that results if the reward offered, or the punishment threatened, is too small and, hence, the compliant behavior is not elicited. Under such circumstances the individual continues to show overt behavior which is in line with his private beliefs, but nevertheless, dissonance will be present. The elements corresponding to his opinions and beliefs will be consonant with the cognitive elements corresponding to his overt behavior, but the latter will be dissonant with the knowledge of the reward he has not obtained or the punishment he will suffer. Here, of course, the dissonance will be greatest if the reward or punishment just barely fails to elicit the compliant behavior. From this point on, the weaker the reward or punishment, the less will be the dissonance.

One should also state for the sake of completeness that the more important the opinions or behavior involved, the greater will be the magnitude of dissonance accompanying forced compliance. In other words, holding constant the weighted proportion of dissonant elements, the greater the importance of the situation, the greater will be the magnitude of the dissonance.

Figure 2 shows graphically the relationships among these variables. Just as in Figure 1 (p. 38), straight lines have been indicated. This does not mean that the predicted relationships are linear but rather that, not knowing the precise form of the relationship, this is the simplest way of indicating the direction of the relationship. In the figure, three curves have been drawn for three different degrees of importance of the opinion involved.

Let us first examine the solid portions of the lines. These indicate the relation between the magnitude of reward or punishment and the magnitude of dissonance when forced compliance *has* occurred. The point along the horizontal axis where these lines reach their peak is, of course, intended to represent that magnitude of reward or punishment which is just barely sufficient to elicit the compliant overt behavior.

The higher the importance of the opinions involved, the greater is the magnitude of reward or punishment necessary to elicit forced compliance and the greater is the magnitude of dissonance that is created. These solid lines are conceptually similar to those in Figure 1 which described the relations for postdecision dissonance. This similarity can be clearly seen if we speak loosely and describe the person

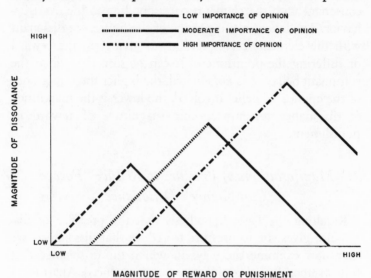

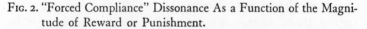

MAGNITUDE OF REWARD OR PUNISHMENT

Fig. 2. "Forced Compliance" Dissonance As a Function of the Magnitude of Reward or Punishment.

The solid portions of every curve refer to situations where forced compliance has occurred; the dashed portions refer to situations where forced compliance has not occurred.

who has shown forced compliance as having made a decision to take the reward or to avoid the punishment, having rejected the alternative of behaving in line with his private opinions.

The dashed lines in Figure 2 indicate the relations between magnitude of reward offered, or punishment threatened, and the magnitude of dissonance when forced compliance *has not* occurred. That is, the reward or punishment has been insufficient to elicit the compliant behavior. These lines are dashed to help us remember that the dissonant and consonant relations are reversed. The elements corresponding to the opinion held privately are now consonant with the elements corresponding to the overt behavior. The latter, in this portion of the figure, are dissonant with the elements corresponding to giving up the reward or suffering the punishment. It can be seen that when the compliant behavior is *not* elicited, the higher the importance of the opinion or belief involved, the lower is the magnitude of dissonance for any specific magnitude of reward or punishment.

Manifestations of Pressure to Reduce "Forced Compliance" Dissonance

Recalling the basic hypothesis that the presence of dissonance gives rise to pressure to reduce that dissonance, we may now examine the ways in which the dissonance that follows upon forced compliance may be reduced. Apart from changing the importance of the beliefs and behaviors involved, there are two ways in which the dissonance may be reduced, namely, by decreasing the number of dissonant relations or by increasing the number of consonant relations. Let us then consider how each of these may be accomplished in a situation of forced compliance.

When the magnitude of the threatened punishment or promised reward has been sufficient to elicit the compliant overt behavior, dissonance is present only as long as the person involved continues to maintain his initial private opinions or beliefs. If following the forced compliance he can succeed in changing his private opinion also, the dissonance may disappear entirely. Thus, for example, if a person whose political ideology is rather conservative is induced to make liberal statements publicly in order to obtain some political favor, the dissonance could be completely eliminated if he actually comes to believe in the liberal statements which he has publicly uttered. Since a situation where reward or punishment is offered to obtain forced compliance may frequently be accompanied by other types of influence, argument, and persuasion, this type of resolution of the dissonance should not be an uncommon one. The act of forced compliance should now predispose the person to be more amenable to exertions of influence which will change his private opinion and hence eliminate the dissonance which exists. Thus one would expect that sometimes forced compliance would be followed by change of private opinion.

One would expect that since the pressure to reduce dissonance depends upon the magnitude of dissonance that exists, a change of private opinion would follow public compliance more frequently when the punishment or reward is relatively weak than when it is too strong. Thus, if one wanted to obtain private change in addition to mere public compliance, the best way to do this would be *to offer just enough reward or punishment to elicit the overt compliance*. If the reward or threat were too strong, only little dissonance would be created and one would not expect private change to follow as often.

Where the threat of punishment or offer of reward is not strong enough to elicit the overt compliant behavior, opinion change in the opposite direction would serve to reduce the dissonance somewhat: if the person changed his private opinion so that he was now even more certain of his initial stand on the matter and saw even more arguments in favor of it, the number of consonant relations would increase and hence the total dissonance would decrease. Thus, it would seem that with respect to obtaining change of private opinion, the offer of reward or punishment which is not sufficient to elicit the overt behavior may be worse than nothing in that it serves to impel the person to increase his original conviction.

The other cognitive elements which may be changed to reduce the dissonance are, of course, those corresponding to the reward or to the punishment. If forced compliance has been elicited, the number of consonant relations may be increased by magnifying the importance of the reward obtained or of the punishment avoided. If this can be accomplished, the total dissonance will be somewhat reduced. For example, imagine that a person walking home at night is approached by a shabbily dressed man who demands some money. Further imagine that the person takes out his wallet and gives the beggar a considerable sum. He then may attempt to convince himself that the shabbily dressed man was really dangerous and would have harmed him greatly if he had not given the money. Similarly, if the reward or punishment was not sufficient to elicit the compliant behavior, the dissonance may be reduced by minimizing the importance of the reward or punishment.

When examining relevant data in the following chapter, we will look for either of these two types of manifestations of pressure to reduce dissonance wherever a situation can be identified in which there was an offer of reward for compliance or a threat of punishment for noncompliance.

Summary

Some data have been presented to document the assertion that public compliance without accompanying change in private opinion occurs when a reward is offered for compliance or when some punishment is threatened for failure to comply. Dissonance inevitably follows such a situation. If public (i.e., forced) compliance is elicited, then the private opinions are dissonant with the cognitive elements corresponding to the overt behavior. If the promised reward or threatened punishment fails to elicit the public compliance, then the knowledge concerning the reward or punishment is dissonant with the cognitive elements corresponding to the overt behavior.

The dissonance thus established, the magnitude of which will be a function of the importance of the opinions involved and of the magnitude of the punishment or reward, may be reduced in either of two ways:

1. Subsequent change of private opinion to make it consonant with the overt behavior.

2. Magnification of the reward or punishment to increase the consonance with the overt compliant behavior.

FIVE

The Effects of Forced
Compliance: Data

The implications of the theory of dissonance which have been elaborated in the preceding chapter would lead one to expect that at least occasionally we should be able to observe forced compliance leading to eventual private acceptance. From casual observation and anecdote, most of us know instances where this seems to be the case. For example, a child who is forced to practice piano may come to accept the necessity of practice; a person moving into a new neighborhood who is forced to conform to certain gardening standards may come to privately accept the opinions and standards which his neighbors have.

There are also rather anecdotal reports from various investigations that seem to point to the occurrence of this phenomenon. Bettelheim (5), for example, reports that some of the internees in German concentration camps, after having been forced to behave in accordance with the opinions and values of the guards, eventually came to accept those opinions and values.

But such knowledge derived from casual or incidental observation is far from sufficient and far from satisfactory.

For the purposes of testing the implications of the theory which has been presented, one would be more satisfied with a demonstration that this phenomenon does occur under controlled conditions. The following would be a desirable set of conditions for the demonstration of this phenomenon:

1. Experimental creation of the conditions which would lead to forced compliance, that is, either offer of reward for compliance or threat of punishment for noncompliance.

2. Unequivocal identification of those individuals who exhibit forced compliance at some time under these circumstances.

3. Evidence that at least some of these persons eventually do show private acceptance even though nothing new is added to the situation.

Data which essentially fit these requirements are available from the experiments conducted jointly by Burdick (9) and McBride (39) which we mentioned in the last chapter (p. 88). It is necessary to describe the details of the procedure in order to see how these requirements are met.

Groups of high school students, ranging from five to seven members each, were organized as discussion clubs. At their first (and only) meeting they were asked to discuss the problem of curfew regulations and their effect on high school athletic events. Each member was asked to write down his opinion as to whether or not curfew regulations should be removed on the nights of high school athletic contests so that those contests could be scheduled later in the evening. After the experimenter collected these statements of opinion (each person had checked either Yes or No), a tally of opinion for the group was handed back to each person. This tally of opinion was fictitious and gave each person the impression that everyone else in the group disagreed with him. They were then asked to discuss the issue by writing notes to one another. The experimenter

collected the notes which were written and delivered prepared notes which urged the recipient to change his opinion.
After fifteen minutes of this note-writing discussion, they
were asked once more to write down their opinion so that
the experimenter could prepare another tally to give to
each one showing just what each person's opinion was.
After collecting these second opinion statements, the experimenter explained that they had no time for further discussion that day and asked them to answer a questionnaire
which they were assured was anonymous. (They were
instructed not to put their names on the questionnaire.)
Among other questions on this questionnaire they were
again asked to state their opinion on the curfew issue.

There was thus obtained (a) an initial private statement
of opinion before they knew the opinions of others, (b) a
second statement of opinion that was made after they knew
everyone else disagreed with them and after influence had
been exerted on them, this second opinion to be made public,
and (c) a third statement of opinion for which they were
assured of anonymity. Thus if a change of opinion occurred
from the first to the second statement and this change was
maintained on the anonymous questionnaire, this indicated
that private change of opinion had occurred by the end of
the experiment. If, however, a change occurred from the
first to the second opinion statement but the third statement
reverted to the initial opinion, this indicated that public
compliance without private acceptance had occurred and
persisted.

The control groups, those in which there was neither
promise of reward nor threat of punishment, were conducted as described above. Certain differences were introduced in the other conditions as follows.

1. Offer of reward for compliance. When subjects were
recruited for these discussion clubs, the experimenter men-

tioned that it might be possible to obtain tickets for them to a university basketball game. When the clubs met, they were told that unfortunately, only enough tickets had been secured so that one person in each group could have a ticket. They were further told that after the discussion they would vote on who should get the ticket to the game. The first two notes given to each person contained no hint of reward. The third note each person in these groups received during the discussion read: "I think that you've put up some of the best arguments here, but I just don't see why you don't change your mind. If you did, I know that I'd vote for your getting the ticket [McBride, p. 41]." The fourth note each one received read: "I just got a note from ———, and we just agreed that if you would only change your mind and be on our side we'd rather you get the ticket than anybody else and we'd both vote for you [McBride, p. 41]."

Thus each person in this condition was offered a reward by others in the group if he would comply and agree with them.

2. *Threat of punishment for noncompliance.* In this condition the possibility of getting tickets to a basketball game was also mentioned to the subjects when they were recruited. When the clubs met, each member was actually given a ticket to an important game. They were told, however, that the experimenter was a bit short on tickets and that anyone who didn't want the ticket should return it. Also, the group would be given an opportunity at the end of the session to vote on whether any particular person in the group should have his ticket taken away. The third and fourth notes which the subjects in this condition received were similar to the notes quoted above except that instead of promising to give the subject the ticket, they threatened to vote to deprive him of his ticket unless he changed his mind. Thus each

person in these groups was threatened with punishment unless he complied and agreed with the others. Actually, all subjects in these experiments were given a free ticket to the game irrespective of the condition.

In the previous chapter, data were presented showing that in both the reward and the punishment conditions there was an appreciable number of persons who showed forced compliance while there were virtually no such persons in the control groups where neither reward nor punishment was offered. It will also be recalled that forced compliance was identified by a discrepancy between what the person stated on a vote which was to be made public to the others in the group and what he stated on an anonymous questionnaire.

In other words, someone who changed his opinion from his initial private statement to the public statement and changed back again on the anonymous questionnaire was judged to have shown forced compliance. Those who changed their minds from the initial statement of opinion to the public vote and maintained this change on the anonymous questionnaire were considered to have truly changed their opinion.

Considering only the three opinion statements, it is not possible to identify whether there were any subjects who, after having shown forced compliance, changed their private opinion too. From the three opinion statements alone, these persons were indistinguishable from others who had been influenced to change their opinion without any intervening forced compliance. But further data are available from the notes which the subjects wrote during the written discussion. In these notes it was occasionally quite clear that a person was showing forced compliance. For example, after receiving a note which threatened punishment for noncompliance, a subject wrote back to the supposed sender of that note saying, "O.K. I changed my mind," and then continued arguing for his original opinion in the notes he sent to others in the group. For these subjects it is clear from their notes that at least for a time they were publicly complying although their private opinion remained unchanged. It is possible to examine whether or not these subjects, by the time of the anonymous questionnaire, had also changed their private opinions. The data for the three conditions are shown in Table 8.

It is clear from an examination of Table 8 that a small percentage of subjects (7 and 6 in the reward and threat conditions, respectively) first showed public compliance without private acceptance and later showed private change

TABLE 8

Instances of Different Types of Opinion Change

Per Cent of Subjects Who Showed

Condition	Only Forced Compliance	Forced Compliance Leading to Private Change	Only Private Change
Reward (N = 135)	14	7	16
Threat (N = 124)	12	6	10
Control (N = 116)	3	0	11

also. This, of course, is true only in the threat and reward conditions. It is of interest to note that the control condition does not differ materially from the two experimental conditions in the per cent of subjects who showed private change of opinion uncomplicated by any forced compliance. These were subjects who had been influenced simply by the persuasive notes they received or by the fact that they perceived so many of their fellows disagreeing with them, or by both. The threat of punishment for noncompliance or offer of reward for compliance seems to have had no material effect on the frequency with which this type of opinion change occurred. The only effect of these variables was to elicit forced compliance from some subjects. A number of these latter, however, end up as persons who have changed privately through the route of eliminating dissonance.

There is, then, some evidence from a controlled situation that the phenomenon we have discussed does occur. While in this experiment the frequency of its occurrence was indeed low, it must be remembered that the whole duration of the discussion was fifteen minutes. Indeed, only about eight to ten minutes elapsed from the receipt of the first note mentioning punishment (or reward) to the answering of the anonymous questionnaire.

In order to illustrate some of the varieties of situations in which forced compliance with resulting dissonance may be elicited, I will discuss two studies which are interpretable along these lines. These studies were conducted in order to determine whether or not inducing a person to speak or argue overtly in favor of some position would, in and of itself, contribute to changing this person's private opinion in the direction of what he had publicly stated.

The first of these studies to be discussed here was reported by King and Janis (31). The subjects in this experiment were male college students. Several months before the actual experiment was conducted, the opinions of these students concerning various aspects of military service for college students were measured. The experiment proper involved presenting each student with a persuasive communication which contained arguments to the effect that (a) over 90 per cent of college students would be drafted within one year after their graduation and (b) the length of military service required of the majority of college students would be at least three years. There were three different conditions under which this persuasive communication was presented to the subjects.

1. Improvisation condition. These subjects, after having silently read the persuasive communication, were asked to make a speech into a tape recorder without further reference to the document they had read. The speech was, of course, to be along the same lines as the document. They were told that the recording of their speech would later be presented to a group of judges who would judge its excellence.

2. Oral reading condition. The subjects in this condition were treated in the identical fashion as those in the improvisation condition except for the fact that they were asked simply to read the document into the tape recorder. Thus in the improvisation condition, the emphasis for the subjects was on the effectiveness with which the arguments were organized and stated in the speech as well as manner of delivery. For the oral reading condition, the subjects simply read the prepared document. The entire emphasis for them was on manner of delivery, intonation, and expression.

3. Control condition. These subjects were asked only to read the persuasive communication silently. Nothing more was required of them. From this condition it was possible to estimate the impact of the prepared document uncomplicated by any overt actions on the part of the subjects. Differences between this condition and the other conditions might be attributable to the fact that the subjects in the other conditions had publicly (to the experimenter and a group of judges via tape recording) uttered the opinions.

Immediately after the experimental session, their opinions concerning the prospects of military service for college students were again measured. The data which King and

Janis present consist primarily of comparisons among the three conditions with respect to change of opinion in the direction advocated by the persuasive communication.

Before examining the results, however, let us examine what one would expect the data to show. As has already been mentioned above, no overt action was forced or elicited at all in the control condition. Consequently, there was certainly no forced compliance involved here and any opinion change which occurred in this condition must be attributed entirely to the persuasive character of the communication itself. The amount of opinion change in this condition serves as a baseline from which to evaluate the amount of opinion change occurring in the other conditions.

But in the improvisation and oral reading conditions, overt behavior was elicited by the experimenter. The subjects were asked to improvise a speech (or to read one) which was to be judged for its excellence. The content of the speech was not, however, in agreement with the private opinions of most of the subjects. Essentially, then, the subjects were offered a reward (winning the contest) to make overt statements which were dissonant with their private opinions. Hence some of the subjects would have shown forced compliance.

Thus in the improvisation condition, some subjects attempted to make a good speech and to offer good arguments in favor of a point of view which they themselves did not hold. There would then have been dissonance between their private opinion and the knowledge of what they were doing. This dissonance, following the theory, could have been materially reduced by changing the private opinion in the direction of accepting the point of view presented in the persuasive communication. One would consequently expect to find appreciably more change of private opinion in the direction advocated in the persuasive communication in the improvisation condition than in the control condition.

The situation created for the subjects in the oral reading condition is quite different. Here they simply read word for word from a script. Compliance with the instructions from the experimenter involved trying to do a good job of speaking with respect to intonation, clarity of enunciation, etc. There is no reason to assume that such overt behavior was dissonant with opinions concerning the prospects for military service which college students face. Consequently, one would not be surprised if the results of this condition were indistinguishable from the results of the control group.

Table 9 (see p. 108) shows the results in terms of the net per cent (per cent changing in the direction advocated by the communication minus the per cent changing in the opposite direction) of subjects in each condition who changed their opinion toward the position taken by the persuasive communication which they had all read. Examination of these data shows that there was more opinion change in the improvisation condition than in the control condition on each opinion item except the fifth one, which deals with personal expectations of being drafted. On the combined index, the difference between these two conditions was significant at the 3 per cent level of confidence. The oral reading condition, however, showed no significant difference from the control condition; the amount of change in the former was actually somewhat lower than in the control condition.

If this interpretation of the data is correct, the increased change in opinion in the direction advocated by the communication in the improvisation condition resulted not from the mere fact that these subjects had to state these opinions overtly but rather because the behavior involved in overtly supporting such opinions was dissonant with existing cognition. One may wonder, however, whether all subjects had such dissonance; that is, some subjects may not have tried

TABLE 9

EFFECT OF ROLE-PLAYING ON OPINION CHANGES FOLLOWING EXPOSURE TO A COMMUNICATION CONCERNING THE PROSPECTS OF MILITARY SERVICE FOR COLLEGE STUDENTS

	Net Percentage Who Changed in the Direction Advocated by the Communication		
Opinion Items	Improvisation Group A (N = 32)	Oral Reading Group B (N = 23)	Silent Reading Control Group (N = 20)
Estimates of required lengths of service for draftees	41	27	5
Estimates of percentage of college students who will be deferred	44	26	25
Estimates of percentage of college students who will become officers	70	47	45
Personal expectations of length of military service	59	46	50
Personal expectations of being drafted	50	26	55
Combined index: per cent influenced on three or more of the five opinion items	87½	54½	65

p = .01

p = .03

Source: Adapted from B. King and I. Janis, "Comparison of the Effectiveness of Improvised versus Non-Improvised Role-Playing in Producing Opinion Changes," *Human Relations*, 1956, 9, 181. Used by permission.

to construct good arguments in favor of the opinion advocated by the document when this did not coincide with their own opinion. Such subjects would not be expected to show change of opinion in the direction of the persuasive communication. In this particular study no such analysis was presented by the authors. A different study by Janis and King (29), however, does present material relevant to this point.

This experiment was essentially similar in its procedures, purposes, and conclusions to the one already described. About four weeks prior to the experimental session, the subjects, all college students, were given a questionnaire which among other things asked their opinions on how many movie theaters would still be in business three years later, what the future available meat supply would be, and how soon they thought a cure for the common cold would be discovered. The following is the authors' description of the essential aspects of their procedure:

The subjects were asked to give an informal talk based on an outline prepared by the experimenter which stated the conclusion and summarized the main arguments to be presented. . . . Each active participant was instructed to play the role of a *sincere advocate* of the given point of view, while two others, who were present at the same experimental session, listened to his talk and read the prepared outline. Each subject delivered one of the communications and was passively exposed to the other two. . . . In all three communications the conclusion specified (in the outline on which the talk was based) an opinion estimate which was numerically *lower* than that given by any of the students on the "before" test. Thus all active participants were required to argue in favor of an extreme position which differed from their initial beliefs [p. 212].

Each of the three talks, of course, dealt with one of the three issues on which earlier opinions had been measured. Immediately after the last talk was completed, these opinions were again measured.

It is apparent that the "active participants" in this experiment were in a situation essentially similar to the subjects in the "improvisation condition" of the previous experiment. The "passive controls" here were comparable to the "control condition." Again, and for the same reasons, one would expect the control subjects to provide a baseline indicating how influential the arguments were in and of themselves. One would expect the "active participants" to show more opinion change than the control subjects since, to the extent that they complied with the instructions to act like sincere advocates, this behavior produced cognition which was dissonant with their private opinions. Table 10 presents the data from the experiment.

An examination of Table 10 makes it clear that for the communications about movie theaters and about the meat shortage, the results are in the same direction as in the previous study. Those who had to make up an argument showed more change than those who simply listened and read the outline. This is not, however, true for the communication about the cold cure (Communication C). The explanation for this, as given by the authors, is:

The active participants who presented Communication C seemed to engage in *less improvisation* than those who presented the other two communications. The Communication C group appeared to adhere much more closely to the prepared outline, making little attempt to reformulate the main points, to insert illustrative examples, or to invent additional arguments [p. 215].

At the conclusion of the experimental session, the subjects were also asked to rate themselves as to how good a job they had done in giving a sincere, organized, and convincing speech. In discussing the relation between these self-ratings and opinion change, the authors state:

For example, among the active participants who presented Communication C, there were 18 students whose self-ratings were comparatively "high" (three to six favorable responses) and 12 cases whose self-ratings were predominantly "low" (zero, one or two favorable responses), 55% of the "highs" as against only 17% of the "lows" showed a sizable net opinion change in the direction advocated by the communications (p = .05). In general,

TABLE 10

CHANGES IN OPINION ESTIMATES FOLLOWING EXPOSURE TO
PERSUASIVE COMMUNICATIONS

Experimental Group	Per Cent Net Change in Opinion Estimates *	
	Slight or Sizable	Sizable
Communication A (movie theaters)		
Active participants (N = 31)	71	45 } p = .01
Passive controls (N = 57)	58	21
Communication B (meat shortage)		
Active participants (N = 29)	62	41.5 } p = .01
Passive controls (N = 57)	52	17
Communication C (cold cure)		
Active participants (N = 30)	53	40 } p > .30
Passive controls (N = 53)	51	45

* The "net change (slight or sizable)" is defined as the percentage changing in the direction advocated by the communication minus the percentage changing in the opposite direction. The "net sizable change" in the case of Communication A was the difference between the percentage who lowered or raised their estimate by 5,000 or more. For Communication B, a sizable change was 25 or more; for Communication C, it was 5 or more.

Source: Adapted from I. Janis and B. King, "The Influence of Role-Playing on Opinion Change," *Journal of Abnormal and Social Psychology*, 1954, **49**, 213. Used by permission.

the comparisons based on all three communications consistently indicate that a greater amount of opinion change occurred among those active participants who rated their oral speaking performances as satisfactory or better [pp. 216–17].

Let us suppose that those subjects who admitted not having done a satisfactory job on their oral presentation of the arguments had, for one reason or another, not complied with the instructions of the experimenter. They had, of course, complied in the sense of having gone through the motions but not in the sense of really having done a good job of it. These subjects, then, had little dissonance between their private opinions and their knowledge of what they were overtly doing and saying. Hence for them, there was less change of opinion in the direction of dissonance reduction.

These studies lend support to the idea that attitude or opinion change is facilitated if a person finds himself in a situation where, by showing compliant behavior, he is engaged in actions which are dissonant with his private opinions. The changes in private opinion which ensue are the end result of a process of attempting to reduce or eliminate this dissonance.

Let us now move on to an examination of a study that bears on the relation between the amount of dissonance that exists after forced compliance and the magnitude of the promised reward or threatened punishment that elicited the compliant behavior. It will be recalled from the previous chapter that theoretically, dissonance should be greatest if the reward offered or the punishment threatened is just sufficient to produce the compliant behavior. The study which will now be discussed is reported by Kelman (30). The data which it provides are sufficiently important to warrant rather detailed description.

Kelman performed his experiment with seventh grade students. The opinion issue with which the study dealt was the preference for one type of comic book over another. These preferences were measured about a week before, and again about a week after, the actual experiment. A careful attempt was made to keep the situations of attitude measurement separate from the experimental situation. In the experiment proper, the experimenter began by giving a talk which opposed one kind of comic book (fantastic hero stories) and favored a different type of comic book (jungle stories). This persuasive communication favored a position at variance with the opinions of some of the subjects and undoubtedly influenced some of them. After the persuasive communication, the experimental conditions, which will soon be described, were created by various reward offers; and the subjects were then asked to write short essays giving their own views on the relative merits of the two different types of comic book stories.

The experiment was conducted by two persons, the first of whom gave the above-mentioned speech favoring jungle stories. The second experimenter then took over and, in giving the instructions for writing the essays, created three experimental conditions. They are as follows:

1. Moderate incentive toward fantastic hero stories. In this condition the subjects were told that the publishers of the comic books would give a free copy of *Huckleberry Finn* to anyone who wrote essays in favor of fantastic hero stories. They were then told to "go ahead and write your own opinions."

2. Low incentive toward jungle stories. Here again they were told of the free book which awaited anyone who wrote in favor of fantastic hero stories. They were also told, however, that if they wrote good essays in favor of jungle stories, they might get a free pass to see the movie of *Huckleberry Finn*. (It had previously been determined by the experimenter that a pass to the movie was generally more attractive to the subjects than a copy of the book.) They were informed that the experimenter only had five such passes to give out, however, so that they might or might not get a pass if they wrote in favor of jungle stories. He ended up by saying, "Remember: if you write in favor of fantastic hero stories, you definitely get a copy of *Huckleberry Finn*. If you write in favor of jungle stories, then you *may* get free passes to a movie. But you run the risk of not getting anything since only five of you can get passes. So take your pick. Now go ahead and write your own opinions [Kelman, p. 193]."

3. High incentive toward jungle stories. Here again, as in the other conditions, the subjects were told of the free book they would get if they wrote essays in favor of fantastic hero stories. But they were then told that if they wrote essays in favor of jungle stories, they would *also* get a free copy of the book and, what is more, would also get a free pass to the movie of *Huckleberry Finn*. They were told there were enough free passes for everyone in the class and they would even be permitted to take off from class time in order to see the movie. The experimenter ended up by saying, "So, remember: write good essays in favor of jungle books and you will not only get a copy of *Huckleberry Finn,* but your whole class will be able to take off time from class and go to see the movie version of it. Now, go ahead and write your own opinions [Kelman, p. 194]."

It is clear that a situation had been created which tended to elicit forced compliance. The experimenter offered rewards to the children if they would write essays in favor of one or another type of comic book. In the three conditions, the magnitude of the rewards which were offered was varied. In each of these conditions, of course, one would expect some persons to have complied overtly while others did not. Actually, in the moderate incentive condition, where the reward was offered if they wrote in favor of fantastic hero stories, 42 per cent wrote in favor of jungle stories. In the low incentive condition, where a slightly more attractive possible reward was offered if they wrote in favor of jungle stories than if they wrote favoring fantastic hero stories, 68 per cent complied. In the high incentive condition, where the reward was very great if they wrote in favor of jungle stories, one finds that 80 per cent of the subjects complied. In short, the offer of a reward did elicit overt compliant behavior in many subjects; the larger the reward offered, the more subjects complied.

Under each of the three conditions described above, some subjects wrote essays in favor of jungle stories, some in favor of fantastic hero stories. Before looking at the data obtained for these six groups, let us first discuss and make specific what one would expect theoretically with regard to opinion change for each of these six groups. We shall begin by discussing those subjects who wrote essays favoring jungle stories.

1. Moderate incentive toward fantastic hero stories. We are considering here those subjects who did not comply. Hence, there would have been some dissonance between the knowledge that they had written favoring jungle stories and the cognitive elements corresponding to favorable characteristics of the free book which they had given up. Their private opinions would, of course, have been consonant with what they wrote. Because of the moderate magnitude of the reward, the dissonance would not be great. We would thus expect a relatively moderate change in private opinion toward greater preference of jungle stories. Such change would decrease the dissonance, but since the dissonance is moderate, the pressure to reduce it would be correspondingly moderate.

2. Low incentive toward jungle stories. Some of these subjects (those who originally favored fantastic hero stories) have written essays in favor of something they do not really believe, in the hope of getting the slightly more attractive reward. The knowledge that they wrote in favor of jungle stories was, for many of these subjects, dissonant with their private opinions and with the knowledge that they have given up a free book. The knowledge of the reward they would get was consonant with what they wrote, but it should be remembered that the compliance was produced by offering a possibility (but only a possibility) of getting a free pass to the movie. Also, in this condition, by writing in favor of jungle stories in order to get a chance at a free pass to the movie, they gave up a free copy of the book. There was very appreciable dissonance for these subjects, and the pressure to reduce it should have been great. Hence, one would expect a large amount of change in private opinion toward favoring jungle stories since such change would reduce the dissonance markedly.

3. *High incentive toward jungle stories.* The knowledge that they wrote in favor of jungle stories was, for some of them, dissonant with their private opinions, but this was the only dissonance involved. The knowledge of the rewards they were to get was consonant with what they had done. The total dissonance is, hence, less than for the comparable subjects in the preceding condition, and we would expect less change in opinion in this group.

The first column of figures in Table 11 shows the average change in opinion from before to after the experimental session. In this table a plus sign indicates change toward more favorable attitudes about jungle stories. It is clear that the theoretical expectations are corroborated. Those who wrote essays favoring jungle stories in the moderate incentive condition showed a small change in opinion; in the low incentive condition, they showed a rather considerable change; and in the high incentive condition, where the dissonance was less because the reward was too great, they showed less change. One would, of course, expect these results to have been even more marked if the data concerned only those subjects in the last two conditions who initially favored fantastic hero stories. Unfortunately, the author did not present the data with reference to initial opinion; what was presented, however, satisfactorily corroborated the theory.

Let us now turn our attention to those subjects who wrote essays favoring fantastic hero stories.

TABLE 11

MEAN OPINION-CHANGE SCORES IN EACH EXPERIMENTAL CONDITION *

		Essays Favoring		
Degree of Incentive	Direction of Incentive	Jungle Stories	Mixed	Fantastic Hero Stories
Moderate	Fantastic hero	+2.62 (29) †	+1.88 (17)	−4.57 (14)
Low	Jungle	+5.49 (47)	+2.30 (10)	+1.89 (9)
High	Jungle	+3.81 (52)	+1.83 (6)	−5.00 (8)

* A positive sign indicates mean change of opinion toward greater preference of jungle stories; a negative sign indicates that the mean change was toward greater preference of fantastic hero stories.

† Numbers in parentheses are the number of subjects.

1. Moderate incentive condition. Some of the subjects in this group undoubtedly wrote essays favoring fantastic hero stories in order to get the free book, thus showing forced compliance. For them, there existed dissonance between their private opinions and what they had done. Since the reward which elicited the forced compliance was not too great, the dissonance would be relatively large. Hence for these subjects, we would expect considerable change in opinion in the direction of increased preference for fantastic hero stories.

2. Low incentive condition. These subjects did not show forced compliance. The possibility of getting a pass to a movie was not sufficient to cause them to comply. Presumably they wrote essays that agreed with their private opinions, and hence, there was no dissonance between these opinions and what they had done. True, they gave up the chance at a pass to the movie, but on the other hand, they received a free copy of the book. There was, then, little dissonance for these subjects and we would expect little opinion change.

3. *High incentive condition.* Here again we are dealing with subjects who did not show forced compliance and for whom there was no dissonance between what they wrote and their private opinions. These subjects, however, did turn down a considerable reward, and this knowledge was dissonant with what they had written. This dissonance could have been somewhat reduced by believing even more firmly than before that fantastic hero stories were better than jungle stories. One would expect these subjects to have shown appreciable opinion change in this direction.

The last column in Table 11 gives the data for these subjects. The subjects who wrote essays favoring fantastic hero stories in the moderate incentive and high incentive conditions did show marked opinion changes in the direction of liking such stories better. The comparable subjects in the low incentive condition showed little change; the small amount of change that existed was actually in the opposite direction.

The column headed "Mixed" shows the data for those subjects who wrote essays not clearly favoring one type of story or the other. It is unclear, of course, what the psychological situation was for these subjects. The data show very slight changes in a positive direction for all the conditions. It is perhaps interesting to note that for every condition the data for this mixed group fall between the averages of the other two groups.

It is instructive to examine the data by comparing those who complied with those who did not comply. Those who wrote essays favoring jungle stories in the moderate incentive condition and those who wrote essays favoring fantastic hero stories in the other two conditions are the ones for whom the offered reward failed to elicit compliance. According to the theoretical curves presented in Figure 2 (p. 93), the direction of the relationship between amount of reward offered and magnitude of dissonance should be negative for those who complied and positive for those who did not comply. Figure 3 (p. 120) shows how the data fit the theory as schematized in Figure 2. The assumption is made in relating the data to these curves that the difference between those subjects who did and those who did not comply can be characterized as a difference in how important the opinion was to them. That is, it would have taken a larger reward to have elicited compliance from those who did not comply. It can be seen in Figure 3 that all the noncompliant groups fall on the positive slope portion of the higher importance curve. The compliant groups all fall on the negative slope portion of the lesser importance curve. Each incentive condition has, of course, a constant position along the scale of magnitude of reward.

For this figure, change of opinion was labeled positive if it was in the direction predicted by pressure to reduce dissonance. The only "negative" change, in this sense, occurs in the low incentive condition for those subjects who did not comply. Here, where theoretically one would have expected a very small change in the direction of increased preference for fantastic hero stories, the actual change was a small one in the opposite direction. It may be seen, however, that in general the obtained data fit the theory rather well.

The theory concerning opinion change following the creation of cognitive dissonance by forced compliance, and the data which have been presented, raise some interesting questions concerning opinion and attitude change. There are several areas of opinion where it is notoriously difficult to

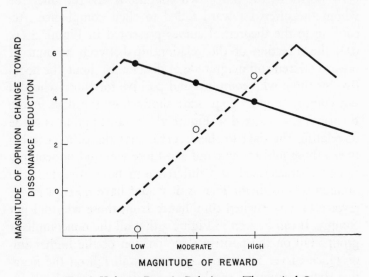

FIG. 3. Kelman Data in Relation to Theoretical Curves.

● Subjects who complied (those who wrote essays favoring fantastic hero stories in the moderate incentive condition and those who wrote favoring jungle stories in the low and high incentive conditions).

○ Subjects who did not comply (those who wrote essays favoring jungle stories in the moderate incentive condition and those who wrote favoring fantastic hero stories in the low and high incentive conditions).

change people. Anyone who has ever engaged in political discussions with persons who did not share their own views will recognize this. And yet, it is also true that there are many instances where people's opinions and attitudes do change drastically in such areas. The suggestion offers itself that perhaps such instances of drastic change of ideology in an area that is highly resistant to change come about only after overt behavior that creates strong dissonance with the existing ideology has somehow been elicited. Once such a state of affairs has been reached, then, far from resisting attempts to influence opinions, the person may welcome them since they help reduce the dissonance thus established.

Deutsch and Collins (12) support this suggestion in a study of changes in attitudes toward Negroes which occurred during residence in an integrated housing project. Living in this integrated project forced whites into contact with Negroes, and undoubtedly, rules of ordinary, polite, neighborly behavior functioned on many occasions to produce overt behavior which was dissonant with private belief. The effect of this, and the general relation between behavior and opinion, is summarized as follows:

If social custom leads one to avoid intimate contact with Negroes, then Negroes are obviously not the kind of people one would like to be intimate with. If Negroes are customarily treated as inferiors, then it is because they are people who are inferior and who should be treated as inferiors. These rationalizations of behavior receive support from the fact that segregation with all its invidious connotations receives official public sanction. Not only do the "best" people avoid social relations with Negroes but the government, the official public, sanctions segregation in law and in public policy. We have seen in our study how the policy decisions of a housing authority may affect the social norms for race relations in the housing project. There is little doubt that public laws and official policies do provide a standard of behavior; by providing a standard favorable to nonsegregated interracial relations they help to stimulate such behavior. *There is evidence in our data that once a change in behavior has occurred, a change in beliefs is likely to follow* [p. 142, italics ours].

The theory of dissonance as applied to situations where forced compliance is elicited, and the specific relevance of this theory to situations such as Deutsch and Collins discuss, have wide implications. For example, the United States Supreme Court ruling on desegregation of schools is a case in point. The theory would imply that in those areas where compliance is obtained, that is, desegregation of schools is carried out, there would occur gradual opinion change toward favoring desegregation among the people. On the other hand, the theory similarly implies that in any area which does not comply, that is, successfully resists desegregation of its schools, attitudes would change in the opposite direction—toward greater favoring of segregation.

Summary

Data from five studies have been presented, all of which are relevant to the theoretical analysis presented in Chapter Four, namely, that dissonance follows from situations which elicit forced compliance and that this dissonance may be reduced by change of private opinion.

The data show that:

1. Following public compliance there is frequently a subsequent change of private opinion over and above what the variables in the situation, not including dissonance, would account for.

2. Taking the magnitude of such opinion change as reflecting the magnitude of the pressure to reduce dissonance, the data fit the hypothesized relations with importance of the issue and with amount of reward used to elicit the compliant behavior.

SIX

Voluntary and Involuntary

Exposure to Information:

Theory

The discussion in this chapter will center about the reasons that, and the conditions under which, persons will actively seek out information. The concern here will be primarily with spelling out the implications which the theory of dissonance has for this type of behavior. There are, however, many other antecedent conditions, apart from the existence of dissonance, which will produce active seeking out of new information. For the sake of somewhat greater completeness and to make it easier to look at the data that will be presented, the discussion in this chapter will digress somewhat from the narrow confines of the theory of dissonance.

Let us develop our thinking on this question with the aid of a hypothetical example. Imagine that a person, reading his newspaper one late afternoon, notices an announcement of a lecture to be given the following evening bearing the title "The Advantages of Automobiles with Very High Horsepower Engines." In the context of this hypothetical illustration the problem with which this chapter concerns itself becomes, Who will voluntarily go to hear this lecture? There are, undoubtedly, some persons who would go to hear this lecture for the same reason that might lead them to attend a symphony concert or see an art exhibition or go to a museum. This does not mean to imply that they would find the lecture entertaining in the same sense that these other activities might be, but rather that acquiring such information, particularly if it is connected with some interest or hobby, seems to function as a satisfaction in itself for many people. Active curiosity and the sheer pleasure of acquiring information for its own sake cannot be ignored in any discussion of voluntary seeking out of new information. This chapter, however, will not discuss these factors further beyond acknowledging their existence and their importance. With reference to the hypothetical example, let us grant that the audience at the lecture will contain a sprinkling of people who came for such reasons and move on to those factors which are of more central concern to this book.

The Possibility of Relevant Future Action

It is perhaps stating the obvious to say that persons will seek out information which is relevant to action they must take. But at the risk of repeating and explicating the obvious, I will devote some space to spelling this out in detail and drawing some implications from it.

If there is no behavior or action in which a person engages or possibly may engage that is relevant to a particular area of information, there will be no motivation from this source to acquire cognition concerning this particular area of information. To return to the example concerning the lecture on automobiles with powerful engines, one might consider a person who does not own a car and does not contemplate owning or driving one. Let us even imagine, if we can, that he has *never* contemplated owning and driving a car and that the very idea is rather strange to him. This may be hard for an American to imagine, but it would not be difficult to find such people in other countries of the world. One would expect this person not to be at all inclined to go hear the lecture concerning automotive engines. The information which this person would expect to acquire from attendance at this lecture would be quite irrelevant to any present or implied future behavior. There simply would be an absence of motivation in him concerning the acquisition of such cognition. He would not be drawn to the lecture, but on the other hand, should circumstances conspire to force attendance on him, he would have no inclination to avoid it actively.

If the area of information is relevant to some impending or possible future behavior for the person, one would then expect to observe considerable motivation to acquire cognitive elements in this area as well as active seeking out of such information. One would further expect that for such a person, this seeking out of information would be rather impartial. He would not select one kind of information to listen to and avoid other kinds. Rather, he would be motivated toward acquiring cognition about all aspects and all alternatives. Let us return once more to the hypothetical example. Consider a person who is contemplating the purchase of an automobile in the near future or who, having decided to purchase one, has not yet decided which kind of car he would like to own. Such a person would be motivated to attend the lecture on high horsepower engines since the information he would thus acquire would be quite relevant to his future behavior, namely, the purchase of an automobile. One would further expect that this person's information-seeking activities within the area of automobiles would not be very selective. He would be just as inclined to attend a lecture stressing the advantages of low horsepower engines as one stressing the advantages of high horsepower engines.

In general, one may say that the preaction or predecision situation will be characterized by extended and nonselective seeking of relevant information. Of course, it is rather rare that there is a pure preaction situation. Most instances will involve mixtures. For example, the person who has decided to purchase a car but has not decided which type of car to buy will actively seek out information concerning various aspects of cars. He will not, however, be nonselective to the extent that he will willingly expose himself to information which would be dissonant with the decision he has already made, namely, that he will purchase a car. This will, of course, be discussed in more detail later in this chapter.

There is one further point to be made about information seeking in a preaction situation before moving on. Along with the nonselectivity of what information he exposes himself to, there will be a lack of resistance to accepting and cognizing any relevant information which comes his way. Thus, prior to the taking of action, many cognitive elements will have been established which may later be dissonant with the cognition corresponding to the action which does ensue.

The Presence of Dissonance

The presence or absence of dissonance in some particular content area will have important effects on the degree of information seeking and on the selectivity of such information seeking. If dissonance exists between two cognitive elements or between two clusters of cognitive elements, this dissonance may be reduced, as has been stated previously, by adding new cognitive elements which produce new consonant relationships. One would then expect that in the presence of dissonance, one would observe the seeking out of information which might reduce the existing dissonance.

The degree to which this kind of behavior manifests itself would, of course, depend upon the magnitude of the dissonance which exists and also upon the person's expectations concerning what content any potential information source would yield. Let us examine the various possibilities in more detail.

1. *Relative absence of dissonance.* If little or no dissonance exists, there would be no motivation (considering this source of motivation alone) to seek out new and additional information. Of course, there would also be little or no motivation to avoid any particular source of information. Thus, returning to the example of the lecture, if a person had recently purchased a car but, strangely, had no cognitive elements at all which were dissonant with what he knew he had done and was doing, this person would have no inclination to either go to this lecture or to avoid it. What is important is that if there is really an absence of dissonance, this lack of motivation to attend or avoid the lecture would be quite independent of whether the car he had just purchased had a high or low horsepower engine.

In a way, the behavior one would observe on the part of this hypothetical person with no dissonance would be identical with the behavior of the person for whom the lecture on advantages of high horsepower engines had absolutely no relevance to any present or future behavior. There is an important difference, however, in that for the latter person, accidental exposure, which he does not avoid, will not introduce dissonance; while for the former, who also does not avoid sources of information, dissonance may be accidentally introduced.

2. *The presence of moderate amounts of dissonance.* The existence of appreciable dissonance and the consequent pressure to reduce it will lead to the seeking out of information which will introduce consonances and to the avoidance of

information which will increase the already existing dissonance. When faced with a potential source of information, a person usually does not know the exact nature of the cognition which he would acquire from exposure to this information source. He must then react in terms of expectations about it. If he is led, for one reason or another, to expect it will produce cognitions which will increase consonance, he will expose himself to the information source. If the expectation is that the cognition acquired through this source would increase dissonance, he will avoid it. It should be pointed out that under most circumstances this kind of action to reduce dissonance is a rather fallible procedure. To the extent that one's expectations may prove wrong, an attempt at dissonance reduction may have the unfortunate result of increasing dissonance.

If a person who has recently purchased a new car, and as a result of the decision has appreciable dissonance, notices the announcement of the lecture on high horsepower automotive engines, one would expect him to be inclined to attend the lecture if the car he has recently purchased has a powerful motor. The title of the lecture would lead him to expect that he would obtain cognition which would be consonant with having purchased the particular car he now owns. If he had purchased a car with low power, however, one would expect him to avoid attending the lecture. This would not simply be a matter of indifference but of active avoidance.

3. The presence of extremely large amounts of dissonance. Let us recall that there is a limit to the magnitude of dissonance which can exist in a system. If two cognitive elements exist in a dissonant relationship, the maximum magnitude this dissonance can have is equal to the resistance to change of the less resistant element of the pair. Similarly, if dissonance exists between one cluster of elements and another cluster, this dissonance cannot exceed in magnitude the resistance to change of the least resistant parts of the clusters. If the dissonance becomes greater than the resistance to change, then the least resistant elements of cognition will be changed, thus reducing the dissonance.

What may one say concerning the seeking out of new information on the part of a person whose dissonance is near to the limit which can exist? Under such circumstances a person may actively seek out, and expose himself to, dissonance-increasing information. If he can increase the dissonance to the point where it is greater than the resistance to change of one or another cluster of cognitions, he will then change the cognitive elements involved, thus markedly reducing or perhaps even wholly eliminating the dissonance which now is so great.

To illustrate this let us return for the last time to the example of the lecture on the advantages of powerful automobile engines. Imagine a person who has bought a low-powered car and, since the purchase, has gradually had more and more cognitive elements introduced which are dissonant with the cognition corresponding to owning and driving such a car. The resistance to changing these latter cognitions is, of course, identical with the resistance of getting rid of that car and purchasing a different one, a procedure which may involve some financial loss together with a public admission of having been wrong. Imagine, however, that his dissonance has increased in magnitude to the point where it is almost equal to his resistance to change and, as a consequence, the notion even occasionally flits through his mind. One may expect that this hypothetical person might go to hear the lecture which he certainly expects will increase his dissonance. Once his dissonance is increased sufficiently, he may bring himself to change, thus eliminating all dissonance in the system at once. It is clear, however,

that one would not expect this voluntary exposure to dissonance-increasing information unless the existing dissonance
is well-nigh at its limit.

Figure 4 presents a graphic summary of the theoretical
relationship between the magnitude of dissonance and the
inclination to seek out new information. Again, as in previous chapters, I have used straight lines to represent seg-

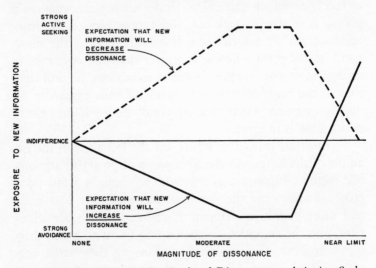

Fig. 4. Relation between Magnitude of Dissonance and Active Seeking of New Information.

ments of the relationship not because I wish to state that
this is the exact function, but rather to emphasize the sche-
matic nature of the graph. The exact function, even if one
knew enough to make an attempt at specifying it, would
naturally depend upon the specification of an exact scale of
magnitude of dissonance.

The figure does, however, show briefly how, depending
upon the expectation of what a source of information will
yield, the exposure to this information source changes as
dissonance increases. If the expectation is that the new in-

formation will probably increase dissonance, there is mostly avoidance of exposure except at very low dissonance and at the limits of dissonance. If the expectation is that the new information will decrease dissonance, there is increasing inclination to seek out that information as dissonance increases until, again, it approaches the limit. Near the limit of possible dissonance we have drawn the curve as descending when the expectation is that the new information will decrease dissonance.

This last, perhaps, needs a further word of clarification. The descending portion of the curve is not implied by, or derived from, any of the previously stated theory but is stated here as an additional hypothesis. In essence I am conjecturing that if the dissonance is so high as to be near the *limit* of possible dissonance in the situation, then even if some new information were to reduce this dissonance somewhat, the person would still be left with a large, uncomfortable amount to deal with. This procedure of adding new consonant elements is, hence, not a very satisfactory procedure for such extreme magnitudes of dissonance. There will, then, be little active seeking out of such new consonance-producing elements. It may be noticed that it is not hypothesized that there will be an avoidance of such new information. The descending portion has been drawn only down to the zero point, namely, indifference—neither active seeking nor active avoidance.

INVOLUNTARY AND FORCED CONTACT WITH INFORMATION

Up to now the discussion in this chapter has focused mainly on voluntary exposure to, or avoidance of, new information. We must, however, also concern ourselves with situations where a person, through no voluntary action on his part, has new information impinge upon him which, if cognized, would increase dissonance.

Considering the discussion up to now in which it has been

pointed out that except near the limits of maximum dissonance, persons will actively avoid dissonance-increasing information, one may well ask about the circumstances under which a person would, involuntarily, become exposed to such new information. Let us examine some of the many circumstances under which this may occur.

1. Accidental exposure. If a system of relevant cognitive elements is characterized by a total or near total absence of dissonance, then, as has already been stated, there should be little or no avoidance of relevant new information which might impinge on the person. Under such circumstances it is quite conceivable, and even likely, that simply through accidental exposure dissonance may be introduced into this largely consonant system. This kind of increase of dissonance through mere accidental exposure is not likely to happen frequently in instances where some dissonance already exists and the person is, hence, wary.

2. Exposure on an irrelevant basis. A person may expose himself to a potential source of cognition for one set of reasons and find, perhaps to his discomfort, that along with the kind of information or opinion which he sought he is also exposed to information which he did not seek and which may be quite irrelevant to the motivation which led him to expose himself to this particular source. This is probably one of the most frequent ways in which dissonance is increased even though there is appreciable dissonance to start with. This is, of course, the type of situation which advertisers frequently try to create, particularly in radio and television advertising. People are attracted to some entertainment and then are also exposed to an advertisement which is usually quite irrelevant to the basis on which the audience was attracted. In this way a person who has, say, recently bought one make of car may find himself listening to someone extol the virtues of a competing make.

3. *Forced exposure.* Sometimes new information and, consequently, new cognition is forced upon a person. This can occur in a variety of ways. Some event or knowledge may be so widespread that it is virtually impossible for a person to avoid knowing it. For example, it would be very difficult to find an adult in the United States who did not know of the existence of nuclear weapons. It also may happen that unforeseen consequences of one's own actions bring about experiences which force the existence of new cognition. For example, a person walking carelessly on an icy street might slip and fall—an event which can hardly fail to make its impact on him. Needless to say, such forced exposure does not always produce dissonance, but in the ordinary course of events it sometimes will.

4. *Interaction with other people.* To the extent that others with whom one interacts do not share one's opinions, these others are a potential source of dissonance. The realization of the potentiality may occur accidentally or on the initiative of others. For example, a person who has just taken some action may tell others about it, perhaps to get support for what he has done or perhaps merely out of enthusiasm. One of his audience may, however, volunteer various items of information and various opinions which are dissonant with the action being discussed. This type of thing probably occurs most frequently when, in trying to reduce dissonance by getting agreement or support from others, one inadvertently creates dissonance in someone else. This will be discussed in greater detail in Chapter Eight.

The foregoing is not intended to be an exhaustive listing of ways in which new dissonance-producing cognition may be created. Nor is it intended that the categories discussed be regarded as mutually exclusive. The intention here is rather to give some impression of the large variety of ways in which it may happen. A person rarely controls his environment sufficiently, or is even able to predict it sufficiently, to protect himself from dissonance-producing cognition. There is never any guarantee that attempts at reducing dissonance will be successful, and it may even happen that the activity which the person initiates, far from reducing dissonance, serves merely to increase it. How, then, would one expect persons to behave when, involuntarily, cognition is introduced which is dissonant with other cognitions which are already present?

Let us consider what the reaction of a person would be if he is forced to read or listen to information or a persuasive communication which, in the ordinary course of events, would produce elements of cognition dissonant with existing cognition. Once these dissonances are introduced one would, of course, expect the same attempts to reduce dissonance which have already been discussed in previous chapters. One might also expect, however, that at the initial moment of impact of the new dissonant cognition, effective processes could be initiated which would prevent the dissonant elements from ever being firmly established cognitively. One might expect to observe such things as attempts to escape or avoid further exposure, erroneous interpretation or perception of the material, or any other technique or maneuver which will help to abolish the newly introduced dissonance and to prevent the further introduction of dissonance.

Some of the variety of ways in which such forcibly introduced dissonances are dealt with are illustrated by Cooper and Jahoda (11). In a number of studies conducted at various times they were concerned with "the reaction of the prejudiced person to anti-prejudice propaganda. What happens when in an experimental situation they are involuntarily confronted with it?" [P. 15.] Cooper and Jahoda conclude from the various studies they have done, that their subjects "prefer not to face the implications of ideas opposed to their own so that they do not have to be forced either to defend themselves or to admit error [pp. 15-16]." The following are the ways they list in which these persons, in an experimental situation, avoid the introduction of dissonance:

1. Initial understanding of the propaganda message followed by a circuitous line of reasoning which ends in misunderstanding. Describing this process which follows the initial correct perception of the propaganda, the authors list these steps: ". . . perceiving the criticism of his position involved in the item; inventing means of disidentification from the special instances of prejudice depicted by the propaganda item; and in the process losing the original understanding of the message. Apparently this process occurs frequently; the unconscious ingenuity of the respondent sets in mainly during the last two steps [pp. 18-19]." In other words, through this process the initial dissonance created by the inadvertent correct perception of the propaganda item is eliminated.

2. Making the total propaganda message invalid. This process apparently occurs most frequently when the initially correct perception has been stated too openly and too distinctly by the subject to permit effective distortion or subsequent misunderstanding. The authors describe the process here as follows: "The respondent accepts the message on the surface but makes it invalid for himself in one of two ways. He may admit the general principle, but claim that in exceptions one is entitled to one's prejudices; or he may admit that the individual item is convincing in itself, but that it is not a correct picture of usual life situations involving the minority group discussed [p. 19]." Here again, the initial dissonance created by the forced exposure is dismissed.

3. Initial misperception in line with existing cognition. Here there is no expression by the subject of initial correct understanding. Cooper and Jahoda describe this situation as

follows: ". . . the prejudiced person's perception is so colored by his prejudices that issues presented in a frame of reference different from his own are transformed so as to become compatible with his own views. Quite unaware of the violation of facts he commits, he imposes on the propaganda item his own frame of reference [p. 20]." Simply from this description it is, of course, difficult to know whether the subject reacted instantaneously to the dissonance or whether, on the other hand, the potentially dissonance-producing information was never cognized. One may speculate that it is the former and that this type of reaction, as contrasted to the first two where the subject does exhibit correct initial understanding, would be shown mainly by persons who already have some dissonance in this opinion area. With already existing dissonance they would be more alert to prevent increase of dissonance and would, hence, perhaps react in this instantaneous manner.

To the extent that the processes described above operate effectively, they should make for the relative ineffectiveness of information or propaganda to which a person is forcibly exposed. Indeed, the forced exposure may succeed in simply marshalling and alerting his defenses against increasing dissonance.

Summary

The endeavor in this chapter has been to examine two major questions:

1. How does the presence of dissonance and its magnitude affect the seeking out or the avoidance of new information?

2. How do persons react when involuntarily confronted with information or propaganda which they would normally have avoided?

From the previously stated general theory of dissonance

and pressures to reduce dissonance, together with the fact that dissonance may be reduced by adding consonant cognitive elements, the implications concerning voluntary exposure to new information may be easily drawn. Dissonance-reducing cognition is sought; dissonance-increasing cognition is avoided.

If a person is involuntarily exposed to information that will increase dissonance, then in addition to the usual procedures whereby he may reduce this dissonance, there are also set up quick defensive processes which prevent the new cognition from ever becoming firmly established.

SEVEN

Voluntary and Involuntary Exposure to Information: Data

The question of who voluntarily seeks or listens to new information is rather an old one. Whenever people consider the problems of dissemination of information, propaganda, advertising, or any other similar endeavor, they are immediately confronted with the questions, Who is reached by such a program? Who listens voluntarily? How can one reach people who would not ordinarily be reached? How can one make sure of reaching those persons for whom the information is expressly intended?

Almost everyone has recognized that there are strong selective factors operating to determine the characteristics of any voluntary audience. One can find frequent assertions concerning this selectivity. Klapper (32), for example, states:

. . . this phenomenon of self-selection might well be called the most basic process thus far established by research on the effects of mass media. Operative in regard to intellectual or aesthetic level of the material, its political tenor, or any of a dozen other aspects, the process of self-selection works toward two manifestations of the same end: every product of mass media (1) attracts an audience which already prefers that particular type of material, and (2) fails to attract any significant number of persons who are either of contrary inclination or have been hitherto uninterested [pp. I-16–I-17].

While such remarks, assertions, and generalizations are abundant, the data to support these statements are relatively lacking. The remainder of this chapter will present some data concerning these questions—data which are not always as compelling as one would wish but which, nevertheless, seem to be the best available. The chapter will conclude with the presentation of the results of an experiment conducted specifically to test the predicted relationship between voluntary exposure to information and magnitude of dissonance.

Preaction Seeking of Information

It will be recalled from the previous chapter that one would expect rather active seeking out of relevant information on the part of persons who are faced with the necessity, or even with the possibility, of action in the future. Although this sounds highly plausible and even obvious, there is nevertheless good reason to want empirical corroboration of such an assertion. There are many data which may be interpreted as seeking out of information in a preaction situation, but most of these data are not very cogent because it is usually impossible to distinguish the direction of causation. For example, one could produce considerable quantities of data to show that persons who vote in national elections are better informed about political issues and events than are those who do not vote. It is possible to interpret such a finding as indicating that those who intend to vote, that is, those for whom there is impending future behavior, seek out relevant information. It is also plausible, however, to propose the opposite direction of causality, namely, that those who become informed about issues and facts become more motivated to go to the polls and vote. This kind of ambiguity of interpretation and concomitant lack of cogency with regard to the hypothesis we are considering is typical of data on such matters. Rather than present a large variety of such data concerning the question on hand, we have selected a pair of studies to discuss, one of which, fortunately, contains a control group which makes the interpretation unequivocal.

During World War II there was a continual information and propaganda campaign in the United States designed to impress people with the dangers of loose talk which might give information to the enemy. This security campaign tried to reach the public through various media. There were appeals on the radio and in the newspapers; there were many posters designed to get this message across. The Office of War Information did several studies to assess the effectiveness of various aspects of this security campaign. Two of these studies have data relevant to preaction seeking of relevant information.

The first of these two studies was a survey of 400 persons in Jacksonville, Florida (57). There had been for some time in this city an intensive local security campaign. The interviewers ascertained from each respondent whether or not he was aware of the local campaign, and each respondent was also asked a question concerning whether or not he felt that he himself possessed useful information which should not be repeated. Table 12 presents the data from the survey. Among those who had voluntarily exposed themselves to the local security campaign, 34 per cent felt that they did possess such information. Among those who were not aware of the local security campaign, only 15 per cent felt that they possessed such information.

In this study there was no control group representing an involuntary audience, and consequently the interpretation is typically ambiguous. One may imagine that those who felt they had, or thought they might have, information which they should not talk about tended more often to expose themselves voluntarily to relevant propaganda. One might also suppose, however, that those who, for one reason or another, were exposed to the security campaign were affected by it so that they recognized the fact that they possessed

TABLE 12

SURVEY OF EFFECTIVENESS OF A LOCAL SECURITY CAMPAIGN

	Number of Respondents	Per Cent of Respondents Who Felt That They Possessed Useful Information
Knew about local campaign	300	34
Did not know about local campaign	100	15

useful information. It may be pointed out, incidentally, that if the former explanation is the correct one, then the security campaign was more effective in reaching precisely those people who were more important for it to reach.

There are two reasons for having included this study in this chapter in spite of the complete ambiguity of interpretation. One reason is to provide a concrete example of this type of causal ambiguity which makes most such data not useful for our purpose. The other reason is to provide comparison to available data from a very similar study which had a control group so that the interpretation can be unequivocal. This next study reported the results of a survey in two towns to assess the effectiveness of a security pamphlet entitled *A Personal Message* (56). The pamphlet described the security cautions to be observed and the reasons for these cautions, and made these points:

1. Enemy agents work by collecting and assembling "bits and pieces" of information, many of which alone are harmless.
2. These bits and pieces are passed on chain-fashion by someone's telling a friend, a cousin, an uncle.
3. The enemy may not know things that even hundreds of people know—unless these hundreds talk.
4. Certain key words summarize the types of information which the enemy is most anxious to get hold of. These key words are: The where—how—when—how many—what kind of troop movements, ship sailings, production, etc.
5. It is safe to talk about what is in the newspapers or on the radio. It is not safe to talk about what you hear from someone, or see yourself.

The survey was conducted in town H and town C. Both towns had a population of about 16,000 people, and both towns were in the state of New York. In town H, *A Personal Message* had been distributed by the Office of Civilian Defense. In town C, the pamphlet had not yet been distributed. In town H, interviews were conducted with 521 relatives of servicemen. In town C, 603 relatives of servicemen were interviewed. Only every sixth person in town C (a total of 100) was given the pamphlet and asked to read it. These persons were interviewed about it the next day. Thus in town H, there were a number of people who had seen the pamphlet during the ordinary course of distribution. There were 78 such people among the 521 respondents. These 78 people, of course, represented a voluntary audience. In town C, there was a sample of 100 people who were each asked by the interviewer to read the pamphlet and, consequently, represented an involuntary audience.

One might expect, in accordance with the hypothesis concerning the seeking of information which is relevant to future action, that persons who had no access to any information which should not be repeated would have had less interest in exposing themselves to the pamphlet. In other words, the information which they might have expected to get from the pamphlet would be irrelevant to any possible future behavior on their part. However, persons who did have access to such information and who either thought that they knew such information or wondered whether they

TABLE 13

SURVEY OF EFFECTIVENESS OF A SECURITY PAMPHLET

Question: "Do you think that you yourself know anything connected with the war which should not be repeated?"

| | | Per Cent Who Responded | |
	Number of Respondents	Yes or Don't Know	No
Town H			
Voluntary audience	78	33	67
Nonaudience	443	18	82
Town C			
Involuntary audience	100	20	80
Nonaudience	503	16	84

knew such information would have tended to expose themselves voluntarily because the cognition they might have acquired by reading the pamphlet would have been relevant to possible future behavior.

The respondents in the survey were asked, "Do you think that you yourself know anything connected with the war which should not be repeated?" Table 13 presents the responses to this question for the four groups of people, namely, the voluntary audience in town H, the nonaudience in town H, the involuntary audience in town C, and the nonaudience in town C. Thirty-three per cent of the voluntary audience either thought they did know such information or else were not sure whether or not they did. This was true of only 20 per cent of the involuntary audience in town C, a difference significant at the 5 per cent level of confidence. The percentages for the nonaudience were 18 and 16.

It is clear from comparison of the percentages for the *involuntary audience* and the *nonaudiences* that reading the pamphlet itself did not make people feel that they had information which should not be repeated. Consequently, one must conclude that the higher percentage of such people among the *voluntary audience* was not caused by reading the pamphlet but rather was itself the cause of reading the pamphlet. In other words, the data support the notion that those people who felt they did know something or were unsure whether or not they did, and hence for whom there was an implied or a possible future behavior, voluntarily exposed themselves more frequently to the pamphlet.

Reduction of Dissonance by Seeking Out Information

Let us now turn again to the major focus of the book, namely, the implications of the theory of dissonance. It will be recalled from the previous chapter that in the presence of dissonance, one would expect active seeking out of information that would produce new cognition consonant with existing cognitions and the avoidance of information that would add to the dissonance. In spite of the vast amount of research which has been done on such problems as radio listenership, newspaper readership, and the like, there is a paucity of data cogent to our hypothesis in the sense that a relatively unambiguous interpretation is possible. As a matter of fact, we were able to turn up only one such study and even here the interpretation is open to objection.

This study, reported by Lazarsfeld (33), concerns the listening audience of a series of educational programs. The following quotation from Lazarsfeld summarizes his findings:

. . . even so-called educational programs are not free from this tendency. Some time ago there was a program on the air which showed in different installments how all the nationalities in this country have contributed to American culture. The purpose was to teach tolerance of other nationalities. The indications were, however, that the audience for each program consisted mainly of the national group which was currently praised. There was little chance for the program to teach tolerance because . . . self-selection . . . produced a body of listeners who heard only about the contribution of a country which they already approved [p. 69].

This certainly is consistent with the hypothesis concerning the active seeking of information which is likely to reduce dissonance. It is quite plausible to assume that members of various minority nationality groups living in America have many cognitive elements that are dissonant with being a member of this minority group. Consequently, from our hypothesis one would expect that they would be highly motivated to listen to a broadcast which they expected would supply information that would produce cognition consonant with being a member of the specific nationality group. Cognition that this nationality group is important in American culture and has contributed importantly to American culture would be consonant with being a member of this group.

Other studies, which may be quoted in profusion, are not even amenable to this degree of unambiguity in interpretation. If one finds, as has been found, that people who are politically liberal tend to read liberal newspapers and that those who are conservative tend to read conservative newspapers, one cannot pin down whether the political disposition leads to selection of the newspaper one reads or whether the newspaper influences opinion. Nor can one say anything about the existence or absence of dissonance in the readers of the various newspapers. Such data are consistent with the implications of the theory of dissonance but certainly do not provide strong corroboration for it.

Another study which is pertinent to the present point has already been discussed in Chapter Three. This is the study by Ehrlich *et al.* (13) which found that the existence of dissonance following the purchase of a new automobile led to the reading of ads which expounded on the virtues of the automobile they had just purchased. This study was discussed in connection with the implications of dissonance theory for postdecision situations. It is also pertinent here, however, since it does deal with voluntary seeking out of information in an attempt to reduce dissonance.

Mixed Characteristics of Voluntary Audiences

Most voluntary audiences will, of course, not be pure in the sense that each member of the audience has been attracted to listen to the information for the same reasons. Any given speech, for example, would probably attract some people in preaction circumstances, some who are attempting to reduce dissonance, and even some who were guided by motives irrelevant to the content of the speech. Most of the studies on the characteristics of audiences do indeed tend to reflect the combined operation of all of these factors. Since in such studies one cannot clearly separate out and pin down the specific motivations involved, these studies do not provide very clear corroborative data. Let us, however, discuss one such study to illustrate the kinds of information obtained and the degree of corroboration which such studies give to the theory in question.

This study is fairly typical of a good deal of research that has been done on the awareness of the public to information or advertising campaigns. Since the public, at least to some extent, can expose itself voluntarily to such information campaigns, the hypotheses which we are considering should be relevant and the effects we have discussed should show themselves in distinguishing between those who have and those who have not exposed themselves to the campaign.

The most relevant data in such studies are reported relationships between information about, or awareness of, some item and some other variable which can be called "interest in the matter." Interest in something is, of course, a very vague term and usually does not refer to anything unambiguous. Sometimes one can plausibly assume that the measure of interest is also a measure of the importance of some implied future behavior or of some existing behavior or reaction. To the extent that such assumptions can be made, the data can be viewed in the light of the present theory.

There is, of course, another difficulty in interpreting such data with reference to this theory. The data which are presented in such studies simply show the relationship between two variables with no indication of the direction of causality. The theory with which we are concerned implies that the presence of dissonance will lead to selective voluntary exposure to information. This type of data can, however, also be interpreted from the other direction of causality. We will discuss one such study, however, in spite of the difficulty of establishing direct and unequivocal relevance to our theory. The study we have selected to discuss is, of course, one in which the above-mentioned difficulties are minimal for this kind of data.

The Survey Research Center (53) reported a study concerning public awareness of one of the campaigns conducted by the American Cancer Society. In addition to questions asking how much they knew about the cancer campaign, respondents in the survey were asked which diseases they considered "most dangerous." Table 14 shows the relationship that obtained between whether or not cancer was named as a "most dangerous" disease and the degree of awareness of the cancer campaign.

Before interpreting this relationship let us consider the feelings and reactions of the persons who named cancer as

TABLE 14

RELATION BETWEEN DEGREE OF AWARENESS OF CANCER
CAMPAIGN AND CHOICE OF CANCER AS A
"MOST DANGEROUS" DISEASE

Degree of Awareness	Per Cent of Respondents Who	
	Named Cancer	Did Not Name Cancer
Very high	11	3
High	34	15
Medium	37	25
Low	9	28
Very low	8	27
Not ascertained	1	2
Total	100%	100%

one of the most dangerous diseases. Seventy-four per cent of them gave as a reason that it is incurable or that it is fatal. Let us imagine, then, that naming cancer as a most dangerous disease indicates some fear of cancer, or at least indicates the presence of an implied future behavior, namely, something must be done to avoid it. If this is true, the relationship that obtained between the opinion of cancer as a most dangerous disease and awareness of the campaign would be consistent with the theory. A campaign by the American

Cancer Society may be expected to provide information about things to do to prevent cancer and may also be expected to provide cognition consonant with a "fear of cancer." We would then expect persons who are afraid of the disease or who have an implied future behavior to expose themselves to the campaign and hence be more highly aware of it than persons who are not afraid of it or who have no implied future behavior. The voluntary audience would have this mixed character, and the data shown in Table 14 undoubtedly reflect both of these factors. It can readily be seen that, interpreted in this way, such data support the theory. It can also readily be seen that an enormous amount of assumption and conjecture is necessary in order to interpret the data at all.

It may strike some readers as strange that people will seek out "frightening" information rather than attempt to reduce the fear. But the point is that if a dissonance exists between knowing one is afraid and other relevant knowledge, and if the fear proves resistant to change, this is precisely what will happen since it does reduce the dissonance. This will be discussed further in Chapter Ten.

Reactions to Involuntary Exposure to Information

Let us now turn our attention to the reactions of a person when he is forcibly exposed to information which, if cognized, would produce or increase dissonance. It will be recalled from the previous chapter that, provided dissonance is already present, the person will be alert to protect himself from the new information. Three studies that provide data concerning these processes will be discussed.

1. The first study is concerned with the avoidance of dissonance by misperception. The quickest and probably the most effective way to deal with the introduction of disso-

nance when forcibly exposed to new information is to mis-perceive or avoid cognizing the stimuli which impinge. It is, of course, well known that people cognize and interpret information to fit what they already believe.

A study by Hastorf and Cantril (24) provides systematic data on the end result of this reaction to involuntary exposure to information which is potentially dissonance-producing. The authors took advantage of an instance in which there were differences of opinion concerning an event in order to study the effect of these different opinions on perception of the event. The initial situation which gave rise to the difference of opinion between two groups of people is best described in the authors' own words:

On a brisk Saturday afternoon, November 23, 1951, the Dartmouth football team played Princeton in Princeton's Palmer Stadium. It was the last game of the season for both teams and of rather special significance because the Princeton team had won all its games so far and one of its players, Kazmaier, was receiving All-American mention and had just appeared as the cover man on *Time* magazine, and was playing his last game.

A few minutes after the opening kick-off, it became apparent that the game was going to be a rough one. The referees were kept busy blowing their whistles and penalizing both sides. In the second quarter, Princeton's star left the game with a broken nose. In the third quarter, a Dartmouth player was taken off the field with a broken leg. Tempers flared both during and after the game. The official statistics of the game, which Princeton won, showed that Dartmouth was penalized 70 yards, Princeton 25, not counting more than a few plays in which both sides were penalized.

Needless to say, accusations soon began to fly. The game immediately became a matter of concern to players, students, coaches, and the administrative officials of the two institutions, as well as to alumni and the general public who had not seen the game but had become sensitive to the problem of big-time football through the recent exposures of subsidized players, commercialism, etc. Discussion of the game continued for several weeks.

One of the contributing factors to the extended discussion of the game was the extensive space given to it by both campus and metropolitan newspapers . . . [p. 129].

In essence, the Princeton newspapers accused Dartmouth of having been deliberately rough and of having deliberately

TABLE 15

Effect of Different Opinions on Perception of an Event

Question: "Do you believe the game was clean and fairly played or that it was unnecessarily rough and dirty?"

Response	Per Cent of Dartmouth Students (N = 163)	Per Cent of Princeton Students (N = 161)
Clean and fair	13	0
Rough and fair	39	3
Rough and dirty	42	93
Don't know	6	4

Question: "Which team do you feel started the rough play?"

Princeton started it	2	0
Both started it	53	11
Dartmouth started it	36	86
Neither or no answer	9	3

set out to injure the Princeton star player. The Dartmouth newspapers contended that the injury to the star player had been an accident and a not unusual one. They further contended that as a result of this accident the Princeton team started to be deliberately rough and dirty. By the time the study was done (a week after the game), opinion in the two schools had crystallized to the extent shown in Table 15.

There was clearly an enormous difference of opinion between students at the two schools. Princeton students almost unanimously felt that it was a rough and dirty game and that Dartmouth started the roughness. Dartmouth students, on the other hand, felt that it was a rough game but not necessarily dirty. Also, they tended to feel that both schools started the roughness.

A film of the football game was shown to about fifty students at each of the two schools. They were provided with a form on which they were asked to check, while viewing the film, any infractions of the rules which they saw. Table 16

TABLE 16

NUMBER OF INFRACTIONS CHECKED WHILE SEEING FILM

Group	Against Dartmouth Team		Against Princeton Team	
	Mean	SD	Mean	SD
Dartmouth students (N = 48)	4.3 *	2.7	4.4	2.8
Princeton students (N = 49)	9.8 *	5.7	4.2	3.5

* The difference between 4.3 and 9.8 is significant at the 1 per cent level of confidence.

presents the data on the average number of infractions they saw in the film.

It is clear from a comparison of Tables 15 and 16 that they managed to see the film in a manner which was consonant with their existing opinions on the matter. The Dartmouth students, who as a group felt the game was less rough and that both teams started the roughness, saw fewer infractions of the rules and an almost identical number of infractions by both teams. The Princeton students, who as a group thought the game was rough and dirty and that Dartmouth started the roughness, saw more infractions of the rules and more than twice as many infractions of the rules by the Dartmouth team as by the Princeton team. The end result was that they managed to avoid introduction, or increase, of dissonance.

2. The second study of reactions to involuntary exposure to information deals with the attempt to invalidate the dissonance-producing information. Even if new information to which a person has been involuntarily exposed is cognized, it is frequently possible to minimize immediately the dissonance thus introduced by invalidating the information in one way or another. Probably the easiest way to do this is simply not to accept the new information as factual.

The recent newspaper and magazine publicity given to the possible relationship between cigarette smoking and lung cancer provided a situation which resembled involuntary exposure to new information. One may well assume that most smokers, whether they wanted to or not, were exposed to this information because of the wide publicity it was given. One may also plausibly assume that the simplicity of the information would have made "misperception" difficult. One might then expect to observe disbelief or skepticism among those for whom this cognition introduces dissonance. One may state with certainty that the knowledge that smoking is conducive to lung cancer is dissonant with continuing to smoke. It is also clear that for most smokers it is not easy to give up smoking. It is among smokers, then, that one would expect to find skepticism concerning the reported research findings.

Relevant data are available from a survey conducted by the Minnesota Poll in February, 1954 (54). In this survey, in addition to questions about smoking habits, each respondent was asked, "There have been some recent reports of scientific studies to learn whether or not cigarette smoking may be a cause of lung cancer. Do you think the relationship between cigarette smoking and lung cancer is proven or not proven?" Of interest to us here is the comparison between those who smoke and those who do not smoke with respect to their acceptance of the link with cancer as proven.

Before presenting the data, however, there are a few points concerning interpretation which should be made. In most instances where one considers the relationship between holding or not holding some opinion and engaging in some behavior relevant to that opinion, the interpretation with respect to direction of causality is bound to be somewhat equivocal. Certainly we will all grant that cognition steers behavior. Consequently, any such relationship between behavior and holding or not holding an opinion could result from this direction of causality. The theory of dissonance, however, predicts the same relation with the causality in the opposite direction. In order to identify clearly the direction of causality then, and eliminate any ambiguity of interpretation, it is necessary to be able to say definitely that at some previous time the behavior existed in the absence of the opinion.

The data which will be presented concerning the opinions of smokers and nonsmokers are, fortunately, capable of unambiguous interpretation with respect to the direction of causality. The opinion in question, namely, whether or not the linkage between cigarette smoking and lung cancer was proven, could not have existed prior to one year before the survey was conducted since before that time there had been no publicity concerning it. If we exclude from the sample all those who report change in their smoking behavior during the last year, we will be left with a sample of persons whose smoking or not smoking existed previous to the impact of the publicity and whose behavior persisted without change. Out of a sample of 585 respondents, there were 32 (slightly over 5 per cent) who reported that within the previous year they either quit smoking (11 persons) or seriously tried to quit but didn't (21 persons). Eliminating these persons from the analysis makes practically no difference in the data and leaves the interpretation quite unequivocal. If there is a relation between smoking and opinion on the lung cancer issue, it cannot be that the opinion determined the behavior. From dissonance theory we would, of course, predict that smokers would evade the impact of this publicity which tends to produce cognition which is quite dissonant with the knowledge that they continue to smoke. We should consequently find that smokers less frequently believe that the link has been proven. Since much of the publicity concerning the matter stressed that heavy smokers were the most vulnerable to lung cancer, one would also expect that the more they smoke, the less they should believe it. Table 17 presents the data.

TABLE 17

Opinions of Respondents Concerning the Linkage between Cigarette Smoking and Lung Cancer

(In Percentage of Total N)

Group	Per Cent Who Thought Linkage Was		
	Proved	Not Proved	No Opinion
Nonsmokers (N = 348)	29	55	16
Light smokers (N = 59)	20	68	12
Moderate smokers (N = 105)	16	75	9
Heavy smokers (N = 41)	7	86	7

Two things are clear from the data. The more people smoked, the more they refused to accept information which would have been dissonant with smoking and the greater the tendency to have a definite opinion on the matter. Thus among heavy smokers, 86 per cent felt it was not proven, while only 7 per cent felt it was proven and only 7 per cent had no definite opinion. The last two percentages increase steadily through moderate and light smokers to nonsmokers. It is certainly clear from these data that persons committed to a given behavior end up rejecting information to which they are exposed which, if accepted, would produce dissonance with their cognition about their behavior.

3. The third study of reactions to involuntary exposure to information is concerned with forgetting the dissonance-producing information. It has probably already occurred to the reader that another way to reduce some newly introduced dissonance is to forget the information to which one was forcibly exposed. This is probably not an easy thing to do since the dissonance-producing information is likely to be salient for the person because of the very fact that it does introduce dissonance. But if the exposure to the new information is relatively brief, and if there are not other reminders of this information in the daily experiences of the subject, one would expect to observe some indication of such selective forgetting.

Wallen (52) conducted an experiment which shows this effect very clearly. The procedure, in brief, was as follows. Each subject was given a list of forty adjectives and was asked to indicate which did, and which did not, describe him. A week later each subject was shown the same list of adjectives with check marks presumably made by someone else who had been rating the subject. These check marks were arranged so that for each subject, half of them agreed with the way the subject had rated himself while the other half disagreed. After forty-eight hours had elapsed, the subjects were asked to recall these fictitious ratings. Each subject was thus forcibly exposed to information which introduced dissonance into his cognition. This assumes, of course, that if a subject regarded himself as, for example, "adaptable" and was then informed that someone who knew him rated him as "not adaptable," these two cognitions are dissonant with one another.

The results of the recall test clearly showed a tendency for the subjects to forget those items of information which introduced dissonance. This is best seen in a comparison of the percentage of errors made in recall for those ratings which had agreed with the subject's own statements and those which had disagreed with how the subject rated himself. In those instances where the subject and the unknown rater both agreed that an adjective did or did not apply, the errors made in recalling the fictitious ratings were 14.5 per cent and 16.7 per cent, respectively. When the two ratings disagreed, that is, the subject said an adjective did apply to himself and the unknown rater said it did not or vice versa, the errors made in recall were 25.6 per cent and 22.3 per cent, respectively. A repetition of the experiment in which recall was delayed for a week showed the same significant tendency to forget those items of information which had introduced dissonance into the subject's cognition.

A number of other findings from this study are also worth mentioning. The experimenter also obtained from the subjects ratings of each adjective in terms of whether or not the subject considered it a desirable trait. There is little indication in the data that the desirability or undesirability of the traits had any effect on recall. The important factor, in this situation at least, was clearly whether or not the two ratings agreed, irrespective of how desirable the subject considered the trait to be. Also of interest are the results from a control group where the second set of ratings were not ratings of the subject, thus not introducing dissonance. There is no indication that, for the control group, the agreement or disagreement between the two sets of ratings had any effect whatsoever on recall.

We may conclude that given sufficient elapsed time between the exposure to the new information and the recall, there is a significant tendency to forget those items of information which introduced dissonance.

Successful Production of Dissonance with Involuntary Exposure

If one puts together the notion that people will tend to avoid exposing themselves to new information which they expect would increase dissonance and the finding that, even if forcibly or inadvertently exposed to such potentially dissonance-increasing information, they will frequently manage to evade its impact by misperception, disbelief, or some other equally serviceable process, we are then led to the conclusion that it is very difficult to change an opinion that already exists if it is consonant with existing behavior or with an existing cluster of attitudes and opinions. This is indeed true. We may, however, ask ourselves about the circumstances under which such change of opinion would occur in the light of dissonance theory.

It seems clear that the avoidance and evasion of material which might produce or increase dissonance depends on anticipations (probably unverbalized ones) about the material or on preliminary assessments of the material. If one could, then, create a situation where the anticipation and the preliminary assessments of some information indicate a reduction of dissonance while the material itself actually increased dissonance, one would expect to obtain more intensified dissonance. Given the successful introduction of dissonance with existing opinions, one would expect to observe more change of opinion; that is, for some persons the dissonance thus introduced would be reduced by changing parts of the existing opinion system.

Ewing (14) reports a study which is pertinent to this

point. Subjects were given a persuasive communication to read, the actual content of which was highly unfavorable to Ford. It was actually more unfavorable to Ford than the initial opinions of any of the subjects. Exactly the same communication, as far as content is concerned, was given to all the subjects. One would then expect that if veridically cognized, this persuasive communication would have introduced dissonance with existing opinions. That is, subsequent to reading the report, there would have existed some cognitive elements which were dissonant with established cognition.

Two conditions were created in the study:

Condition I: For the subjects in this condition the persuasive communication was introduced with, "Numerous people have pointed out that Ford represents 'Big Business' at its worst. However, some of the following facts hardly justify this view [p. 80]." In other words, these subjects were led to expect that the persuasive communication would present content favorable to Ford. Thus, those whose opinions were already favorable to Ford would not have expected dissonant information and would not have protected themselves psychologically.

Condition II: For the subjects in this condition the persuasive communication was introduced so as to give an opposite expectation: "Numerous people have pointed out that Ford represents 'Big Business' at its best. However, some of the following facts hardly justify this view [p. 80]." These subjects, then, were led by this introduction to expect that the communication would contain content unfavorable to Ford. Those whose opinions were already favorable, while being forced to read the communication, would have been alert in defending themselves against the introduction of dissonance. It is worth while to repeat that actually the content was identical for both conditions and was more unfavorable to Ford than the opinions of the subjects. If Condition I was successful in beguiling the subjects and, hence, producing dissonance, one would expect more opinion change following the reading of the communication than in Condition II.

Before reading the persuasive communication, each subject indicated his opinion concerning the issue involved. Immediately after reading the communication the subjects were again asked to record their opinions. Two days later they indicated their opinions on the issue for the third time.

Table 18 presents the data from this experiment. They show that where the stated intent of the propagandist

TABLE 18

NET CHANGE OF OPINION AFTER READING PROPAGANDA

	Net Change of Opinion from	
	First to Second Statement	Second to Third Statement
Condition I: Stated intent of propaganda agrees with subject	2.37	.15
Condition II: Stated intent of propaganda disagrees with subject	1.35	− .92 *

* A negative sign indicates that the net change of opinion was in a direction away from the actual content of the propaganda.

was favorable to Ford (the subjects being generally favorable) and the content of the communication was unfavorable, the propaganda succeeded in changing subjects' opinions toward more unfavorable notions about Ford. Moreover, this change of opinion persisted to the third measurement. Where the content of the propaganda and the stated intent of the propagandist were both unfavorable to Ford, the change was much less and was almost completely nullified after two days had elapsed. The difference between the two groups was statistically significant far beyond the 1 per cent level of confidence for the total change of opinion from first to third measurement. The data corroborate our theoretical implication that where the expectation and initial impression of the subjects was to expect information consonant with their existing opinions (by having the stated intent agree with their opinions), the propaganda was successful.

The interpretation that the stated intent did function in this way was further supported by subjects' responses concerning whether they felt the propaganda was biased or unbiased, logical or not, in agreement with or opposed to own observations, and authoritative or of doubtful validity. Table 19 shows the percentage of responses which were

TABLE 19

PERCENTAGE OF FAVORABLE REPORTS OF THE CHARACTERISTICS
OF THE PROPAGANDA

Extent to Which Original Opinion Was More Favorable than Actual Content of the Communication	Condition I		Condition II	
	N	Per Cent of Favorable Reports	N	Per Cent of Favorable Reports
Almost none	4	0	5	100
Small	25	36	41	22
Moderate	13	50	26	15
Large	26	55	24	8

favorable (unbiased, logical, in agreement with own observation, and authoritative) for various degrees of difference between the subjects' own initial opinions and the opinion represented by the actual content of the propaganda.

It is clear that the actual content of the propaganda did not determine whether or not the subjects evaluated its characteristics favorably. The two groups read exactly the same content. Yet the percentages evaluating its characteristics favorably in Conditions I and II went in exactly opposite directions in relation to the difference between their initial opinion and the actual content of the propaganda. What seems to be the determining factor is the stated intent. For Condition I, the stated intent was close to the original opinions of those who differed very much with the actual content, while for Condition II, the stated intent was close to the original opinions of those who differed little or not at all with the actual content. The percentage of favorable evaluations of the characteristics of the propaganda, then, depended very much upon how close the original opinion of the subject was to the stated intent of the propaganda. The greater the difference between these two, the smaller was the percentage of favorable evaluations.

An Experiment on Exposure to Information

We have now discussed at great length the implications which the theory of dissonance has for the behavior of persons when confronted with the possibility or the necessity of exposing themselves to information or propaganda. We have also presented the results of a number of studies which are consistent with the implications of the theory. Some of the studies discussed are, however, equivocal with respect to interpretation. I consequently designed and, with the help of Danuta Ehrlich and Peter Schönbach, conducted a laboratory experiment specifically to test the whole range of the relationship between dissonance and exposure to information.

It is worth while to review briefly the specific implications of the theory for this type of behavior. For the sake of simplicity, the review here will restrict itself to consideration of dissonance between knowledge of what one is doing and other cognitions under circumstances where behavioral cognition is resistant to change because the behavior itself is difficult to change. The following would be expected:

1. If existing cognition is wholly or mostly consonant with the knowledge about behavior in question, there will be no motivation (from this source) to acquire information. In these circumstances, then, one should observe little or no voluntary exposure to information. On the other hand, there should be no active avoidance of information either.

2. If there is appreciable dissonance between general cognition and the behavioral elements in question, there should be active effort to reduce the dissonance and to avoid increase of dissonance. Thus, if a source of information is viewed as potentially decreasing dissonance or providing new elements consonant with the behavior, persons should expose themselves to this source. If the source of information is viewed as potentially increasing dissonance, there should be active avoidance of exposure to the information.

3. If the dissonance becomes greater than the resistance to change of behavior, the behavior should change. In this manner the dissonance is eliminated and what was dissonant with knowledge about the old behavior is, of course, consonant with knowledge about the new behavior. If the dissonance is so large that it is *almost* sufficient to overcome the resistance to changing the behavior, one may expect that the easiest way to eliminate the dissonance is temporarily to increase it sufficiently so as to change the behavior. Under these circumstances one would expect persons *to expose themselves to dissonance-increasing information*. However, this would occur only in instances of extremely large, near maximum, dissonance. The maximum dissonance that can

be produced between any two cognitive elements is, of course, equal to the resistance to change of that element which is less resistant.

This brief summary is simply a restatement, in words, of what was stated graphically in Figure 4 (p. 130). In order to test these theoretical implications, an experiment was designed to fulfill the following requirements:

1. The individual subject should be in a situation where he engages in continuing behavior which has some appreciable resistance to change. It must, however, be clear that change is possible.

2. Events in the environment should be manipulated experimentally so as to produce, for some persons, cognition consonant with the knowledge of this behavior and, for others, cognition dissonant with the knowledge of this behavior.

3. At a certain time each subject should be given the opportunity to acquire further information relevant to his behavior.

The essential design of the experiment was simple. A gambling situation was devised in which the subject had to make a choice as to which side he wanted to play on. In order to introduce resistance to change, a penalty was introduced for changing sides. By manipulating the likelihood of the subject's winning or losing, consonance or dissonance could be introduced.

A total of 108 subjects were used in the experiment. They were all male undergraduates of the University of Minnesota who volunteered for the experiment. Each experimental session was conducted with one subject at a time.

When the subject arrived he entered the experimental room and met the experimenter who also introduced him to the observer. The observer subsequently took no part in the experiment. His job was to record all remarks the subject made during the course of the experiment and to record the time the subject spent exposing himself to new information. The experimenter told the subject:

Before we start I would like to explain that we are studying people's behavior in gambling situations. We have designed a two-person card game especially for this study and the two of us are going to play against each other.

In this game, the two sides are not even: one is much better than the other. After you familiarize yourself with the rules of the game, which are typed on this sheet (the instruction sheet is pointed to) you will be asked to make a choice between those two sides, that is, between Player A and Player B. Incidentally, we will play for money and we actually start you with two dollars and fifty cents which you may consider payment for your participation in this experiment. Whatever you win, you can take away with you. Whatever you lose will remain with us. (The money is placed before the subject at this point. He is also given the instruction sheet.)

Why don't you now read the description of the game. If you have any questions about the instructions, don't hesitate to ask them.

The instruction sheet which the subject then read is reproduced below:

Description of the Game:
There are two players in this game: Player A and Player B. Before each game, the cards will be shuffled, cut, and seven cards will be dealt out on the table, face up. The values of the seven cards will then be added up. The cards count: ace, one point; deuce, two points; three, three points; and so on up to ten. Tens and picture cards count ten points each. The maximum total for seven cards would be, of course, seventy.

Whenever the total number of points is 48 or less, Player A wins. Player A always wins the exact amount of his wager. (You will be asked to state how much you want to bet before each game.) At 49 points nobody wins. Player B wins if the cards add up to 50 or more. His possibilities of winning are as follows: from 50 to 54 points he wins the exact amount of his wager; from 55 to 59 he wins twice the amount of his wager; from 60 to 64 he wins four times the amount of his wager; and from 65 to 70 he wins eight times the amount of his wager.

Thus when the total number of points is:

48 or less	Player A wins and Player B loses;
49	Neither of the players wins or loses;
50–54	Player B wins and Player A loses 1–1;
55–59	Player B wins and Player A loses 2–1;
60–64	Player B wins and Player A loses 4–1;
65–70	Player B wins and Player A loses 8–1.

After the subject had read the description of the game, the experimenter continued as follows:

We are going to play thirty games altogether. That is, thirty times the cards will be shuffled and seven cards dealt out, face up, on the table. Before each game, you will be asked to bet. You can bet anywhere from five to twenty-five cents each time.

To make this game as fair as possible, you will be allowed to switch once during the thirty trials if you want to. What I mean is that you can change once to the other side at any time. If you do decide you want to change sides it will cost you one dollar, however, to do so. Consequently, as you see, it is very important for you to make the correct choice before we start playing.

From our experience we know that it is not too difficult to make the correct choice as long as you take enough time to consider it carefully. Take your time now and think it through before making your decision. Here is paper and pencil which you may use for any calculations you would like to make.

After the subject announced his decision, the experimenter made sure that he was fairly confident about it. The subject was then handed a sheet of paper on which the numbers *one* through *thirty* were indicated. He was told that instead of passing money back and forth across the table he could keep a record of his winnings and losses on each trial so that at any time he would know how much money he had. The experimenter then produced the cards and they were ready to start playing. Before each trial the subject was asked how much he wanted to bet on that trial. The experimenter then shuffled the cards and asked the subject to cut them before turning seven cards over.

After twelve trials, the experimenter produced a graph purporting to show the cumulative probabilities of all possible scores from 10 to 70. The experimenter told the subject that from the graph, he could calculate the exact probability of various scores and could thus find out exactly which side was better and how much better. Actually, the graph given to the subject, if interpreted correctly, would have told each subject that he was playing on the losing side. A different graph was used, of course, depending on which side the subject was playing. The experimenter explained carefully how to use the graph, giving examples of calculations from it. The experimenter tried to make sure that the subject understood the graph sufficiently to use it. The subject was then told:

This graph belongs to you from now on. You may use it or not use it; it is entirely up to you. You may spend as much time with it as you choose. Whenever you are ready to start playing again, just let me know.

The experimenter then waited until the subject indicated that he was finished looking at the graph and wanted to resume play. The observer recorded the exact amount of time that the subject voluntarily spent looking at, or calculating from, the graph. When the subject stopped looking at the graph, the experiment was concluded. The experimenter then questioned the subject about various things and explained the purpose of the experiment to him. Each subject kept $2.50 in payment for his participation.

Let us recapitulate by pointing out how the above procedure produced the desired situation.

Creating resistance to change of behavior. The subject, believing one side of the game was more advantageous than the other, made a choice as to which side he wanted to play on. The experimenter, by stressing the fact that it was possible to decide correctly, and by stressing that the subject could do it correctly if he thought it through, made it difficult for the subject to admit later on that he was wrong and, consequently, difficult for him to change. To add to this difficulty, it was stressed that while he was permitted to change at any time he liked, such change would cost him a dollar.

Producing cognition consonant or dissonant with knowledge of his behavior. The behavior in question here was, of course, continuing to play on the side of the game which the subject initially chose. By the twelfth trial there had been produced a large range of gains and losses. Subjects who had been winning a lot had experiences impinging on their cognition which tended to tell them that the side they were on was indeed the better side—cognition which was certainly consonant with the knowledge that they continued to play on that side. On the other hand, subjects who had been losing often had acquired a lot of information about the game which was quite dissonant with the knowledge that they continued to play on the side originally chosen. In other words, there was experimentally produced a wide range of degree to which the person's relevant cognition was dissonant with his knowledge about his behavior.

Introducing an opportunity to acquire information. The graph, when presented to the subject at the end of the twelfth trial, was clearly and obviously an opportunity for the subject to obtain further information about the situation. He was told that this graph would give him the correct picture of the probabilities in the game he was playing. His expectations of what kinds of things the graph would tell him would, of course, be somewhat dependent upon his experiences with the game thus far. This point will be further elaborated in specifying the predictions from the theory of dissonance.

RESULTS

The major result of the experiment can, of course, be embodied in a curve showing the relationship between the magnitude of consonance or dissonance present in the cognition of the subject at the time he was presented with the graph and the amount of time he spent looking at that graph. The measure of time, it will be recalled, was obtained by having the observer measure, with a stop watch, how long the subject spent looking at the graph. There was undoubtedly much error involved in this measure. Some subjects could obtain as much information in one minute as less adept subjects could obtain in perhaps five minutes. The measure of degree of dissonance also presented a bit of a problem. It is clear that winnings or losses are related to consonance since they reflect the person's experiences in the situation. Since the wager was allowed to vary, however, it was deemed most desirable to take the difference between the amount of money the subject had at the end of the twelfth trial and the initial $2.50 that he started with, and divide this figure by the average amount of that subject's wagers over the twelve trials. The data showing the relation between these two measures are shown in Table 20 and in Figure 5.

It is clear that the amount of time the subject spent looking at the graph is a rather complicated function of the

TABLE 20

Relation between Dissonance and Time Spent Looking at Graph

Intervals on Dissonance Scale (Winnings per Average Wager)	Number of Subjects in Interval	Average Time Spent on Graph (In Seconds)	Standard Deviation of Time Scores
+ 3.0 and greater	7	90.7	63.6
+ 2.99 to + 1.00	15	178.3	121.0
+ 0.99 to − 1.00	9	173.3	129.1
− 1.01 to − 3.00	14	308.5	141.1
− 3.01 to − 5.00	18	239.9	195.5
− 5.01 to − 7.00	7	94.1	43.3
− 7.01 to − 9.00	3	43.0	23.6
− 9.01 to −11.00	4	122.5	110.3
−11.01 to −13.00	6	155.5	46.8

measure of dissonance. It is actually a composite of the two curves shown in Figure 4 (p. 130). Since the subject's expectations of what information the graph will yield depend on his previous experience with the game, the data change from following the curve of "dissonance-reduction-expectation" to "dissonance-increase-expectation." This shift in ex-

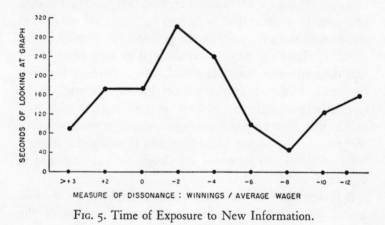

Fig. 5. Time of Exposure to New Information.

pectation occurs at about —5.00 on the abscissa of Figure 5. Let us review briefly how this obtained relationship fits the predictions from the theory of dissonance.

1. It was predicted that if the relation between cognition and behavior was largely consonant, there would be little or no motivation to acquire information by looking at the graph. As expected, on the positive end of the dissonance scale the amount of time spent looking at the graph was not very great. In other words, where the experience of the subject had produced cognition consonant with his knowledge about his behavior, he did not spend very much time looking at the graph. One may regard this part of the prediction as being only *partially* confirmed, however, because if there were little or no motivation to look at the graph, averages around 175 seconds seem a bit too large. One would have expected the time spent looking at the graph to have been even lower. I will return to this point later.

2. It was predicted that when the relation between cognition and knowledge about behavior was dissonant there would have been considerable time spent on the graph if the subject hoped he could obtain information in this manner that would reduce the dissonance. We do indeed find that for moderate values of dissonance (—1.00 to —5.00) the amount of time spent on the graph reaches a peak. These persons, through their experience with the game, had acquired a moderate amount of cognition which was dissonant with continuing to play on the side originally chosen. It was possible, however, for them to hope that the graph would tell them that they were actually on the correct side. If they found such information in the graph it would have reduced dissonance, and they consequently spent considerable time searching for such information.

3. It was predicted that when the relation between cognition and behavior was dissonant there would be an active

avoidance of the graph if the graph were perceived as yielding information which would probably increase the dissonance which already existed. Those subjects who were fairly extreme on the scale of dissonance (-5.00 to -9.00) had had experience with the game which had introduced considerable dissonant cognition. Furthermore, these subjects had had experience which had been consistent enough so that they expected the graph would contain information which would further increase the dissonance which they were struggling to get rid of. They, consequently, avoided looking at the graph. The average amount of time these subjects spent looking at the graph was low indeed.

4. It was predicted that if the dissonance between cognition and knowledge of behavior became so large as to be close to the magnitude of the resistance to change of the behavior, then the easiest way to eliminate the dissonance would be to increase it temporarily to a point where it was greater than the resistance to change of the behavior. Then switching to the other side of the game would eliminate the dissonance. One may imagine that the value of -12.00 on the dissonance scale was certainly close to the magnitude of resistance to change, since this represented losing twelve times the average amount of the wager in twelve trials. And we find, indeed, that as the value of dissonance approached this point, the amount of time they spent looking at the graph increased.

To repeat, comparing Figure 5 with the theoretical curves presented in Figure 4, it may be seen that one would obtain exactly the data actually obtained if one assumes that at some point of moderate dissonance the expectations of the subjects change from expecting dissonance reduction to expecting increase of dissonance.

Since the relationship is so complicated, it is worth while

to point out that the variation of time spent looking at the graph in relation to variation in dissonance is statistically significant beyond the 1 per cent level of confidence using a nonparametric analysis of variance. Testing the differences between adjacent intervals also shows that the initial rise, subsequent drop, and final rise are each statistically significant at the 5 per cent level of confidence.

Given the high level of overall significance and the significance, or near significance, of the adjacent differences tested, we may be quite confident that the obtained shape of the function between the dissonance measure and the time spent looking at the graph is not due to chance.

Let us return, now, to a further consideration of the relatively high values of average time on the positive end of the dissonance scale. Since, theoretically, one would expect little or no motivation to seek out information here, one would have expected these values to be considerably lower unless other factors entered. One can, indeed, clearly identify one complicating factor which made these values unusually high. It will be recalled that the graph which was shown to the subjects, if viewed correctly, would have told each one that the side of the game he had initially chosen was wrong. There would then have been a number of subjects on the positive side of the dissonance scale who, looking briefly at the graph simply because the experimenter gave it to them, would have seen it correctly and thus have had some dissonance introduced into a system which had been quite consonant. This really corresponded to involuntary exposure. If this is correct, one would expect that those who, while looking at the graph, said something indicating correct perception of some part of the graph would have taken considerably longer to look at it than the others. This should be true, however, only for those on the positive side of the dissonance scale. Table 21 presents the average time for those two classes of subjects grouped in intervals large enough to avoid very low numbers of cases.

It is clear from the data in Table 21 that for those subjects on the positive side of the dissonance scale (including the interval containing the zero point) those who indicated some correct perception did look at the graph longer. The difference here was significant beyond the 5 per cent level of confidence (tested nonparametrically). Subjects on the negative side of the dissonance scale showed a slight dif-

TABLE 21

RELATION BETWEEN PERCEPTION OF GRAPH AND
TIME SPENT LOOKING AT IT

Intervals on Dissonance Scale	Subjects Who Indicated Correct Perception		Others	
	N	Mean Time	N	Mean Time
+10.99 to − 1.00	14	200.5	17	121.3
− 1.01 to − 5.00	15	247.3	17	289.8
− 5.01 to −13.00	11	109.3	9	112.1

ference in the opposite direction. These differences did not even approach significance. It seems clear, then, that the surprisingly high average time found on the positive end of the scale was indeed a result of dissonance introduced by the graph itself.

If the interpretation of the data in terms of dissonance theory is correct, then there should be some supporting evidence in the spontaneous comments of the subjects and in the number of subjects who decided to switch after seeing the graph.

Let us look first at certain spontaneous comments made by the subjects while looking at the graph. For each subject a judgment could be made as to whether or not they mentioned some *incorrect* perception of the graph, that is, that they saw the graph as telling them that the side of the game they were on was the better side. From dissonance theory one would expect this most frequently among those subjects who either consulted the graph to reduce their dissonance (interval from —1.01 to —5.00) or avoided the graph for fear it would increase their dissonance (interval from —5.01 to —9.00). Such remarks showing incorrect perception do occur for 26 per cent of the subjects in these two intervals. Among those who have been winning, and hence have little or no dissonance, only 16 per cent of the subjects made such comments indicating incorrect perception. Among those in the last two intervals (—9.01 to —13.00) where the subjects presumably are increasing their dissonance temporarily in order to change, there is not a single instance of comment showing incorrect perception of the graph.

According to the theory one would also expect to find that most subjects in the last two intervals (—9.01 to —13.00) switched from one side to the other after looking at the graph. Actually, 60 per cent of these subjects changed sides after seeing the graph as compared to 35.7 per cent of the other subjects on the negative side (—1.01 to —9.00). Of course, there are very few persons on the positive side (only 10 per cent) who changed sides after seeing the graph. While neither the differences with respect to incorrect perceptions nor the differences with respect to changing sides are statistically significant, they are consistent with the theory. One might well ask, however, why only 60 per cent of the subjects in the last two intervals changed when the theory would expect all of them to change. It must be remembered that it cost the subject one dollar to change sides and it is precisely these extreme losers who had very little money left at the end of the twelfth trial. Most of them still had more than a dollar left but not very much more. A number of these said that they felt like changing after seeing the graph, but with the little money they had left, they couldn't afford the dollar. Others may have felt this way but did not say it.

Summary

This chapter has dealt with data concerning one aspect of the process of dissonance reduction, namely, obtaining new cognition which will be consonant with existing cognition and avoiding new cognition which will be dissonant with existing cognition.

It has been shown that much of the data concerning selectivity in exposure to propaganda, information, and mass media can be interpreted along the lines of attempted dissonance reduction. Unfortunately, most such data are causally equivocal and cannot be regarded as providing strong corroboration for the theory of dissonance.

The data concerning reactions of people when involuntarily exposed to new information are, fortunately, more adequate. When dissonance exists, persons will be able to evade the impact of dissonance-increasing information, even when forcibly exposed to it, by various means such as misperception, denying its validity, and the like. If persons do not expect a source of information to produce dissonant cognition and, hence, are not alert to avoid the dissonance, the information will have more impact.

The interaction between the amount of dissonance which exists and the expectation concerning some particular source of new information in determining whether or not a person will expose himself to, or avoid, this source of information is made particularly clear by the results of an experiment designed to test these implications of the theory.

EIGHT

The Role of Social Support: Theory

The social group is at once a major source of cognitive dissonance for the individual and a major vehicle for eliminating and reducing the dissonance which may exist in him. On the one hand, information and opinions which are communicated to him by others may introduce new elements which are dissonant with already existing cognition. On the other hand, one of the most effective ways of eliminating dissonance is to discard one set of cognitive elements in favor of another, something which can sometimes only be accomplished if one can find others who agree with the cognitions one wishes to retain and maintain. Processes of social communication and social influence are, hence, inextricably interwoven with processes of creation and reduction of dissonance.

The most convenient way to elaborate the implications of the theory of dissonance for social processes, and for the role which social support plays in the reduction of dissonance, is to first outline, in brief, some theory concerning social influence processes which I have already published (15, 17). I do not intend, however, merely to recapitulate this theory of social influence but rather to recast it and, perhaps, make it more powerful by relating it to the theory of dissonance.

The existence of disagreement among members of a group on some issue or some opinion, if perceived by the members, certainly produces cognitive dissonance. Let us examine this a bit more closely to see what, specifically, is dissonant with what. I wish to assert, here, that the cognitive elements corresponding to some opinion the person holds would be dissonant with knowing that another person holds a contrary opinion. If a person looks at a plot of grass and sees that it is green, this knowledge is dissonant with knowing that another person, not color-blind, claims it is brown. Designation of the relations between such cognitive elements as dissonant is, of course, consistent with the conceptual definition of dissonance. The cognition that another person says a particular patch of grass is brown would *not* follow from one's seeing it as green. Similarly, if a person is convinced that cold northern winters are very healthful and invigorating, these cognitive elements are dissonant with knowing that someone else considers them simply unlivable.

What factors affect the magnitude of the dissonance which is established by such open expression of disagreement? Here one finds that the same variables which have been previously discussed as affecting the magnitude of dissonance are again the important ones to consider. But let us be more specific. The total dissonance introduced into a person's cognition by the knowledge that someone holds a contrary opinion will, of course, depend upon how many existing cognitions are consonant with the cognitive elements corresponding to the opinion in question. The larger the number of consonant relations involving this opinion, the less will be the magnitude of the dissonance introduced by the disagreement. By number of consonant relations we mean, as previously discussed, a summation weighted by the importance of the elements involved in the relation. This leads to the specification of two major variables which affect the magnitude of dissonance created by disagreement with others.

1. To the extent that objective, nonsocial, cognitive elements exist which are consonant with a given opinion, belief, or knowledge, the expression of disagreement will produce a lesser magnitude of dissonance. Thus, where the content of the opinion concerns "testable physical reality," there will be little dissonance created by social disagreement. If a person believes that glass is fragile, there are so many cognitive elements, acquired experientially, which are consonant with this belief that there will be relatively little dissonance if someone else utters a contrary view. On the other hand, if a person believes in reincarnation, there are very few, if any, cognitive elements corresponding to "physical reality" which are consonant with this belief; and the expression of a contrary opinion will introduce a greater total dissonance into his cognition.

2. The larger the number of people that one knows already agree with a given opinion which he holds, the less will be the magnitude of dissonance introduced by some other person's expression of disagreement. Since knowing that someone else holds the same opinion is consonant with holding that opinion oneself, the more people who agree with an opinion, the more cognitive elements there are which are consonant with the cognition corresponding to that opinion. If, then, one member in a group disagrees with a person's opinion while there are several who agree, the magnitude of the total dissonance created for the person will be less than if only the disagreement existed.

The magnitude of the dissonance, of course, will also be

affected by those variables that affect the importance of the cognitive elements involved in the dissonance. The more important the elements, the greater will be the magnitude of the dissonance. One must then, in the context of social disagreement, identify the variables that will affect the importance of the cognitive elements corresponding to knowledge of what others believe.

One such variable is, of course, the relevance of the disagreeing person, or the group in which the disagreement is voiced, to the opinion at issue. The more relevant the person or group to the opinion, the more important will be the cognitive elements corresponding to knowledge about the opinions of these others, and the greater will be the dissonance set up by the expression of disagreement. If the person voicing disagreement is seen as expert or very knowledgeable on such matters, the dissonance between knowledge of his contrary opinion and one's own opinion will be greater. If the opinion on which disagreement is voiced is important to, or especially relevant to, the group in which the disagreement is voiced, the dissonance will likewise be greater. Relevance here means that the opinion is within the realm of content matter with which the group usually concerns itself.

Another variable which clearly will affect the importance of the cognitive elements, and hence the magnitude of the dissonance, is the attractiveness of the person voicing the disagreement or of the group within which it is voiced. This variable, when referring to the group, has frequently been called cohesiveness, denoting the sum total of attractions that pull the members to, and keep them in, the group. It is plausible to assume that the dissonance between one's own opinion and knowledge of a contrary opinion voiced by some other person is greater if the other person is important to one in some sense or if the group is important or attractive.

One other factor which will affect the magnitude of the dissonance must be mentioned here, namely, the extent of the disagreement itself. If one person says "black" and another says "white," the disagreement, and the dissonance in the cognition of each, will be greater than if the disagreement is between "black" and "dark gray." Consider, for example, a person who is convinced that the only way to deal with juvenile delinquents is strict discipline and harsh punishment for any infraction of the rules. If a friend of his voices the opinion that the discipline must be reasonable and that the punishment should be mild and take cognizance of mitigating factors, some dissonance will be created for the person. The dissonance would be much greater, however, if this friend voiced the opinion that the only way to deal with juvenile delinquents was to shower them with love and kindness. We are actually dealing here with dissonance between clusters of cognitive elements. The larger the number of dissonant relations between the elements in the two clusters, the greater will be the total dissonance.

The Reduction of Dissonance Stemming from Social Disagreement

According to the theory, when there is dissonance there will be corresponding pressures to reduce the dissonance, the magnitude of these pressures depending upon the magnitude of the dissonance. Here again, the ways in which dissonance reduction may be accomplished are similar to those that have already been discussed in other contexts. Three methods for reducing dissonance stemming from social disagreement readily suggest themselves.

1. The dissonance may be reduced, or perhaps even eliminated completely, by changing one's own opinion so that it corresponds more closely with one's knowledge of what others believe. Changing one's own opinion will effectively reduce dissonance only, of course, if there are not many persons who already agree with one's original opinion (who would then be disagreeing after the opinion change). This is completely analogous to changing existing cognition in other contexts.

2. Another way of reducing the dissonance would be to influence those persons who disagree to change their opinion so that it more closely corresponds to one's own. This is, of course, analogous to changing the environment and thereby changing the cognitive elements reflecting that environment. In the context of dissonance stemming from social disagreement, this is a major manifestation of pressure to reduce dissonance. These first two methods, taken together, represent the usual sort of influence process which results in movement toward uniformity in groups in the presence of disagreement. Thus, recasting the theory of influence processes in terms of dissonance theory makes it quite easy to derive movement toward uniformity.

3. Another way of reducing dissonance between one's own opinion and the knowledge that someone else holds a different opinion is to make the other person, in some manner, not comparable to oneself. Such an allegation can take a number of forms. One can attribute different characteristics, experiences, or motives to the other person or one can even reject him and derogate him. Thus if some other person claims the grass is brown when I see it as green, the dissonance thus created can be effectively reduced if the characteristic of being color-blind can be attributed to the other person. There would be no dissonance between knowing the grass is green and knowing that a color-blind person asserted

it was brown. Similarly, if one person believes that flying saucers are space ships from other planets and some other person voices the opinion that flying saucers, as such, do not even exist, the resulting dissonance in the cognition of the former may be reduced if he can believe that the latter is a stupid, ignorant, unfriendly, and bigoted individual.

Since all three of these processes, namely, changing one's own opinion, attempting to influence others, and attributing noncomparability to others, may potentially reduce dissonance, one would expect to see all of them intensified in degree as the magnitude of the dissonance increased. Thus, as the magnitude of difference of opinion increased, as the relevance of the opinion to the group increased, as the attraction to the group increased, and as the number of other cognitive elements consonant with the opinion decreased, one would expect greater tendencies to change one's own opinion in response to disagreement, greater effort expended at influencing those who disagreed (especially those who disagreed most), and a greater tendency to make those who disagreed noncomparable. In short, returning once again to the basic theory, the pressure to reduce dissonance will be a function of the magnitude of the dissonance.

This much is recasting of previously published theory, the derivations of which have been well substantiated by experimental work. Let us very briefly review the results of this experimental work before proceeding to elaborate further implications of the theory of dissonance for social influence processes.

Several experiments have shown that the magnitude of dissonance affects the manifestations of pressure to reduce dissonance in the theoretically predicted direction. In the presence of disagreement in a group, increasing the attraction of the members to the group increases the attempts on the part of the members to reduce the dissonance occasioned by the disagreement. Back (2) has shown experimentally that both the tendency to change one's own opinion and the degree to which one tries to influence others increase as the attraction of the members to the group increases. In his experiment, Back dealt with groups composed of two persons who had never met one another before. In half of his groups, instructions were given to each subject which were oriented toward making the group and the other member of the group very attractive to him. In the other groups, the instructions were oriented toward making the group less attractive to the member. Otherwise the procedure was identical in all groups. Each of the two subjects in each group was individually shown a set of pictures before being brought together. Each one was asked to write an interpretation of the pictures. They were then brought together and allowed to discuss the matter as long as they liked. When they finished their discussion, they were separated and again asked to write down their interpretation of the pictures.

The degree to which each subject's opinion changed in response to the discussion was measured by examining the extent to which his second interpretation differed from his first one in the direction of his partner's interpretation. The data show that the average number of such changes of one's own opinion in the direction of bringing it closer to the opinion of the partner was greater in the groups of high attraction than in those of low attraction. In other words, as the magnitude of the dissonance created by the disagreement increased (because the person voicing the disagreement, or the group in which it was voiced, was more attractive), there was more change of opinion toward reducing this dissonance.

By careful observation of the discussion between the two subjects in each group, Back was also able to obtain measures of the degree to which they tried to influence one another. The data showed, again, that the greater the attraction to the group, the greater was the degree to which the members tried to influence one another. In other words, the greater the magnitude of dissonance, the stronger the attempt to reduce this dissonance by changing the opinion of the person who disagreed.

An experiment by myself and others (18) corroborated these findings by Back in a somewhat different context. In this experiment, groups of six or seven persons were employed. Again, some of the groups were made highly attractive to the members, while other groups were instructed in a way calculated to make the group less attractive. The discussion in these groups, concerning opinions about a labor-management dispute, was conducted entirely in writing. In this way a complete record of who wrote to whom, and about what, was obtained. The perception of disagreement in the group—that is, each person's perception of how many disagreed with him and how much—was also controlled in all groups by falsifying the "opinion census" which was handed to each subject purporting to tell him what each other person in the group thought about the issue. The results showed that in the high attraction groups there was more change of own opinion than in the low attraction groups. The data also showed that the subjects in the high attraction groups wrote more words attempting to influence those who disagreed than did comparable subjects in the low attraction groups.

Schachter (46) reported an experiment which was primarily concerned with reduction of dissonance by means of derogating those who voiced disagreement. Groups of subjects were brought together ostensibly for the first meeting of a club interested in problems of juvenile delinquency. Half of these clubs were made to appear very attractive to the members while the other half, otherwise treated identically, were made to seem considerably less attractive, both in terms of how well they expected to like others in the club and how attractive the activities of the club would be to them. At their first meeting they were asked to discuss a case study of a juvenile delinquent which was written so that all subjects were inclined to feel that this particular delinquent needed love and kindness. In each club there were three members who, unknown to the subjects, were paid participants. These three appeared in every group and their behavior was standard in all groups. One of these always voiced an opinion which agreed with the opinions of the subjects; another always started out with the opinion that this particular delinquent in the case study needed harsh punishment, but as the discussion progressed, changed his mind so that he ended up agreeing with the subjects; the third paid participant consistently throughout the discussion held to the disagreeing opinion that harsh punishment was the best thing. These roles were rotated among the paid participants so as to cancel out any systematic personality differences among them.

The major measures obtained were the degree to which, at the end of the discussion, the subjects indicated derogation of these three persons and indicated they would rather not have them continue as members of the club. In none of the conditions was there any evidence of derogation or rejection of the person who always agreed with the group, nor of the one who started out disagreeing but ended up agreeing. But there was evidence of derogation and rejection of the persistent disagreer. What is more, the degree to which the persistent deviant was rejected was greater in the high attraction than in the low attraction groups. In other words, there was evidence that reduction of dissonance was attempted through rejection of the person who voiced disagreement and that the extent to which this occurred depended upon the magnitude of the dissonance created by this disagreement.

In the same experiment, Schachter also varied the relevance which the issue had for the group. Some of the groups, as stated above, came together in order to discuss juvenile delinquency. Other groups, however, came together for a quite different purpose but were asked, as a favor to the experimenter, "just this once" to discuss the case of the juvenile delinquent. It would never happen again, they were assured. Otherwise these groups were treated in exactly the same manner as the others. The results show that when the issue is largely irrelevant to the group, and hence the magnitude of dissonance created by the expression of disagreement is less, there is less rejection of the persistent deviant.

There are also data from experimental work which show that the larger the number of existing cognitive elements which are consonant with an opinion, the less is the magnitude of total dissonance introduced by the knowledge that someone else disagrees. Hochbaum (26), for example, performed an experiment in which half of the subjects in his groups were given prior evidence that their opinions on certain kinds of issues tended to be valid. When later faced with disagreement from others on this kind of issue, they showed considerably less change of opinion than did those who did not have this prior evidence. The same effect was shown in somewhat different form in the previously mentioned experiment by myself and others (18). In this experiment, those who knew that some others in the group agreed with them were considerably less affected by disagreement than were those who thought that all the others disagreed with their own opinion. This point seems so obvious, however, that there is little to be gained in documenting it further.

The remaining evidence to be reviewed here concerns the

relationship between the extremity of the disagreement which is voiced and the magnitude of dissonance created by this disagreement. Experiments reported by myself and Thibaut (20) and by Gerard (23) both indicate that the magnitude of dissonance and the manifestations of the pressure to reduce the dissonance increase as the extremity of the disagreement increases. In both these experiments, groups of subjects were asked to discuss an issue which was chosen so as to produce a wide range of initial opinion in each group. The discussions were carried on by means of writing notes to one another so that the data on who attempted to influence whom would be easily and reliably obtained. Both experiments showed that the great majority of the communications attempting to influence others to change their opinions were directed toward those who disagreed most extremely with the communicator. In other words, the attempts to reduce dissonance by changing the opinions of those who disagreed were strongest in the direction of those disagreements which created the greatest dissonance.

Let us now return to further consideration of the implications of dissonance for social influence and communication processes. The theory that has been stated so far in this chapter has dealt with the social process which goes on in an effort to reduce dissonance which has been introduced by the open expression of disagreement in a group. One may also, however, examine how a person with cognitive dissonance which has arisen outside the social group reacts if he is exposed to an influence process within the group. It seems clear that a social group is a potential resource for the reduction of dissonance, irrespective of how and where the dissonance has arisen. By obtaining social support for some opinion, the person thus adds cognitive elements which are consonant with that opinion and thus reduces the total magnitude of dissonance.

One would consequently expect that if a person has appreciable dissonance between two clusters of cognitive elements, he would initiate communication and influence processes with other persons in an attempt to reduce this dissonance. He might attempt to obtain knowledge that others agree with his opinion, thereby adding new consonant cognitive elements. He could do this by finding others who already agree, or by influencing others to agree. At any rate, the existence of dissonance in persons would be one of the determinants of what issues and topics are brought up in social interactions and thus become relevant issues to groups.

For example, if a person has recently bought a new car, and has the usual postdecision dissonance, one would expect him to communicate about his recent purchase to other people he knows. If he knows someone else who owns an identical car, one would certainly expect him to inform that person of his purchase since he would then be confident about obtaining cognition consonant with his decision. He even might hope to get agreement from owners of different cars that the car he bought is a very good one. If, however, some friend of his proceeded to exclaim that the car the person had just purchased was very poor, one would expect considerable persuasive discussion to ensue.

As has already been hinted in the last paragraph, in addition to determining the content of communication and influence processes among persons, that is, what topics are talked about, the existence of dissonance will also affect the direction of communication, that is, to whom one talks. If, except for the dissonance produced by disagreement from others, most of the cognitions relevant to a certain opinion are consonant with that opinion, a person's communication and attempted influence will be exerted mainly toward changing the opinions of those who have voiced disagreement. Furthermore, these influence attempts will be directed mainly toward those persons within a group who disagree most, since these greater disagreements correspond to the large dissonances in his cognition. If, however, there is already considerable dissonance between the cognitions corresponding to some opinion and many existing cognitive elements, the direction of influence exertion will be less simple. On the one hand, the dissonances produced by the open expression of disagreement from others may be reduced by attempting to influence those who disagree; but on the other hand, the already existing cognitive dissonance may be reduced in magnitude by communication from those who already agree with the opinion in question, thus adding more cognitive elements consonant with the opinion. One would then expect that, not considering the dissonance introduced by the expression of disagreement in a group, when the relevant cognitions are largely consonant, communication (attempted influence) would be directed mainly at those who disagree with one. But when there exists appreciable dissonance among the relevant cognitions, there will be tendencies to communicate with, especially to listen to, those who already agree with the opinion one holds.

Since in the presence of dissonance there is pressure to reduce dissonance (and to avoid further increase of dissonance) and since disagreement and agreement from others can increase or reduce existing dissonance, there are some things one can say about the circumstances under which attempted influence will or will not be successful. In general, influence exerted on a person to change his opinion so that dissonance is reduced will be more successful in changing that opinion than influence which would produce an increase of dissonance. In short, if a person already has an appreciable number of cognitive elements which are dissonant with an opinion that he holds, it will be easier to influence him to change his opinion in a direction which will make it consonant with those other cognitive elements than to change his opinion in the other direction. Consider a person who smokes heavily and believes that smoking is rather harmful to his health. It will be easier for other people to persuade him that smoking is not at all harmful and that the data which purport to show that it is harmful are inadequate, than it will be to persuade him that smoking is not only "rather harmful" but is positively lethal.

From the foregoing discussion we see that in the presence of dissonance, a person frequently will attempt to obtain social support for the opinions he wishes to maintain. If social support is obtained, the dissonance will be materially reduced and perhaps even eliminated. If, however, such agreement from others is not forthcoming, then the dissonance may persist or even be increased. When such social support is sought in an attempt to reduce dissonance, the success of the attempt is equivalent to the success of a social influence process. Let us, then, inquire into the determinants of whether or not an individual, attempting to reduce cognitive dissonance, is successful in obtaining social support.

The most obvious circumstance in which persons will receive social support for some opinion they wish to maintain is, of course, if those they talk to already happen to have that same opinion. If this is not the case, one may expect an influence process to ensue. The situation is again rather simple if it should happen that the opinion brought up is quite irrelevant to existing cognition in these other persons. Under these circumstances, little or no dissonance is introduced for the other persons and the resistance on their part to changing their opinion should not be very great. Imagine, for example, a parent who is a strict disciplinarian but knows many things, including the reactions of his own children, which are dissonant with believing that strict discipline is good and with knowing that he maintains strict discipline. He may attempt to reduce this dissonance by convincing others that strict discipline is a fine thing. If his friends happen to be childless, and if this opinion is not relevant to other opinions they hold, he will be able to influence them quite easily.

The more usual instance is one where the opinion is relevant to the cognitions of the other persons. Under these circumstances, as mentioned before, the greatest resistance to changing their own opinion should exist in those persons for whom the expression of disagreement creates or increases dissonance. Whether or not opinions change when this is the case will, of course, depend upon whether the dissonance created becomes sufficiently large to overcome the resistance to change of the opinion. Whose opinion changes will likewise depend upon the magnitude of the dissonance in each person's cognition. It is clear that since the dissonance created by such disagreement is greater when the groups are more attractive and when the opinion is relevant to the group, one would expect more change of opinion in such groups than in others. Whether the person who initiates the influence process in an attempt to reduce dissonance obtains agreement, and hence dissonance reduction, or suffers increased dissonance perhaps to the point of changing his own opinion, depends then on the outcome of a complex interaction.

There is one type of circumstance of dissonance reduction by obtaining social support which is particularly interesting and which we will discuss in some detail. Social support is particularly easy to obtain when a rather large number of persons who associate together are all in the same situation —that is, they all have the same dissonance between cognitions which can be reduced in the same manner. Let us, for example, consider a group of people who, unlikely though it may be, have all purchased the same make of new car at the same time. It will clearly be an easy matter for these people to persuade each other that this make of car is indeed very superior and an altogether wonderful piece of machinery. When a situation occurs where the identical dissonance exists in a large number of persons, one may observe very startling and curious mass phenomena.

Let us proceed by first considering the kinds of circum stances that will give rise to identical cognitive dissonance for many persons. We will then analyze the manifestations one would expect to observe as a result of the pressure to reduce this dissonance and of the special circumstance that social support in the reduction of this particular dissonance is easy to obtain.

Sometimes an event may occur which is so compelling in its nature as to produce almost identical reaction or behavior in everyone for whom the event has relevance. At the same time, many persons may have existing cognition which is dissonant with the cognitions corresponding to their reaction to the compelling event. If such a circumstance arises, there will then be a large number of people having almost exactly the same cognitive dissonance. Natural disasters or the threat of such, for example, can produce such uniform reactions. As an illustration, the threat of a serious flood could cause a whole community to evacuate their homes. All of these persons will have similar cognitions corresponding to the inconveniences they suffer by this action. Such cognitions will be dissonant with having evacuated, and this dissonance will be present in the cognition of all or most of the persons. Whatever mechanisms develop and are used by these persons for reducing the dissonance will, very likely, be equally satisfactory for most of them, and consequently, the attempted dissonance reduction will easily obtain social support. They may, for example, convince each other that the threatened flood is certain to come and will be catastrophic, or they may attempt to persuade one another that the inconveniences are really pleasurable delights.

Uniform dissonance in a large number of people may also be created if undeniable and incontrovertible information impinges which is dissonant with a very widely held belief or opinion. For example, many people might be utterly convinced that if the opposition political party wins a given election, economic ruin will descend upon the country. The opposition party may then win the election, and not only does economic ruin not descend, but the economic situation may even get better. There will then exist, for these persons, a dissonance between their knowledge of what happened economically and their opinions about the abilities and policies of the party in power. Another illustration may be given in the area of religion. It was very widely believed, for example, that the year A.D. 1000 would usher in the long-awaited millennium. The uneventful expiration of this year must have introduced considerable and uniform dissonance in the cognitions of those persons who held the belief. In this type of situation again, with a large number of persons who associate with one another and suffer from the same cognitive dissonance, social support for consonant cognitions would be very easy to obtain. Before proceeding to discuss the somewhat unique manifestations of pressure to reduce dissonance in such circumstances, let us describe one other type of situation which may, on occasion, produce widespread and uniform cognitive dissonance.

Groups and organizations sometimes commit themselves to a certain course of action. At the time the action is taken, of course, most of the persons in the group or organization undoubtedly have cognitions which are mainly consonant with the action. Future developments, occurring either independently or as a consequence of the action, may then produce new cognitions which are dissonant with the knowledge that the action was taken and that it continues. Under such circumstances, similar dissonances will exist for all or most of the members of the group. Here, of course, the uniform dissonance may not be widespread in the sense that a very large number of persons have the same dissonance. But it may be true that a large proportion of the persons a given individual knows may have the same cognitive dissonance which he himself possesses. For example, a group of twenty or thirty families may buy a tract of land for the purpose of building homes and establishing a co-operative community. In the course of doing all this, numerous items of information may be forthcoming which produce cognition dissonant with the knowledge that they have bought the land and are continuing in the endeavor. The expense of bringing utilities to the land may be very high, the cost of building the houses may exceed expectations, the condition of the roads, never before considered, may suddenly appear as a serious thing. In such circumstances where the persons are committed to the course of action in the sense that it would be impossible or very difficult to change their behavior, the pressure to reduce dissonance will be directed mainly toward changing the cognitions which are dissonant with the action and toward acquiring new cognitions consonant with the action. Again, since all or most of the persons in the group have the same dissonance, social support for the attempted reduction of dissonance will not be difficult to obtain.

The above discussion of types of situations in which the identical cognitive dissonance would exist simultaneously in many persons is not meant to exhaust all the possibilities for this kind of occurrence. The point is, however, that this sort of thing, while perhaps infrequent, is not terribly rare. Under such circumstances all of the mechanisms of reducing dissonance which we have already discussed will come into play, of course. Our particular interest in these circumstances arises from the fact that under such special conditions a number of manifestations of pressure to reduce dissonance occur which are unique to this kind of situation. These manifestations are usually labeled as mass phenomena. The following discussion will attempt to show that these mass phenomena, on a conceptual level, are no different from the other manifestations of pressure to reduce dissonance which have already been discussed. The difference here is that with social support so easy to obtain, the magnitude and scope of the ensuing effects are sometimes quite dramatic.

The Occurrence of Widespread Rumors

The word "rumor" is usually used in connection with items of information which are transmitted verbally from person to person. Frequently, there is the connotation in the word "rumor" that the information thus transmitted is false. The truth or falsity of the item of information will not concern us here, however. What is of interest are the conditions which must pertain for an item of information or a rumor to become widespread. A number of such conditions seem clear and obvious. Once the content of the item of information exists in someone's cognition (perhaps arising simultaneously in several persons), there must be something which will impel this person to tell it to someone else or to several other people. For the rumor to continue spreading and become widespread, it is furthermore necessary that a sufficient number of the hearers of the rumor also feel impelled to tell others about it. It is then clear that for the rumor to spread widely a large number of persons, in direct or indirect contact with one another, must be in similar circumstances; that is, they must be similarly affected by the item of information with regard to telling others about it.

The implication is not intended that the *only* circumstance in which these conditions will be satisfied and rumors will spread widely is the existence of uniform dissonance among a large number of people. Indeed, there are undoubtedly other factors which may cause rumors to spread widely, such as extensive uncertainty about the future among people who are in similar circumstances. The purpose is, however, to demonstrate that the existence of widespread, uniform dissonance is *one* circumstance that will give rise to rumors which will spread widely and that, furthermore, where rumors arise and spread in an attempt to reduce dissonance, one can predict certain things about the nature and content of the rumors.

Let us examine this a bit more closely. Imagine that some undeniable information has impinged on the cognition of many people creating dissonance in all of them between the cognitive elements corresponding to this information and some opinion or belief which they all hold. If the opinion or belief is not very resistant to change, it may simply be discarded in favor of a different opinion or belief, thus eliminating the dissonance. If, for one reason or another, there is strong resistance to changing the belief, then there are two ways in which the dissonance may be reduced. Persons may attempt to change the cognitive elements corresponding to the new information (in essence, denying the validity of it), or they may attempt to acquire additional cognition consonant with the belief in question. Any attempt in either of these two directions that is reasonably satisfactory will, during discussions with others having the same dissonance, meet with social support. This social support enables the new cognition which is consonant with the belief to be accepted by the persons, thus reducing the dissonance. The content of these cognitions, transmitted in this manner, may spread quite easily and have the appearance of a widely accepted rumor.

Denial of Reality

It sometimes happens that a large group of people is able to maintain an opinion or belief even in the face of continual definite evidence to the contrary. Such instances may range all the way from rather inconsequential occurrences of short duration to phenomena which may almost be termed mass delusions. For example, many readers will have witnessed a group of people who, having planned a picnic for Sunday, discredit the weather report which predicts rain for that day, supporting one another during the process. They may then go on the picnic and perhaps continue to believe the rain will not come all the time that the clouds are gathering. This belief, which contradicts the evidence of reality, may sometimes persist up to the very moment when the rain starts falling. Likewise, groups of scientists have been known to continue to believe in certain theories, supporting one another in this belief in spite of continual mounting evidence that these theories are incorrect.

The examples given are purposely rather prosaic because it must be emphasized that we are discussing a phenomenon that occurs in persons who are in good contact with reality. That is, the impact of reality is very strong, exerting powerful pressure on the cognition to correspond veridically. For such persons it is very difficult to maintain opinions and beliefs that are contradicted by reality. One may well ask, then, under what circumstances such denial of reality will occur.

Let us imagine a person who has some cognition which

is both highly important to him and also highly resistant to change. This might be a belief system which pervades an appreciable part of his life and which is so consonant with many other cognitions that changing the belief system would introduce enormous dissonance. Or it could be a cluster of cognitive elements corresponding to some very important action the person has taken, an action to which he has committed himself in such a way that changing the action is almost impossible. Let us further imagine that an event occurs and impinges on this person's cognition creating strong dissonance with the existing cognition. If, under these circumstances, attempts at reduction of dissonance by acquiring new cognitive elements consonant with the original cognition are unsuccessful, one would expect an attempt to be made to deny the validity of the event which gave rise to the dissonance. This, however, is difficult to do if the reality is rather unequivocal and impinges directly on the cognition of the person. If, for example, a person were walking in the rain and getting wet, it would be extremely difficult for him to convince himself that it was not raining. Reality which impinges directly on people does, for most of us, have a very compelling quality.

The attempts of the person in whom the dissonance exists will, however, lead him into discussions with others about the validity of the event. If the person walking in the rain were to attempt to deny the reality of the rain, assuming that for some reason the cognition of rain introduced a very strong dissonance for him, he might say to his companion that perhaps it wasn't raining at all but rather that the wind was blowing drops off leaves of trees—drops which had collected in a previous rain. His companion, however, being quite responsive to the impact of reality, would probably reject this notion quite strongly unless he himself was suffering from the identical dissonance. He then would want to believe it too. It is only when quite a large number of persons who associate with one another have the identical dissonance which cannot be resolved in easier ways, that by supporting one another they may actually be able to maintain the opinion that it is really not raining at all. If everyone believes it, it most certainly must be true.

Mass Proselyting

It is undoubtedly already apparent to the reader why and how proselyting activities may be manifestations of pressure to reduce dissonance. Certainly, large-scale proselyting activities are conceptually no different in nature from isolated instances of one person attempting to influence another to agree with some opinion. If such influence attempts, or such large-scale proselyting, are successful, the new converts or adherents to the opinion or belief system introduce added consonance, thus reducing existing dissonance with the belief system. It remains for us, however, to inquire into the conditions under which the existence of dissonance and the pressure to reduce it will manifest itself in mass proselyting activities.

Let us again consider a situation where a number of persons who associate with one another hold a set of beliefs which are, for one reason or another, very important to them and highly resistant to change. And, once more, let us consider the situation which arises if an event occurs or some information impinges on the cognition of these persons which creates a very powerful dissonance with the belief system, a dissonance which is, however, not strong enough to cause the entire belief system to be discarded. Let us further specify that the information creating the dissonance is unequivocal and undeniable—that is, so compelling in its nature that the validity cannot be denied.

In short, we have postulated the existence of an extremely strong dissonance between two clusters of cognitive elements, each cluster being highly resistant to change and, hence, remaining unchanged. In other words, the dissonance under these conditions cannot be reduced by changing the elements of cognition which are involved in the dissonance. It can only be reduced by adding new cognitive elements consonant with the belief system.

As stated previously, one would expect persons with such a dissonance to seek out others suffering from the same dissonance in an attempt to obtain support for new cognitions consonant with the belief system. Such new cognitions may involve explanations of the dissonance-producing event, new reaffirmations and new evidence consonant with the belief system, and the like. We have already seen that when associating with others who have the identical dissonance, it is highly likely that support for these new cognitions will be forthcoming. In the unhappy event that a person with such a dissonance is surrounded by persons who will not support these attempts at reducing dissonance, the dissonance may very likely be increased by these nonbelievers to the point where the person discards the belief system. If, however, he is surrounded by fellow believers with the same dissonance, this dissonance will be reduced to some extent and the belief will be retained.

If the initial dissonance is, as we have postulated, extremely strong, it is not likely that the dissonance will have been reduced to any pronounced degree by the above procedures. The ingenuity of the human being in devising explanations, rationalizations, new "evidence," and the like, while great, is still limited. The dissonance between the belief system and the undeniable event, although smaller in relation to all the new relevant consonant cognitions, will still remain. How, then, may still more elements of cognition be added which are consonant with the belief system so as to still further reduce the dissonance? Clearly, this may be done by persuading more and more persons that the belief system is true, that is, by proselyting and obtaining converts. Thus, under such circumstances one would expect to observe more or less large-scale proselyting to manifest itself in attempting to reduce dissonance. If such persons could persuade the whole world of the correctness of their beliefs, the dissonance would undoubtedly be rendered negligible.

The following two chapters will present data relevant to the role which social communication and influence processes have in creating and reducing dissonance.

NINE

The Role of Social Support: Data on Influence Process

The content area which encompasses social communication and influence processes is, indeed, very large, both in terms of its range and the amount of relevant data which exist. I have no intention, in this chapter, of giving a thorough presentation of all the data in this area which can be interpreted or explained in terms of the theory of dissonance. Clearly, if it is correct to say that holding one opinion is dissonant with the knowledge that someone else, generally like oneself, holds a contrary opinion, then much of the data on influence in face-to-face groups and effect of mass media can be interpreted in line with the theory. The fact that people tend to associate with others who agree with them, the fact that people read newspapers which already support their existing views, etc., can all be seen as instances of dissonance reduction or as avoiding increase of dissonance. But such instances are not very compelling with respect to the theory of dissonance.

What I will attempt to do in this chapter is to present that evidence from the area of social communication and influence process which is most relevant to the theory of dissonance and for which alternative explanations are more difficult to devise. The data to be presented can be grouped roughly under two headings: first, data showing that opinion change which occurs in the presence of social communication is predominantly of a nature which reduces dissonance, and second, data showing that the existence of dissonance leads to the initiation of, and modification of, influence and communication processes.

Influence Processes Leading to Reduction of Dissonance

Let us examine first the overall implications of the theory of dissonance in relation to social support. As stated in the preceding chapter, the existence of dissonance in a person leads to a process of social communication by which he attempts to reduce the dissonance. He will try to find persons who agree (or try to influence persons to agree) with those cognitions he would like to acquire in order to reduce the dissonance. To the extent that his efforts are successful, one should find that over a period of time, opinion change which reduces the dissonance has taken place. In other words, if a person had two opinions which were dissonant with one another, it is more likely that one of these two opinions would change than if the two opinions were consonant with each other.

In examining data relevant to this point, there is always the problem of determining a priori whether two given opinions are or are not dissonant with each other. Granted that there are many instances where it would be difficult to do this, there are, nevertheless, instances which are quite clear. Let us look at two examples of opinion change where, after a period of time has elapsed, one can compare persons who initially held two dissonant opinions with persons who held consonant opinions. Lipset *et al.* (37) present opinion-change data for a sample of 266 persons who were interviewed twice (August and October) during the presidential election campaign of 1940. Both times the respondents were asked questions to ascertain whether they considered themselves Democrats or Republicans and whether they were for or against Willkie. Table 22 presents the data from this study.

Certainly, with respect to these data, the a priori designation of dissonance and consonance is clear and unequivocal. Being in favor of the Republican candidate follows from,

TABLE 22

CHANGES IN OPINION ACCORDING TO INITIAL DISSONANCE

Opinions on First Interview	Per Cent Who Changed Some Opinion on Second Interview	
Republican for Willkie (N = 135)	4.4	Initial consonance
Democrat against Willkie (N = 72)	5.6	
Republican against Willkie (N = 35)	34.3	Initial dissonance
Democrat for Willkie (N = 24)	50.0	

and is consonant with, considering oneself a Republican. Being against the Republican candidate is dissonant with considering oneself a Republican. Similarly, considering oneself a Democrat is dissonant with being for the Republican candidate and consonant with being against that candidate. Looking at the first column of numbers, it is clear that, as one would expect, the great majority of persons did have opinions which were consonant with one another. Out of the 266 persons who were interviewed, only 59 initially held dissonant opinions. Likewise, as expected, there turned out to be very little change of opinion among those persons whose initial opinions were consonant with one another.

Only about 5 per cent of these persons changed either their opinion concerning Willkie or their general political affiliation during the two-month period between the two interviews.

In contrast, there were a very large number of persons who, initially holding opinions which were dissonant with one another, changed their opinion over the two-month period: 34 per cent in the case of Republicans against Willkie and 50 per cent in the case of Democrats for Willkie. All of the persons with initially dissonant opinions who changed their opinion changed in the direction of reducing the dissonance. There were twenty-four such persons. Two of them changed their political affiliation to bring it in line with their candidate preference, and the other twenty-two changed their candidate preference to bring it in line with their political affiliation. It is not surprising, of course, that the cognitions concerning political affiliation were more resistant to change than the cognitions concerning candidate preference.

Another example of the same type of opinion change may be taken from a study reported by Blau (6). This study was concerned with opinion changes among a sample of 944 Cornell University students who were interviewed in the spring of 1950 and again in the spring of 1952. Among other things, Blau obtained data concerning orientation toward international affairs—that is, whether the respondents advocated the use of power or advocated international co-operation as the most effective means of preventing war. He also obtained data on the general political beliefs of the persons interviewed, mainly reflected in whether they had supported the Progressive, Democratic, or Republican party in 1948. The author demonstrated that liberal political ideology was consonant with favoring co-operation in international affairs in the sense that these two sets of opinions were generally found together. Likewise a conservative political ideology went together with favoring the use of power in international affairs. This same judgment concerning consonance between opinions could also be made on the basis of the explicit content of things advocated by the three political parties in 1948. Blau proceeded to show that the changes in opinion which did occur over the two-year period were, indeed, largely in the direction of dissonance reduction. Thus, in his words,

The distribution of the scores on orientation toward international affairs hardly changed between 1950 and 1952. This similarity, however, conceals compensating changes in opposite directions. One-fifth of these 944 students shifted toward a more cooperative disposition, and about as many (18 per cent) became more power-oriented.

An examination of these changes reveals a strain toward consistency. A progressive political philosophy is associated with a cooperative orientation, as has been shown. . . . Since a power orientation was inconsistent with a progressive ideology, the students who endorsed very progressive political programs were most constrained to become increasingly favorable toward international cooperation. Among the third-party followers who, in 1950, had not been advocates of international cooperation, 47 per cent moved toward a more cooperative orientation. Among the corresponding groups of Democrats and Republicans, only 27 and 32 per cent, respectively, moved in this direction [pp. 209–10].

Once more there is evidence that shifts of opinion which do occur over time tend to be in a direction which reduces dissonance. Blau also reported the same type of shift of opinion in the direction of "greater consistency" for other content. For example, over the two-year period, conservative students tended to shift away from thinking that world government was highly important in the prevention of war, while liberal students tended to change toward increased acceptance of world government. In this case the changes in the direction of reducing dissonance occurred just as often even though the prevailing trend in the sample as a whole was away from reliance on world government.

Demonstrating that shifts of opinion which do occur over time tend to reduce dissonance is not sufficient, however. The major point to be made is that obtaining *agreement from others* is one of the major ways in which such dissonance reduction may be accomplished. In both of the above sets of data it is plausible to suppose, of course, that during the period of time intervening between the two interviews, the people did talk about these issues with others around them. Thus one would expect that someone who was a Democrat and thought Willkie was the better of the two available candidates would, in attempting to reduce this dissonance, try to persuade himself that perhaps Willkie was not so good. If he could find others who would tell him that Willkie was not an able person or that Willkie had certain specific undesirable characteristics, he would then have been able to change his opinion concerning Willkie. Consequently, one would expect that one of the major determinants of whether or not change of opinion in the direction of dissonance reduction occurs would be the availability of other persons who could support the new and consonant opinion.

The study by Blau presented some data relevant to this further point. Blau compared change of opinion among those who had few social contacts with opinion change among those who had many social contacts. It is certainly clear that if a person has very few social contacts it would be correspondingly more difficult for this person to find others who would agree with the things he wants to believe. A person with many social contacts, being able to find such others more easily, should more frequently be able to change his opinion so as to reduce the existing dissonance. Blau does, indeed, find that those students who had difficulty making friends, and those who were not members of existing campus groups, changed their opinions over time less frequently than did those who belonged to campus groups or had no difficulty making friends. For example, with regard to cooperative versus power orientation in international affairs, Blau says:

Changes in the orientation toward international affairs also indicate that students who are integrated into significant groups on their campus are more prone to shift their opinions than are others. For example, fraternity members were more likely to change their orientation, regardless of the direction of this change, than independent students [p. 211].

And again, with respect to changes in attitudes toward world government, a similar finding is reported:

A third of the students who reported that they had difficulty making friends changed with the trend, away from world government, in contrast to almost half (48 per cent) of those who found it easier to make friends. . . .

However, there is some evidence to suggest that *any* shift of opinion, against the trend as well as with the trend, is related to a student's integration in the college community. The differences found were small, but they reveal a coherent pattern . . . [p. 211].

In short, the data support the theoretical expectations. For both of these opinion areas the changes which did occur were mainly in the direction of reducing dissonance, and those who had more social contacts were more likely to have changed their opinion.

While the data discussed thus far in this chapter are consistent with the theoretical expectations, there is one particularly important variable left uncontrolled which makes the degree of confirmation of the theory of dissonance somewhat less than might be desired. Specifically, in the studies which have been reported there is no control over, nor any measure of, the amount of influence, and the direction of this influence, exerted on the persons who do change their opinions. For example, considering the data on changes of opinion among those whose political affiliations were dissonant with their attitudes toward Willkie, one might offer an alternative explanation of the obtained results. One might plausibly maintain that Republicans associate primarily with other Republicans and that Democrats associate primarily with other Democrats. If this were the case, then a Republican who was opposed to Willkie would be exposed mainly to pro-Willkie opinions since that was the prevailing opinion among his associates. Similarly, a Democrat who was for Willkie would be exposed mainly to anti-Willkie opinions from his associates. If this were true it would not be surprising to find that such influence would be successful in a number of cases and that these persons would change their opinion in a direction that looked like greater consistency. The point is that the direction of influence to which these persons were involuntarily exposed might well have been different for the two groups.

The same kind of alternative explanation might be offered for the Blau data although it has somewhat less plausibility there. For example, the indication that fraternity members changed their opinion in either direction more frequently than nonfraternity members is difficult to account for by an explanation involving different content of influence from others because of the prevailing opinions among that person's associates. This finding almost forces one to accept some selectivity on the part of the person whose opinions are dissonant, either with respect to whom he talks about the matter, or with respect to the direction of influence attempts from others to which he will more readily respond, or both. Thus these data provide a somewhat greater degree of confirmation for these implications of dissonance theory.

Nevertheless, it would have been highly desirable to have had some control over the direction of influence exertion on these persons whose opinions changed. Ideally, one would want to compare data on opinion change for persons whose opinions initially were dissonant with data for persons whose initial opinions were consonant, under circumstances where all persons had been exposed to exactly the same influence attempts from others. Under such controlled circumstances the interpretation of the results would be unequivocal. There is, of course, little possibility of this kind of precise control in field studies such as those we have been discussing. I will, however, describe a laboratory experiment conducted by McGuire[1] which does precisely fulfill these conditions.

In this experiment, ninety-two college students participated in two sessions spaced one week apart. At the first session they were told that they were to answer a questionnaire which was part of a study to determine students' views on various matters pertaining to university planning. The questionnaire consisted of twenty-four different statements or propositions. These statements consisted of eight sets, each made up of three syllogistically related propositions; that is, two were premises and the third a conclusion which logically followed from the first two. Each of the twenty-four statements concerned the occurrence of some future event or contingency. The following is an example of one syllogistically related set of three statements used by McGuire:

[1] I should like to thank Dr. William J. McGuire for making his raw data available to me for the purpose of the analysis I shall describe.

1. The government will adopt the student-draft policy that will be in the best interest of the nation as a whole.

2. The student-draft policy that will be in the best interest of the nation as a whole is to defer all students at least until the completion of their education.

3. The government will adopt the policy of deferring all students at least until the completion of their education.

The particular syllogistic sets used were constructed so that, insofar as possible, neither of the two premises taken alone would be likely to suggest the conclusion to the subject. In addition, four of the conclusions stated a desirable outcome for the subjects, as in the example given, while the other four conclusions stated an undesirable outcome. The twenty-four statements were arranged on the questionnaire in the following manner: the sixteen premises (two from each set) came first, arranged in a random order with the restrictions that no two premises from the same set had fewer than three other statements intervening, nor were presented on the same page of the questionnaire. Following the premises came the eight statements representing the conclusions, arranged in random order. For the subjects, of course, there was no distinction between premise and conclusion—there were simply twenty-four statements.

Along with each of the twenty-four statements was a scale on which the subject was asked to rate the likelihood of the occurrence of the stated event. This scale consisted of five-inch horizontal lines marked off by short vertical lines every half inch. These short vertical lines were labeled from right to left by the numbers 0, 10, 20, . . . , 90, 100. Near the 0 was written "Very Improbable End" and near the 100 was written "Very Probable End." The subjects were told to draw a line through the scale at that point which expressed their opinion of the probability of the statement's being true.

The second session took place one week later. At this session the subjects were each given four persuasive communications to read. This was immediately followed by another administration of the questionnaire consisting of the twenty-four statements which have already been described. Each of the persuasive communications which the subjects were given to read consisted of the reply of a fictitious Dr. Harold Wilson to a question asked him during a press conference reportedly held on the occasion of his election to the presidency of the National Association of University Administrators, a fictitious organization. Each communication consisted of the interviewer's question and Dr. Wilson's 150- to 200-word reply. In each instance the question directly concerned one of the premises of the eight sets and each reply consisted of a one-sided argument of a reasonable and plausible nature. The reply argued for the likelihood of the occurrence of the event. In other words, to the extent that the persuasive communication was effective, the subject would increase his rating of the probability of the event actually occurring.

In all, eight such persuasive communications were used, one for each of the syllogistically related sets, although each subject saw only four of them. The four which a subject saw always consisted of two concerning a premise related to a desirable conclusion and two concerning a premise related to an undesirable conclusion. Equal numbers of subjects were exposed to each of the persuasive communications.

Before examining the results, let us consider how this experiment satisfies the conditions which were previously specified. If, for example, concerning the three statements in one set, a subject indicated that he felt each of the premises was highly likely and, at the same time, felt that the conclusion which followed logically from these premises was highly unlikely, it would be plausible for us to conclude that cognitive dissonance existed for this person. I do not wish to imply here that dissonance exists if the probability asserted for the conclusion is not exactly equal to the product of the probabilities asserted for the two premises. First of all, even logically, the probability of the conclusion could be higher than the product of the probabilities of the two premises because other possible premises may also imply the same conclusion. Also, I do not desire to assert that each person thinks with precise logic about probabilities. What is plausible to assert, however, is that:

1. Among those persons for whom the stated probability of the conclusion is *greater* than the product of the probabilities of the two related premises there will be some who have cognitive dissonance which can be reduced by increasing the probability of one of the premises. Being affected by the persuasive communication would, hence, *reduce* dissonance for these persons.

2. Among those persons for whom the stated probability of the conclusion is *less* than the product of the probabilities of the two related premises there will be some who have cognitive dissonance which can be reduced by lowering the probability of one of the premises. Being affected by the appropriate persuasive communication would, hence, *increase* dissonance for these persons.

It is clear, then, that on the basis of the responses to the first questionnaire, one can identify groups of persons, some of whom had cognitive dissonance that could be reduced by change of opinion in one direction, and some of whom had cognitive dissonance which could be reduced by change of opinion in an opposite direction. Since all of the persuasive communications argued for increasing the probability of the premise to which it was directed, these communications would help reduce dissonance only for *some* of those who were exposed to it.

Let us now look at the results. Table 23 presents the data on change, from the first to the second questionnaire, of the probability of those premises with which the communications were concerned. These data are based on only those instances where the probability of the conclusion did not change more than .10 from the first to the second

TABLE 23

Changes in Probability of Those Premises Related to the
Persuasive Communications

	Probability of Conclusion on First Questionnaire	
	Greater than the Product of the Probabilities of the Two Related Premises	Less than the Product of the Probabilities of the Two Related Premises
Desirable conclusions		
Exposed to communication	+12.4	−5.0
Not exposed	+ 1.6	−8.1
Undesirable conclusions		
Exposed to communication	+20.0	+1.3
Not exposed	+ 5.9	−5.0

testing. Clearly, any dissonance which existed on the first questionnaire could have been reduced by changing the opinion about the likelihood of either of the premises or of the conclusion. Since we are interested in looking at the change in those premises with which the communications were concerned, it is advantageous to restrict consideration to those instances where at least one of the other avenues of dissonance reduction is ruled out. Ruling out both of the other avenues of dissonance reduction, that is, considering only those instances where neither the conclusion nor the premise not involved in the persuasive communication changed, would have resulted in too few cases for analysis.

Let us look first at the data for those instances where the subject did not receive a persuasive communication related to a particular premise. In these instances, as one would expect simply from the pressure to reduce dissonance, there was a slight change over a period of time (one week) in the direction of dissonance reduction, both for the instances where the premise is related to a desirable conclusion and where it is related to an undesirable conclusion. When the probability of the conclusion was "too high" on the first questionnaire, the probability of the premise increased, on the average, 1.6 and 5.9 by the second questionnaire. Where the probability of the conclusion was "too low" initially, the probability of the premise had decreased, by the time of the second questionnaire, 8.1 and 5.0.

Let us now look at the comparable changes for those instances where the subjects *were* exposed to a communication arguing for the high probability of a premise. In those instances where being influenced by this communication would have reduced dissonance, that is, when the probability of the conclusion was "too high" on the initial questionnaire, the subjects were, indeed, influenced by the persuasive communication. For the premises related to desirable and undesirable conclusions, the average changes in the probability of the premise after reading the communication were +12.4 and +20.0, respectively. In other words, the subjects were strongly influenced by the communication when such influence reduced dissonance. The comparable changes for those instances where being influenced by the communication would have increased dissonance were −5.0 and +1.3. That is, if being influenced would have increased dissonance, persons remained uninfluenced by the same communications that had so pronounced an effect on the others. It is also interesting to note that the desirability or undesirability of the related conclusion had little or nothing to do with the extent to which the communication was effective. It was effective only when it served to reduce dissonance and ineffective otherwise.

In short, here are data collected under controlled circumstances which show clearly that under identical conditions, attempted influence is more effective on persons for whom it reduces dissonance. These data, considered together with the less well-controlled field studies which have been discussed, strongly support the implications from dissonance theory.

Dissonance Leading to Initiation of Influence Processes

Let us now turn our consideration to the effect of the existence of dissonance on the social communication process. Up to now the discussion has dealt with the results of this process and has shown that dissonance reduction does occur through the attainment of social support. The existence of dissonance should also lead to seeking social support, and so one should be able to detect some effects on the communication process. One of the most obvious effects, as stated in the preceding chapter, is the initiation of communication with others concerning some issue. Just as the existence of dissonance following a new car purchase, for example, leads the new car owner to read ads concerning the car he has just purchased, the dissonance should also lead him to initiate discussions with others concerning cars and this car in particular. In this way he can hope to find others who agree that the car he purchased is wonderful or, failing this, persuade others that this is so.

Specifically, one would expect the existence of cognitive dissonance to be accompanied by heightened communication concerning content relevant to the cognitive elements involved in the dissonance. One would also expect the reduction of dissonance to be accompanied by a lessening of discussion and communication about these content areas.

Data relevant to this prediction are extremely scanty. There have been hardly any studies that have dealt with the initiation of communication or, indeed, even with the general level of communication among persons under circumstances where one can unequivocally, or even plausibly, infer the existence or absence of specific dissonance. The data from the studies which will be presented are, consequently, more illustrative and suggestive than conclusive.

Some pertinent data are found in a study reported by Baxter (3) in which a number of persons were interviewed periodically during the election campaign of 1948. Particular attention was given to the collection of data concerning the extent to which the respondents engaged in spontaneous, informal discussions with others about politics and the election. The panel of respondents was interviewed in June, 1948, for the first time. In addition to determining the extent of their discussions concerning politics and the election, each respondent was asked how interested he was in the present election and whether or not he was doing anything for his party in this election campaign. Table 24 presents the data obtained.

Examination of the first part of this table shows that among those who were not doing anything for the party there was a "common sense" relationship between the degree of interest in the election and the extent to which they talked about it. Those who were more interested talked about it more. But among those who said they were doing something for the party this "common sense" relationship was missing.

Here, those with low interest in the election talked about it as frequently as those with high interest. This latter finding is perhaps understandable if one assumes that cognitions corresponding to being uninterested in the election are probably dissonant, for most people, with the cognitive elements corresponding to the knowledge that they are working for the party in this election, and if one also assumes that, counteracting the tendency for high interest to lead to more talking, there is a tendency for those with cognitive dissonance (the low interest group) to talk about the elec-

TABLE 24

RELATION BETWEEN DISSONANCE AND INITIATION OF COMMUNICATION

	Per Cent of Respondents Who Talked Politics
Not doing anything for party	
High interest in the election (N = 487)	38
Low interest in the election (N = 217)	14
Doing something for party	
High interest in the election (N = 40)	65
Low interest in the election (N = 19)	68

tion with others in an attempt to reduce their dissonance. If they can get others to tell them that the election is actually very important and convince themselves of this, then the dissonance between their working for the party and their low interest would be reduced or even eliminated.

There is, of course, one further fact we can look for in the data to support this interpretation. If, indeed, the absence of relationship between interest in the election and talking politics among those who are doing something for the party results from the attempts to reduce dissonance on the part of the low interest category, one should be able to find some evidence of such dissonance reduction. Specifically, if these people were successful in reducing their dissonance, one should find them changing their interest in the election over a period of time. Table 25 presents the relevant data from the June and from the October interviews.

It will be seen from this table that in June the proportion of persons having high interest in the election was almost identical for those who were and those who were not doing anything for the party—68 and 69 per cent, respectively. For those who were not doing anything for the party this percentage remains virtually unchanged over a four-month period from June to October. For those who were

TABLE 25

	June	October
Not doing anything for party	69	73
Doing something for party	68	88

doing something for the party, however, the expected shift in opinion in the direction of dissonance reduction does indeed occur. By October the percentage who said they had high interest in the election had increased to 88. I would like to state once more, however, that while the results of this study are perhaps relevant to the implication from dissonance theory that the existence of dissonance will lead to the initiation of social communication processes, and while the obtained results are certainly consistent with this, the number of cases on which the data are based is so small, and there are so many uncontrolled factors operating, that the results certainly cannot be regarded as conclusive.

Let us now return to the Blau study, since there are

also some data presented in that report which are relevant to the present point. It will be recalled that Blau found that opinion changes over a two-year period were mainly in the direction of increasing the consistency among opinions, or in our terms, reducing dissonance. One of the areas of opinion which showed such change was attitude toward the Germans. In relation to changes on this attitude, Blau presented data concerning the initiation of social communication. On the interview the following question was asked: "Do you ever get as worked up about something that happens in politics or public affairs as you do about something that happens in your private life?" It is, perhaps, safe to assume that if a respondent answers Yes to this question, it means that he gets aroused to the point where he discusses it with others and argues about it. If the answers to this question do reflect the extent to which the respondents initiate discussion about such matters, then the theoretical implications are clear. One would expect the existence of cognitive dissonance related to political and public affairs to lead to talking about these matters, and hence, persons who had such dissonance should more often answer Yes to the above question than would those who had little or no dissonance in these areas. Furthermore, there are clear implications for change over a period of time with respect to this matter. If, indeed, as the author asserts, most changes were in the direction of reducing dissonance, then those persons who changed their opinion over the two-year period, having (on the average) less dissonance by the time of the second interview than at the time of the first one, should likewise show a decrease in the tendency to answer Yes to the above question. Those subjects who did not change their opinion on some specific issue over the two-year period, having the same amount of dissonance (on the average) at the time of both interviews, should show no decrease or increase in the tendency to answer Yes. It is with respect to this derivation concerning change that some data presented by Blau are of interest.

Table 26 presents data on the relation between responses to the question reflecting the degree to which they talked about politics and public affairs and whether or not they changed their opinion concerning Germans over the two-year period. It clearly shows that those who changed their opinion concerning Germany, presumably in the direction

TABLE 26

RELATION BETWEEN CHANGES IN ATTITUDE TOWARD GERMANS
AND TALKING POLITICS AND PUBLIC AFFAIRS

Answer to Question *		Per Cent Whose Attitude toward Germans	
In 1950	In 1952	Changed Decidedly (N = 192)	Remained the Same (N = 317)
No	Yes	8	14
Yes	No	29	18
Same answer both times		63	68

* The exact question asked was: "Do you ever get as worked up about something that happens in politics or public affairs as you do about something that happens in your private life?"

of greater consonance, did decrease the extent to which they got worked up about relevant content and, presumably, the extent to which they initiated discussions about it. Only 8 per cent who said they did not get worked up about these matters in 1950 said they did in 1952. Changes in the other direction amount to 29 per cent. Among those who did not change their opinion concerning Germans there is also no change, on the average, in the extent to which they got worked up about related matters, the changes from No to Yes and from Yes to No being about equal. Once more, one finds the results quite consistent with what would be expected from dissonance theory. Also, once more, it is clear that many assumptions have to be made to interpret the data in this light, and consequently, the results are far from conclusive with respect to the theory.

One other set of data, this time from a controlled laboratory investigation, adds to our confidence in the results of the Blau study since the same kind of decrement in communication was observed after persons changed their opinions. This study, reported by Festinger, Gerard, Hymovitch, Kelley, and Raven (18), was conducted as follows. Groups of about seven persons, previously strangers to one another, were assembled in the laboratory. Each person was given a case study which was supposed to be an actual record of a labor dispute. They were told to read it and that they would presently discuss this matter among themselves. Immediately after reading the case study, each subject was asked to indicate, on a slip of paper, his opinion as to the behavior of the union representatives in the future negotiation meetings. This opinion was indicated on a seven-point scale ranging from (1) "They will be . . . totally resistant to compromise proposals" to (7) "They will comply with counterproposals . . . immediately making the necessary concessions in order to reach agreement."

After a suitable interval (presumably for tabulating the opinions), each person was given a tally showing the (fictitious) distribution of opinion in the group. The subjects we are concerned with for present purposes were each handed back a tally showing that everyone else in the group held an opinion different from their own, either two or three points removed from their own opinion as indicated on the scale. The subjects were then asked once more to indicate their opinion on the seven-point scale. After these second opinions were collected, the group proceeded to discuss the issue by means of writing notes to one another. Consequently, data are available concerning the extent to which the subjects initiated communication with others during the discussion. This is adequately reflected by the number of words they wrote to others during the first ten minutes of discussion, because during this brief period no notes were delivered and so all communication was self-initiated.

Table 27 presents the data on the number of words communicated by those subjects who did *not* change their

TABLE 27

AVERAGE NUMBER OF WORDS WRITTEN PER PERSON

	Attraction to the Group	
	High	Low
Subjects who do not change	95	75
Subjects who change	76	58

opinion immediately after seeing the fictitious tally of opinion and by those subjects who *did* change their opinion at that time. The subjects were further separated according to whether they were in highly attractive or less attractive groups. The attraction to the group was experimentally manipulated in this study.

It is clear from an examination of these data that for both the high and low attraction conditions, those subjects who had changed their opinion before the discussion initiated less communication than subjects who still held their original opinion. The information obtained by the subjects from the fictitious tally certainly was dissonant with the opinion they held. Those who reduced this dissonance by changing their opinion were then less impelled to communicate with others about it. In the high attraction groups, where the dissonance created by the knowledge of disagreement from others would have been greater, the initiation of communication was, of course, also greater.

None of the three studies we have discussed above, considered individually, provides strong corroboration for the implications of the theory of dissonance concerning the initiation of communication. Taken together, they certainly support it. The existence of dissonance seems to lead to the initiation of social communication, and the reduction of dissonance is followed by a lessening of such communication.

We may now turn our attention to the selectivity of social communication which arises by virtue of the existence of dissonance. In other words, with whom will persons communicate when attempting to reduce existing dissonance? As stated in the previous chapter, when the dissonance is mainly between cognition corresponding to one's own opinion and the knowledge that others hold a contrary opinion, the direction of communication is clear. Under these circumstances one way to reduce the dissonance is to change the opinions of those who disagree. When, however, in addition to the above dissonance there also exists dissonance between the cognition corresponding to the opinion the person holds and other information which does not fit with this opinion, then the situation is more complex. The latter dissonance can be reduced by discussing the matter with persons who already agree with the opinion one holds. Thus one would expect, on theoretical grounds, that given a largely consonant set of cognitions corresponding to a given opinion, the presence of disagreement will lead mainly to communicating with those who disagree. Given already existing serious dissonance among the cognitions corresponding to the opinion, however, the presence of disagreement in a group will lead to tendencies to talk to those who agree as well as to those who disagree. One would thus expect, in the latter case, to find a higher incidence of initiating communications with those who already agree.

Brodbeck (8) conducted an experiment which was specifically designed to test this derivation. The first session of this experiment was conducted with groups of approximately twelve subjects, all strangers to one another. On arrival, the subjects were told that they were participating in a nationwide study for the (fictitious) National Council for Adult Education. The study was concerned with the attitudes of adults on issues which were considered important. The issue to be considered in the session in which they were participating was the use of wire tapping by law enforcement agencies. (This issue was chosen for the experiment because student opinion was nearly half for and half against wire tapping.) The subjects were told that they would later have an opportunity to discuss the issue among themselves but that first they were to indicate their present opinion concerning it. They were then handed a slip of paper on which they were asked to check whether they were for or against wire tapping, and they were also asked to check, on a six-point scale, how confident they were that their opinion was right. This scale varied from "I am absolutely certain of the opinion I expressed above" to "I am completely uncertain about whether my opinion is right or wrong."

After these statements of opinion and confidence had been collected, the experimenter, in order to stimulate discussion among the subjects, told them that they were to hear a tape-recorded speech on the issue by the (fictitious) president of the National Council for Adult Education. As a matter of experimental control, two speeches had been prepared, one giving a very strong argument in favor of wire tapping and one giving a very strong argument against it. For half the groups the former speech was played while the latter was played for the other half. Which speech was used in which groups is immaterial to our purpose. The important thing is that some subjects in each group heard a persuasive communication which asserted that their own opinion was correct while some subjects in each group heard a persuasive communication which asserted that their own opinion was wrong.

When the speech was finished, each subject was once more asked to indicate on a slip of paper whether he was for or against wire tapping and how confident he was in his opinion. This essentially concluded the first session of the experiment.

Before describing the second session, which proceeded immediately, let us analyze what has happened so far. Within each group there are now some persons whose dissonance (if they ever had any) among cognitions relevant to their opinion about wire tapping has been reduced by a speech they heard. These are the subjects who heard a speech strongly supporting the opinion they already held. I will refer to these as the *consonant subjects*.

Within each group there are also some persons for whom dissonance was either created or increased among cognitions corresponding to their opinion on the issue. These are subjects who listened to a speech given by an "authority" which argued strongly against the opinion they held. Of course, the speech would not have created or increased dissonance equally for all of these subjects, some people being more affected by this kind of persuasive communication than others. It would seem, though, that if the confidence they expressed in their opinion decreased after hearing the speech opposed to their own views, this would be an indication that the speech introduced considerable dissonance. Thus those subjects who heard a speech opposed to their opinion and, while holding to the same opinion, lowered their confidence will be referred to as the *strongly dissonant subjects.* Those subjects whose confidence remained the same after hearing the persuasive communication opposed to their own opinion will be referred to as the *weakly dissonant subjects.*

The groups used for the second session, which followed immediately, consisted of eight subjects, four of whom held an opinion in favor of wire tapping and four of whom held an opinion against wire tapping. These eight were selected from the original twelve subjects in the following manner:

1. Four were *consonant subjects.* If there were more than four available, four were selected at random. There were five groups in which there were only three consonant subjects available, and in these groups, a subject who had switched opinion after hearing the speech was included so that the second session group of eight persons would still have four opinions on each side of the issue. When this was done, the other subjects, of course, did not know that one of them had switched his opinion.

2. Four were *dissonant subjects.* All who were *strongly dissonant,* that is, had lowered their confidence, were included. The balance was made up by random selection among the *weakly dissonant* subjects. Most groups included only one or two strongly dissonant subjects.

Those subjects who were not used for the second session were led out of the room, presumably to hold a discussion separately. The experimenter placed in front of each of the eight remaining subjects a placard which stated his present opinion: "in favor of wire tapping" or "opposed to wire tapping." Each subject could see everyone else's placard and it was clear that the group was evenly divided on the issue. The experimenter then asked them to list on a slip of paper the two persons they would most prefer to discuss the issue with if they split up into pairs to carry on the discussion. They then proceeded to have a general group discussion about the issue for twelve minutes after which they were asked once more to write down their opinion and the confidence they had in their opinion. This concluded the experiment.

Table 28 presents the data on whether or not they indicated that, if they split up into pairs, they would like to listen to someone who already agreed with them. It

TABLE 28

RELATION BETWEEN DISSONANCE AND DESIRE TO LISTEN TO SOMEONE WHO AGREES WITH OWN OPINION

Per Cent of Subjects Who

	Chose Person Who Agreed (One or Both Choices)	Did Not Choose Person Who Agreed
Strongly dissonant (N = 27)	56	44
Weakly dissonant (N = 51)	41	59
Consonant (N = 75)	34	66

is clear from an examination of the data that the results were in line with our theoretical expectations. Of those who entered the second session having heard a speech which supported their own opinion and, consequently, having largely consonant relations among their cognitions, only 34 per cent indicated any desire to listen to someone who already agreed with them. Most of them wanted, exclusively, to discuss the matter with those who disagreed. Of those who entered the second session with weak dissonance, 41 per cent showed some desire to listen to someone who already agreed with them. The comparable percentage for those who had strong cognitive dissonance was 56. In short, the greater the magnitude of dissonance already existing when one is made aware of disagreement within the group, the greater is the tendency to seek support from those who already agree with one's own opinion.

It will be remembered that the subjects next proceeded to have a face-to-face discussion in the total group of eight persons. One may, then, ask what effect participating in the discussion and listening to others express themselves during the discussion had on the opinion of those whose confidence had been reduced by the speech they heard— that is, those who already had strong dissonance before the group discussion. If, indeed, the data just presented indicate that these persons were looking for support from those who already agreed with them in order to reduce the dissonance created by the speech, one would expect that they would also have listened selectively to the discussion in the group, paying more attention to, and putting more credence in, those statements which supported their opinion than to those statements which did not support it. If this is true, one would expect that following the discussion, they would have been able to reduce their dissonance, thereby recovering confidence in their opinion. This, of course, should have been more readily true of those who indicated they wanted to listen to someone who already agreed with them.

This expectation is borne out by the data. Of the fifteen strongly dissonant subjects (confidence reduced by the speech) who indicated they wanted to listen to someone who already agreed with them, only four showed the same confidence after the discussion as they had immediately after having heard the speech. Six of the fifteen recovered their confidence completely after the discussion—that is, they had a confidence in their opinion equal to the confidence they had *before* hearing the speech. The other five subjects in this category actually *overrecovered* their confidence during the discussion—that is, these five subjects indicated a confidence in their opinion following the discussion which was actually higher than the confidence they had *before* listening to the disagreeing speech.

Of the twelve subjects whose confidence had been reduced by the speech but who had not indicated that they wanted to listen to someone who already agreed with them, only three recovered their confidence completely. The other nine either had the same confidence that they indicated after the speech or recovered their confidence only partially. Thus, of all those subjects whose confidence had been reduced by listening to a disagreeing speech, more than half recovered their confidence at least completely after a group discussion even though the participants in the discussion split equally in opinion on the issue. For these persons the group discussion completely nullified the impact of the speech. It is interesting to note that there was not a single instance in the entire experiment where the group discussion further lowered the confidence of someone whose confidence had already been lowered by hearing the speech.

There are some interesting implications here for the problem of the impact of the mass media on the opinions and attitudes of persons. The direct impact on a person of a persuasive communication via the mass media is probably seldom strong enough to cause a complete about-face on an opinion which he holds. More often the direct impact is to create some doubts in the mind of the person. To the extent that this person talks about the matter to selected others following his exposure to the mass media, it is quite likely that his doubts will be erased. The mass media may be expected to be most effective under circumstances where there is something to prevent the ready reduction of the dissonance which is created by the exposure to these media. Thus, for example, one would expect the mass media to be more effective with respect to content about which people do not talk readily than with respect to content which is frequently the subject of discussion. Similarly, one would expect the mass media to be more effective with persons who are relatively isolated socially than with those who have many social contacts.

TEN

The Role of Social Support: Data on Mass Phenomena

Mass phenomena are frequently so striking and dramatic in quality that one tends to think of them as exclusively so. There is also a tendency to seek explanations of these striking phenomena which match them in dramatic quality; that is, one looks for something unusual to explain the unusual result. It may be, however, that there is nothing more unusual about these phenomena than the relative rarity of the specific combination of ordinary circumstances that brings about their occurrence.

In discussing mass phenomena in this chapter, I am at somewhat of an advantage because I am not attempting to deal with or to explain all, or even a large number, of mass phenomena. As was discussed in Chapter Eight, the concern here is with finding and analyzing instances where, for one set of reasons or another, a number of people who are in contact with one another all suffer from the same cognitive dissonance. Under such circumstances, the striking and dramatic aspects of mass phenomena exist not because something exceptional or unique is brought into the situation, but only because social support is particularly easy to find in the pursuit of dissonance reduction. Theoretically, it should make little difference whether the dissonance is truly widespread, resulting in a mass phenomenon involving very large numbers of people, or whether the dissonance is shared by a relatively small number of people—provided that in the latter case, social support is still easy to come by. This chapter will, hence, focus on situations where a number of people suffer the identical dissonance rather than on the resulting phenomenon. Thus, the discussion will, on occasion, deal with dissonance that affects relatively few people, and the resulting phenomena may be prosaic as well as dramatic.

One further word concerning the nature of the data with which the chapter will deal and what may be expected from it. In previous chapters when presenting and discussing data, I have been concerned with the cogency of the data to the hypotheses, that is, whether there were or were not equally plausible, and equally simple, alternative explanations of the data. Whenever there were data collected with relative precision under controlled conditions, this was a question which could be discussed fruitfully. There are, to my knowledge, no data on mass movements which have been collected under controlled conditions. For any of the studies to be reported in this chapter, an ingenious person can think of other explanations which could not be refuted by the data. Hence in this chapter I shall be more concerned with the question of whether or not the data are really consistent with the theory of dissonance. That is, does the theory of cognitive dissonance adequately derive the results? If indeed it does, though other explanations may be advanced, then it is significant that the same theory is able to deal both with the results we have discussed in previous chapters and the more complicated phenomena under question here.

Dissonance Reduction Through Rumors

If a person has a strong reaction of fear which persists, the cognition corresponding to this reaction would be dissonant with the cognition that "there is nothing to be afraid of." If such dissonance exists for a person, the pressure to reduce the dissonance will frequently be manifested by an attempt to acquire some cognitive elements which are consonant with the fear reaction. This would, of course, be especially true if the fear reaction could not be turned off at will. For example, a child who for one reason or another is afraid may tell his parents that there are creaking noises in the house indicating the presence of burglars. It does not help satisfy or calm the child to assure him that the noises are quite harmless and that there is nothing to be afraid of. On the contrary, it upsets the child to be thus "reassured." Perhaps it would be more reassuring to the child to be helped in his attempt to acquire cognition consonant with his fear reaction. Other writers have, of course, recognized this type of problem. Freud (22), for example, writes:

We are not used to feeling strong affects without their having any ideational content, and therefore, if the content is missing, we seize as a substitute upon another content which is in some way or other suitable . . . [p. 314].

Murray (40) points to very much the same thing in discussing the results of a small experiment he conducted. Five girls, all about eleven years old, rated each of thirty photographs of people in terms of how benign or how malicious the person appeared. Each photograph was rated once after a pleasant experience and again after having been frightened. Although the number of subjects is too small and the conditions of the experiment too haphazard for the results to be very conclusive, there is a clear tendency for the children to rate the people in the photographs as more "malicious" after they have been frightened. In other words, being afraid, and knowing one is afraid, leads to a tendency to acquire cognition consonant with this fear. In this case it led to a tendency to see other persons as frightening. Murray states:

It was as if the subjects, experiencing an emotion without adequate stimulus, sought something in the external world to justify it—as if the idea had come to mind: "there must be malicious people about." The result of this was that the photographs appeared to change in the direction of adequacy as stimuli [p. 324].

There are natural events which, if they occur, produce fear reactions in people—for example, various types of disasters. There are also some kinds of events which produce similar fear reactions even though they are not accompanied by visible disaster—for example, earthquakes. Even people who live in earthquake areas like California and are quite sophisticated about such things are frightened by the tremors of an earthquake. But most often, following an earthquake there is no visible damage or destruction which would produce cognition which is consonant with this fear reaction. It is, of course, pure speculation, but one may imagine that the mass media, by publicizing the instances of damage which do occur, and by comparing the magnitude of the given earthquake to the worst earthquakes of the past, thus reminding people of the danger involved, may be performing an important function of reducing dissonance.

I have discussed earthquakes as an example because a relevant study exists concerning rumors following an earthquake. This study is reported by Prasad (44) who systematically recorded the rumors which were widely current immediately following an especially severe quake in the province of Bihar, India, on January 15, 1934. The quake itself, a strong and prolonged one, was felt over a wide geographical area Actual damage, however, was quite localized, and for a period of days, communication with the damaged area was very poor. The rumors were collected among people living in the area which received the shock of the earthquake but which did not suffer any damage. We are, then, dealing with communication of rumors among people who felt the shock of the earthquake but who did not see any damage or destruction.

While Prasad reports little concerning the emotional reactions of these people to the quake, it is plausible to assume that these people who knew little about earthquakes had a strong reaction of fear to the violent and prolonged quake which they felt. One may also assume that such a strong fear reaction did not vanish immediately but probably persisted for some time after the actual shock of the quake was over. But let us consider, for a moment, the content of the cognition of these persons. When the earthquake was over, this strong fear reaction persisted even though they could see nothing different around them—no destruction, no further threatening things. In short, a situation had been produced where a large number of people had the identical dissonance, namely, between cognition corresponding to the fear they felt and the knowledge of what they saw around them which added up to the cognition that there was nothing to be afraid of.

If this widespread identical dissonance did exist for all these persons, one would expect it to have been easy for them to obtain social support for cognitions consonant with the fear they felt. Actually, this was clearly reflected in the data which Prasad reported. The vast majority of the rumors which were widely circulated and believed were ones which, if believed, provided cognition consonant with being afraid. One might even call them "fear-provoking" rumors, although, if our interpretation is correct, they would more properly be called "fear-justifying" rumors. The following are a fair sample of these rumors which Prasad collected:

The water of the River Ganges disappeared at the time of the earthquake, and people bathing were imbedded in sand [p. 130].

There will be a severe cyclone at Patna between January 18 and January 19 [p. 130]. [The earthquake occurred on January 15.]

There will be a severe earthquake on the lunar eclipse day [p. 131].

A flood was rushing from the Nepal borders to Madhubani [p. 131].

January 23 will be a fatal day. Unforeseeable calamities will arise [p. 132].

There will be a Pralaya (total deluge and destruction) on February 26 [p. 132].

It is clear that a goodly number of rumors that arose and were widely circulated predicted terrible disasters to come. To the extent that any of these rumors were accepted and believed, they provided cognition consonant with being afraid. For these rumors to have become widespread it was necessary for a large number of persons to have had the same dissonance which would be reduced by acceptance of these rumors.

If the explanation in terms of widespread identical dissonance and the pressure to reduce it is correct in accounting for the prevalence of these disaster rumors, there is one clear implication, namely, that if rumors had been collected among persons living in the area of destruction, few, if any, of such "fear-justifying" rumors would have been found. Those persons directly in the area of destruction caused by the earthquake were, undoubtedly, also frightened. Indeed, their fear reaction would very likely have been even stronger than the reaction of persons who merely felt the shock of the quake. But for these persons in the area of destruction, no cognitive dissonance would have been created. The things they saw around them—the destruction, the wounded and killed—produced cognition which was certainly consonant with feeling afraid. There would have been no impulse to acquire additional cognition which would fit with the fear. Disaster rumors of the type so prevalent *outside* of the area of destruction should, consequently, have been absent *inside* the area of destruction.

Unfortunately, Prasad presented no data on rumors which circulated inside the area of destruction following the earthquake. There is, however, another study reported by Sinha (49) which partially answers this question, although not as satisfactorily as might be desired. This study reported a careful collection of rumors following a disaster in Darjeeling, India—a disaster which was fully comparable to the earthquake in terms of destruction and loss of life but which, unfortunately for purposes of comparison, did not arise from an earthquake but from a landslide. Nevertheless, it must have produced considerable fear among the people. Sinha, in describing the disaster, stated:

There had been landslides before, but nothing like this had ever happened. Loss of life and damage to property were heavy and extensive. . . . In the town itself houses collapsed and victims lay buried under the debris. . . . Over a hundred and fifty persons lost their lives in the district, about thirty of them in the town itself. Over a hundred were injured. More than two hundred houses were damaged and over 2000 people were rendered homeless [p. 200].

Again, in a comment which is especially important from the point of view of regarding this study as providing a comparison for the Prasad study, Sinha compared the two disasters directly in saying:

There was a feeling of instability and uncertainty similar to that which followed the Great Indian Earthquake of 1934 [p. 200].

There was, however, one important difference between the study reported by Prasad and the one reported by Sinha. While the rumors following the earthquake were collected among persons outside the area of destruction, the rumors which Sinha reported were collected from persons in Darjeeling who actually were in the area and witnessed the destruction. Since for these people there would have been no dissonance (what they saw and knew was quite consonant with being afraid), one would not expect "fear-justifying" rumors to have arisen and spread among them.

Actually, in Sinha's report there was a complete absence of rumors predicting further disasters or of any type of rumor that might be regarded as supplying cognition consonant with being afraid. Some of the rumors represented a slight exaggeration of the actual damage while others were even of the hopeful variety. The following are a sample of the rumors which did exist in Darjeeling:

Many houses have come down on the A——— road. (Only one house had actually collapsed on this particular road [p. 201].)

It has been announced that the water supply will be restored in a week [p. 203].

It will take months before the water supply is resumed [p. 203].

There are extensive floods in the plains. . . . Many bridges have been washed away [p. 204].

There was widespread belief that there had been a slight earthquake which had helped in producing the damage. (There had actually been no earthquake.)

The remarkable thing about these rumors was the lack of serious exaggeration, the presence of a few that were even hopeful, and the complete absence of "fear-provoking" or "fear-justifying" rumors.

The contrast between the rumors reported by Sinha and those reported by Prasad is certainly strong. If the situations in which these two authors collected the rumors were indeed comparable except for whether or not the rumors were collected in the area of destruction, then the difference in the nature of the rumors between the two studies is consistent with what would be expected from our discussion.

I have chosen to discuss the Prasad and Sinha studies of rumor in some detail not only because the data are consistent with the theory of dissonance, but also because they do not agree entirely with so-called common sense. After all, why should the occurrence of an earthquake impel people to spread and believe rumors which are frightening?

Many other studies of rumors report data which are consistent with both the theory of dissonance and with common sense. For example, Sady (45) reported on rumors which circulated in one of the Japanese relocation camps during World War II. It was clear that the Japanese, who were arbitrarily moved to these relocation camps, saw this as an act of hostility directed toward them by the United States. It was also quite clear that any cognition corresponding to being treated well or shown friendliness by the officials of the camps was dissonant with the cognition that the United States was hostile to them. There were, accordingly, persistent rumors which provided cognition consonant with the perceived hostility—rumors which persisted in spite of, or more appropriately because of, attempts on the part of the camp officials to improve living conditions. Rumors that were widely current included reports that many people were dying because of the heat and that their bodies were taken away secretly at night, and that the site for the relocation center had been deliberately chosen so that as many as possible of the evacuees would die.

The reaction, as far as rumor went, to a specific attempt at improvement of conditions in one relocation center is well illustrated by the following example. During the first summer at the Poston Relocation Center, temporary medical clinics operated because the regular hospital was not yet finished. When the hospital was opened, these temporary clinics were closed and a twenty-four-hour home-call service for emergencies was started. This was widely publicized by the officials. It represented a clear improvement in the medical services offered in the camp. Cognition corresponding to knowing that the authorities were improving medical service was certainly dissonant with knowing these authorities were hostile. The rumor arose, and was widely accepted, that the doctors were not going to make any more home calls at all. No matter how serious the condition of the patient, he would have to be brought to the hospital in order to see a doctor. Thus what was accepted by the people were "facts" consonant with knowing the authorities were hostile.

Another example, of a very obvious nature, may be taken from an experiment by Schachter and Burdick (47). These authors attempted to plant rumors and to study the extent of their spread in a small private school. Part of the procedure was to have the principal of the school, in an utterly unprecedented action, remove a girl from the class without any explanation beyond saying that the girl would not be back that day. As might be expected, some rumors spontaneously arose concerning the reason that this girl had been removed from the class. The data show that those who liked the girl who had been removed tended to initiate rumors of a favorable character (she had been singled out for some honor, and the like) while those who disliked the girl tended to initiate rumors of an unfavorable nature (she had been caught cheating). Clearly, the content of the rumors initiated by these persons is such as to be consonant with their overall opinions of the girl.

Let me here re-emphasize that I do not mean to imply that all rumors are manifestations of attempts to reduce dissonance. As was stated in Chapter Eight, there are many other sets of circumstances that will cause rumors to start and to spread. Dissonance that is present identically for many persons is just one of these sets of conditions. I would also like to add a thought concerning the obvious and common sense nature of some of the rumors that have been given above as examples. In many instances, indeed perhaps in most, what seems obvious and corresponds to common sense may indeed be correct. In order to test a theory and its derivations, one usually appeals to instances which are not obvious so as to rule out alternative explanations. If the theory has any validity, however, it should also be consistent with a large body of data which are obvious. Certainly a theory which elegantly handles some nonobvious aspect of behavior, but is inconsistent with much that we know of an obvious sort, is not a very satisfactory theory.

Maintaining Invalid Beliefs

It is quite difficult for people who are ordinarily responsive to reality to maintain beliefs which are clearly invalid. By the term "invalid" I do not mean here a belief which is *possibly* wrong, but rather one which has been, and continues to be, directly and unequivocally disconfirmed by good evidence such as actual events which impinge on the persons who hold the belief. What has been described in the last sentence corresponds, of course, to a cognitive dissonance.

When such clear and unequivocally disconfirming evidence impinges on a person, the cognition corresponding to this knowledge is dissonant with the belief he holds. When such a state of affairs exists, the most usual and ordinary way of eliminating the dissonance is to discard the belief rather than to attempt to deny the evidence of one's own senses. For example, if a person believed that it was impossible for objects heavier than air to fly, he would undoubtedly discard this belief on seeing an airplane in the sky—or at least after riding in one.

But there are circumstances in which this does not happen—that is, even in the face of clearly disconfirming evidence, the belief is not discarded. One is told, for example, that there are gamblers who continue to believe in the validity of certain "systems" for winning at roulette in spite of steady losses using the system. One is also told that there are instances of scientists continuing to believe in the validity of a theory long after it has been disproved by clear experimental evidence. What, however, are the circumstances under which this will happen—that is, under what conditions will the attempts at dissonance reduction focus on denying the evidence of reality rather than on discarding the belief? As discussed in Chapter Eight one would expect this to happen under the following circumstances: the belief is difficult to change, and there are a sufficient number of persons with the identical dissonance so that social support is easily obtainable.

Let us illustrate this specifically by discussing an example reported by Sady (45). During World War II, some Japanese in the United States, when given the opportunity, requested that they be repatriated to Japan at the end of the war. Those who were citizens of the United States and requested repatriation thereby renounced their citizenship. For all of them, citizen or not, the request for repatriation was an irrevocable act. At the end of the war they were to be returned to Japan. Apparently one major difference between the many who did not request repatriation and the few who did was the belief they held concerning the outcome of the war. While the majority of Japanese in the relocation centers believed and hoped that the war would end in a negotiated peace, most of those who requested repatriation firmly believed that Japan would win the war.

In other words, there was a group of persons who firmly held a belief, namely, that Japan would win the war, and had taken certain irrevocable actions on the basis of this belief. For any of these persons, the knowledge that he had requested repatriation and would return to Japan at the end of the war was consonant with the belief that Japan would win the war. Furthermore, those who requested repatriation were heavily committed to this belief because they could not change their minds about repatriation.

Events occurred, however, which introduced cognition which was dissonant with this belief—dissonant identically for all those holding the belief. News began to appear concerning Japanese reverses in the war. Eventually, news and photographs of the Japanese surrender were circulated in the relocation centers, and the news was, of course, accepted and believed by the vast majority. Those who had requested repatriation, however, by supporting one another in an attempt to eliminate the dissonance introduced by this information, rejected the evidence of the Japanese surrender. It was dismissed as American propaganda, and those who had requested repatriation continued to believe that Japan had won the war. It is doubtful that such a belief could have persisted in the face of all the disconfirming evidence if social support had not been so easily obtained among the people who suffered the same cognitive dissonance.

It is interesting to note that even on the way back to Japan on an American ship these persons continued to believe that Japan had won the war and that Japan was forcing the United States to return them. It was apparently only after landing in Japan and seeing the actual destruction and the American occupation troops that the belief was finally discarded. Unfortunately, the only evidence for this comes from a newspaper dispatch from the Associated Press (55):

BITTER DISAPPOINTMENT MARKS RETURN HOME OF NISEI
WHO WISHED THEY HAD STAYED IN U.S.

Why 95% of those who came back to Japan on the ship with me thought that Japan had won the war: They thought it just a bunch of American propaganda that Japan surrendered and believed that they were being brought back to Japan because the Japanese had won the war and were compelling the Americans to transport them.

It is clear that for a considerable time, these people, by supporting one another, were able to deny the validity of evidence contrary to a belief they needed to maintain.

Mass Proselyting

Let us turn, now, to examining data where there is evidence concerning the social process which arises when social support is easily obtainable. Again, we will look for situations where a belief that is very difficult to discard is held, and where cognition dissonant with this belief is introduced by the unequivocal evidence of one's own senses. Specifically, if the belief is very difficult to discard, and if the cognition dissonant with the belief is also very difficult to discard, obtaining social support will be one of the major means of reducing the magnitude of the dissonance. Under such circumstances, the introduction of an identical dissonance into the cognitions of many people will lead to two observable manifestations of the pressure to reduce the dissonance by obtaining social support. First, there will be an increase in giving and obtaining support among those suffering the identical dissonance. Second, there will be an increase in the attempts to persuade new people that the belief is, after all, valid.

In principle, the phenomenon discussed here is no different from what one observes in a person who buys a new car, has some experiences with it which are not altogether to his liking, and proceeds to try to convince his friends that the make of car he just purchased is the most wonderful thing on the market. The only difference is that where there are a number of people having the same cognitive dissonance, the phenomenon may be much more spectacular, even to the point where it is possible to withstand evidence which would otherwise be overwhelming. This results in an apparent paradox, namely, that after being exposed to evidence of one's own senses which unequivocally demonstrates a belief system to be wrong, people proceed to proselyte more vigorously for the belief system.

There is a type of movement which has occurred with fair frequency in recent history and which fits the conditions thus far specified and where, hence, one would expect to observe an increase in proselyting and in seeking social support following an unequivocal disconfirmation of a belief system. Some of the millennial and messianic movements which have existed in the past are examples of this type of movement. While the data concerning the amount of proselyting in these movements are in most instances exceedingly scanty, it is worth while to describe some of them briefly. Typically, those movements which are relevant to our purposes here have the following characteristics:

1. A belief or set of beliefs is held with conviction by a number of people.

2. The belief, at least in part, has sufficient implication

for the affairs of the daily world so that the believers take action in accordance with the belief.

3. The action is sufficiently important, and sufficiently difficult to undo, that the believers are, in a very real sense, committed to the belief.

4. At least some part of the belief is sufficiently specific and concerned with the real world so that unequivocal disproof or disconfirmation is possible.

5. This possible disconfirmation actually occurs, usually in the form of the nonoccurrence of a predicted event within the time limits set for its occurrence.

6. The dissonance thus introduced between the belief and the information concerning the nonoccurrence of the predicted event exists in the cognitions of all the believers, and hence, social support in attempting to reduce the dissonance is easily obtained.

Let us look briefly at one of the relevant historical movements to see how it fits these conditions and to see, to the extent that evidence exists, how adherents reacted to the dissonance. The Millerite movement of the nineteenth century, since it is one of the best documented instances, is most suitable for our purposes.

In the early part of the nineteenth century, William Miller, a New England farmer, reached the conclusion that the Second Advent of Christ ushering in the millennium would occur in the year 1843. This conclusion was based on the literal interpretation of statements in the Old Testament together with a variety of assumptions concerning calculation of time. Although Miller talked about the impending event for many years, belief in his conclusion was rather slow in spreading. Gradually, however, he succeeded in convincing a number of people, and one of these in particular, Joshua Himes, gave the beliefs enormous impetus by organizing a movement. A newspaper was started, conferences of ministers were called, books and pamphlets were printed and distributed, camp meetings were held, and by the beginning of the year 1843 there were a large number of people who firmly believed that that year would mark the end of the world as they had known it.

Here, then, was a situation with all of the characteristics we have discussed. A large number of people were convinced that the Second Advent would occur in 1843. There were clear implications for action here which these believers in Miller's prophecy engaged in. At a minimum it involved spreading the belief and enduring the scoffing of an unbelieving and hostile world; at a maximum it meant neglecting one's worldly affairs entirely, giving one's money to the movement and, in effect, pauperizing oneself—consequences which were certainly immaterial as long as the Second Advent would indeed occur when and as predicted. In short, most of the people who believed were also committed to the belief. It would not be easy, under these circumstances, to discard the belief. The belief was also specific enough so that confirmation or disconfirmation would be unequivocal; the Second Advent either would or would not actually take place during the specified period.

One may, then, inquire concerning the reactions of these people when the year 1843 drew to a close and the Second Advent had not occurred as predicted. This reaction may be succinctly summarized as follows:

1. Initial bewilderment. This was undoubtedly symptomatic of the existence of the dissonance. These people were in a situation where they continued to maintain a belief and also knew that the prediction was incorrect, two cognitive clusters which were certainly dissonant.

2. An attempted rationale for the failure of the prediction. This rationale, when supported by all the other believers, reduced the dissonance somewhat. In this instance

the rationale consisted, essentially, in changing the date before which the Advent was to occur.

3. An increase in proselyting for the belief. In order to further reduce the dissonance, they tried to persuade more and more persons that the belief was correct.

Sears (48) describes these occurrences as follows:

Then a fluttering of doubt and hesitation became apparent in certain communities, but soon these were dispelled when it was recalled that as far back as 1839 Prophet Miller had stated on some occasion, which had been forgotten in the general excitement, that he was not *positive* that the event would take place during the *Christian* year from 1843 to 1844, and that he would claim the whole *Jewish* year which would carry the prophecy over to the 21st of March, 1844.

Having accepted this lengthening of the allotted time, the brethren who had assumed the responsibility of sounding the alarm entered into their work with renewed energy and outdid themselves in their efforts to terrify the army of unbelievers into a realization of the horrors that awaited them and to strengthen the faith of those already in the ranks [pp. 140–41].

This new and increased fervor continued unabated, and when March 21, 1844, came and went without the Second Advent having occurred, there was a repetition of the previous reaction. There was strong and severe disappointment of short duration, but soon the energy and enthusiasm returned to, and indeed even exceeded, its previous level. Nichol (42) and Sears (48) describe the reaction as follows:

The year of the end of the world had ended, but Millerism had not. The prediction of the Millerites had failed, but so also had the predictions of their enemies, who had confidently forecast that when 1843 came to a close the Millerites would become infidels, burn their Bibles, and do numerous other ungodly things, because of their disappointment. But the Millerites did none of these. Though some who had been only lukewarm in the movement fell away from it, many maintained both their faith and their fervor. They were ready to attribute the disappointment to some minor error in calculating chronology [Nichol, p. 206].

But in spite of the failure of the prophecy the fires of fanaticism increased. The flames of such emotions cannot be quenched at will; like all great conflagrations they must burn themselves out. And so it was in 1844. Instead of decreasing, the failure seemed to excite even greater exhibitions of loyalty to the expectation of the impending Judgment Day [Sears, p. 147].

By the middle of July, 1844, the movement had reached a new fever pitch, and the energy expended to spread the belief was greater than ever. This even included tours to new territory, going as far west as Ohio, to convert new people to the belief. Also about this time, more and more currency was being given to a new predicted date, namely, October 22, 1844. In the period from mid-August to the new predicted date, things reached an incredible pitch of fervor, zeal, and conviction.

It is strange to contemplate that the result of two successive disconfirmations of the prediction had simply increased the conviction that the Second Advent was near at hand and had increased the time and energy that was spent convincing others of the truth of the prediction. But no matter how resistant to change a belief system is, dissonance may mount to a point where it will be discarded—where the dissonance can no longer be reduced to a point where it is tolerable. Three successive disconfirmations were sufficient finally to do this for the Millerites. When October 22, 1844, came and went without the Second Advent, the belief was finally discarded and the movement came to a quick and sudden end.

To the extent that one can ascertain the relevant facts, other movements of similar character also behaved in a similar manner, namely, an increase of proselyting activity following the disconfirmation of a strongly held belief to which the adherents were committed. Data on these other movements are, however, so scanty that I will not describe them here. Rather I will proceed to describe a study reported by Festinger, Riecken, and Schachter (19) which was based on direct observation of a similar movement. The authors observed the movement as participants for approximately two months preceding and one month succeeding the unequivocal failure of a prediction which was based on a belief to which these persons were committed. During this period of observation, data were collected concerning each instance of proselyting so that adequate comparison could be made of the level of proselyting before and after the disconfirmation of the prediction. But let us start by briefly describing the general character of the movement with which the study was concerned.

The movement, if such it can be called considering the relatively small number of persons who were involved in it, centered around a woman who received written messages from a number of the Guardians who lived in outer space. Her adherents, numbering twenty-five to thirty persons, believed completely in the validity of these messages and in the things they said. Most of the messages were "lessons," that is, they were expositions of various aspects of a set of beliefs. They explained about the life of the gods on other planets, different spiritual vibration frequencies on different worlds, reincarnation, and the like. The beliefs thus expounded, and accepted by the adherents, were not original. They were rather an eclectic combination of the doctrine of various sects and groups such as the "I Am" movement, the theosophists, and the like. The group that gathered around the woman who received the messages were, for the most part, upper middle-class people who were well educated. The reasons that these people, who led normal lives and filled responsible roles in society, accepted this set of beliefs and accepted the validity of the messages are unknown and outside the scope of our interest here. Our interest in this group arises because the messages from the Guardians brought these people some astounding news, namely, that on a given date, just before dawn, a cataclysmic flood would engulf most of the continent. Here was a prediction, based on the belief in the validity of the messages from the Guardians, which was specific enough to be capable of unequivocal disconfirmation. Let us then examine those aspects of the behavior of the adherents which are relevant to us here, namely, their conviction in the belief, the degree to which they were committed to the belief, the level of proselyting for the belief before and after the date for which the cataclysm was predicted, and the degree of social support they offered one another.

The level of proselyting for the belief system was relatively low before the date for which the cataclysm was predicted. This level varied from time to time from a few instances of active publicity seeking at one extreme to great secrecy at the other extreme. Immediately after the prediction of the cataclysm was received in the messages from the Guardians, there was a brief spurt of activity designed to spread the word and, undoubtedly, to attract adherents. This occurred about three and a half months before the fateful date. The woman who received the messages gave two or three talks to a group of people, and one of the other adherents sent two press releases to an assortment of newspapers around the country announcing the impending event. This flurry of active proselyting subsided quickly, and for most of the subsequent period before the cataclysm, the adherents were content to study the "lessons" from the Guardians and make whatever preparations were needed. There seemed to be no desire at all to attract new believers. Those who were chosen to be saved would undoubtedly join the group of their own accord and, even if they did not, would be saved individually when the time came. Those who were not chosen were intended to perish in the flood, but even this was of no consequence; it merely involved a loss of their material bodies. Their spirits would be transported to other planets of appropriate vibration frequency for them.

If anyone came to members of the group to ask about the belief system, they were treated cordially; questions were answered but there were not any attempts to convince or convert. If anyone came back again, it was on their own initiative. There were also times when the group imposed secrecy concerning various aspects of their beliefs and of their preparations for the cataclysm. Outsiders, for example, could not discover what they were doing in preparation for the flood, and members of the group were frequently cautioned against talking to those who were not chosen. Members were also cautioned against revealing to outsiders the content of messages from the Guardians. This lack of interest in attracting new believers, amounting at times to a positive aversion for publicity, was dramatically illustrated by a series of events which occurred just a few days before the flood was due.

One of the adherents, a physician, had held a post in the student health service of a college. The college administration, for reasons connected with his beliefs, had requested his resignation. For the newspapers this apparently was wonderful material. The fact that the physician had resigned and the content of the prediction of cataclysm made headlines all over the country. This occurred only five days before the flood was due, and the group was besieged by newspapermen clamoring for interviews. What might have been a heaven-sent opportunity for anyone interested in spreading the word and attracting potential believers was, for these people, a source of pain, irritation, and embarrassment. They avoided the persistent newspapermen as much as possible, usually refused interviews with a brief "no comment," and were greatly troubled by the whole affair. The newspapers, however, continued to write stories about the group, particularly those newspapers in the city in which the group was located. Many people who read the stories in the newspapers did phone or come to the house seeking further knowledge. The group of believers, however, treated these visitors very casually, refusing admission to the house to many, and not seriously attempting to attract anyone. Those who were chosen would be saved anyway.

So much, in brief, for the level of proselyting in the days preceding the coming cataclysm. Let us turn our attention now to the evidence one can muster concerning the conviction of these people and the extent to which they had committed themselves to their belief, that is, taken actions in accordance with it—actions which were difficult to undo, hence making it difficult for them to discard the belief system. There was, indeed, a range of conviction in the group. The conviction ranged from slight skepticism (quite rare in the group) to extreme and utter conviction (the prevalent state of affairs). Those who were slightly skeptical were the very few persons who had been brought into the group more or less against their will, or at least without any volition on their part. Thus, for example, the seventeen-year-old daughter of one of the leaders of the group, while a member because of circumstances, occasionally expressed skepticism. But by and large, if one were to characterize the degree of conviction in the group as a whole, it was complete faith in the belief and in the validity of the messages from the Guardians.

As in other movements such as these, there was a close connection between the degree of conviction and the degree to which committing actions were taken in accordance with the belief. If one really accepted the prediction that the world, as one knew it, was to come to an end on a certain day at a certain time, one did not go about one's business as usual. At a minimum such a person neglected affairs of the world which, in the light of what was about to happen, were very unimportant. At a maximum such a person flouted his disdain for this world and the things concerning it. The people in this group did all of these things. Many quit their jobs, discarded possessions which they used to hold dear, and were careless of their money. After the fateful day they would have no need of these things. Hence, it is plausible to contend that for most of the people in the group, giving up the belief would have been no easy thing. It would have left them jobless, poor, exposed to scorn, and faced with having to build their lives all over again.

The disconfirmation of the prediction did, of course, occur. But let me relate a bit about the circumstances. For some time it had been clear to the people in the group that those who were chosen were to be picked up by flying saucers and evacuated from this planet before the cataclysm occurred. Some of the believers, these mainly college students, were advised to go home and wait there individually for the flying saucer that would arrive for each of them. This was reasonable and plausible since the date of the cataclysm happened to occur during an academic holiday. Most of the group, including the most central and most heavily committed members, gathered together in the home of the woman who received the messages and waited there for the arrival of the flying saucer. For these latter, disconfirmation of the prediction, in the form of evidence that the messages were not valid, began to occur four days before the predicted event was to take place. A message informed them at that time that a saucer would land in the back yard of the house at 4:00 P.M. to pick up the members of the group. With coats in hand they waited, but no saucer came. A later message told them there had been a delay—the saucer would arrive at midnight. Midst absolute secrecy (the neighbors and press must not know) they waited outdoors on a cold and snowy night for over an hour and no saucer came. Another message told them to continue waiting, but still no saucer came. At about 3:00 A.M. they gave up, interpreting the events of that night as a test, a drill, and a rehearsal for the real pickup which would still soon take place.

Tensely, they waited for the final orders to come through —for the messages which would tell them the time, place, and procedure for the actual pickup. Finally, on the day before the cataclysm was to strike, the messages came. At midnight a man would come to the door of the house and take them to the place where the flying saucer would be parked. More messages came that day, one after another, instructing them in the passwords that would be necessary in order to board the saucer and in preparatory procedures such as removal of metal from clothing, removal of personal identification, maintaining silence at certain times, and the like. The day was spent by the group in preparation and in rehearsal of the necessary procedures, and when midnight came, the group sat waiting in readiness. But no knock came at the door; no one came to lead them to the flying saucer.

From midnight to five o'clock in the morning the group sat there struggling to understand what had happened, struggling to find some explanation that would enable them to recover somewhat from the shattering realization that they would not be picked up by a flying saucer and that, consequently, the flood itself would not occur as predicted. It is doubtful that anyone alone, without the support of the others, could have withstood the impact of this disconfirmation of the prediction. Indeed, those members of the group who had gone to their homes to wait alone—alone in the sense that they did not have other believers with them—did not withstand it. Afterward, almost all of them became skeptics. In other words, without easily obtainable social support with which to begin reducing the dissonance, this dissonance was sufficient to cause the belief to be discarded in spite of the commitment to it. But the people who had gathered together in the home of the woman who received the messages could, and did, provide social support for one another. They kept reassuring one another of the validity of the messages and that some explanation would be found.

At fifteen minutes before five o'clock that morning an explanation that was at least temporarily satisfactory was found. A message arrived from God which, in effect, said that He had saved the world and stayed the flood because of this group and the light and strength they had spread throughout the world that night.

The behavior of these people from that moment onward presents a revealing contrast to their predisconfirmation behavior. These people, who had been disinterested in publicity and had even avoided it, now became avid publicity seekers. For four successive days, finding a new reason each day, they invited the press into the house, gave lengthy interviews, and attempted to attract the public to their ideas. The first day they called all the newspapers and news services, informed them of the fact that the world had been saved, and invited them to come and get interviews. The second day a ban on having photographs taken was lifted, and the newspapers were once more called to inform them of this fact and to invite them to come to the house and take pictures. On the third day they once more called the press to inform them that on the next afternoon they would gather on their front lawn to sing and that it was possible a space man would visit them at that time. What is more, the general public was specifically invited to come and watch. And on the fourth day, newspapermen and about two hundred people came to watch the group singing on their front lawn. Gone was the predisconfirmation secrecy. There were almost no lengths to which these people would not go now to get publicity and to attract potential believers in the validity of the messages. If, indeed, more and more converts could be found—more and more people who believed in the messages and the things the messages said— then the dissonance between their belief and the knowledge that the messages had not been correct could be reduced.

The conviction of those persons who had met the disconfirmation together did not seem to waver at all, at least on the surface. Indeed, the need for social support to reduce the dissonance introduced by the disconfirmation was so strong, and the social support so easily forthcoming from one another, that at least two of these persons, who before had occasionally shown some mild skepticism concerning certain aspects of the beliefs, now seemed completely and utterly convinced of the validity of it all. Throughout the time that the authors maintained contact with these people, they continued to believe. The sudden change to almost frantic seeking of publicity represented one of the few signs that in spite of the rationale for the disconfirmation and in spite of the social support they could give one another, appreciable dissonance persisted. With sufficient social support available so that they could manage to retain the belief to which they were so heavily committed, and with the clear and unequivocal knowledge that the prediction had been false, almost the only avenue for further dissonance reduction was to obtain more cognition consonant with the belief in the form of knowing that more and more people also accepted their beliefs and the messages as valid.

ELEVEN

Recapitulation and Further Suggestions

The various definitions, assumptions, and hypotheses which constitute the theory of cognitive dissonance have been stated in the five theoretical chapters of the book. In an effort to provide a brief summary of the theory, I will restate some of these definitions, assumptions, and hypotheses in as organized a manner as seems feasible.

The basic background of the theory consists of the notion that the human organism tries to establish internal harmony, consistency, or congruity among his opinions, attitudes, knowledge, and values. That is, there is a drive toward consonance among cognitions. In order to deal with this notion in a somewhat more precise manner, I have imagined cognition to be decomposable into elements or, at least, clusters of elements. The following theoretical statements have been made about the relations among these cognitive elements:

1. Pairs of elements can exist in irrelevant, consonant, or dissonant relations.

2. Two cognitive elements are in an irrelevant relation if they have nothing to do with one another.

3. Two cognitive elements are in a dissonant relation if,

considering these two alone, the obverse of one element follows from the other.

4. Two cognitive elements are in a consonant relation if, considering these two alone, one element follows from the other.

Starting from these definitions, a number of situations have been denoted as implying the existence of cognitive dissonance.

1. Dissonance almost always exists after a decision has been made between two or more alternatives. The cognitive elements corresponding to positive characteristics of the rejected alternatives, and those corresponding to negative characteristics of the chosen alternative, are *dissonant* with the knowledge of the action that has been taken. Those cognitive elements corresponding to positive characteristics of the chosen alternative and negative characteristics of the rejected alternative are *consonant* with the cognitive elements corresponding to the action which has been taken.

2. Dissonance almost always exists after an attempt has been made, by offering rewards or threatening punishment, to elicit overt behavior that is at variance with private opinion. If the overt behavior is successfully elicited, the person's private opinion is dissonant with his knowledge concerning his behavior; his knowledge of the reward obtained or of the punishment avoided is consonant with his knowledge concerning his behavior. If the overt behavior is not successfully elicited, then his private opinion is consonant with his knowledge of what he has done, but the knowledge of the reward not obtained or of the punishment to be suffered is dissonant with his knowledge of what he has done.

3. Forced or accidental exposure to new information may create cognitive elements that are dissonant with existing cognition.

4. The open expression of disagreement in a group leads

to the existence of cognitive dissonance in the members. The knowledge that some other person, generally like oneself, holds one opinion is dissonant with holding a contrary opinion.

5. Identical dissonance in a large number of people may be created when an event occurs which is so compelling as to produce a uniform reaction in everyone. For example, an event may occur which unequivocally invalidates some widely held belief.

Thus far, dissonance and consonance have been defined as "all or none" relations—that is, if two elements are relevant to one another, the relation between them is either dissonant or consonant. Two hypotheses have been advanced concerning the magnitude of dissonance or consonance.

1. The magnitude of the dissonance or consonance which exists between two cognitive elements will be a direct function of the importance of these two elements.

2. The total magnitude of dissonance which exists between two clusters of cognitive elements is a function of the weighted proportion of all the relevant relations between the two clusters which are dissonant, each dissonant or consonant relation being weighted according to the importance of the elements involved in that relation.

Starting with these hypotheses about the magnitude of dissonance, a number of operational implications seem clear.

1. The magnitude of postdecision dissonance is an increasing function of the general importance of the decision and of the relative attractiveness of the unchosen alternatives.

2. The magnitude of postdecision dissonance *decreases* as the number of cognitive elements corresponding identically to characteristics of chosen and unchosen alternatives *increases*.

3. The magnitude of the dissonance resulting from an at-

tempt to elicit forced compliance is greatest if the promised reward or threatened punishment is either *just sufficient* to elicit the overt behavior or is *just barely not sufficient* to elicit it.

4. If forced compliance is elicited, the magnitude of the dissonance *decreases* as the magnitude of the reward or punishment *increases*.

5. If forced compliance fails to be elicited, the magnitude of the dissonance *increases* as the magnitude of the reward or punishment *increases*.

6. The magnitude of the dissonance introduced by the expression of disagreement by others *decreases* as the number of existing cognitive elements consonant with the opinion *increases*. These latter elements may correspond either to objective, nonsocial items of information or to the knowledge that some other people hold the same opinion.

7. The magnitude of the dissonance introduced by disagreement from others *increases* with *increase* in the importance of the opinion to the person, in the relevance of the opinion to those voicing disagreement, and in the attractiveness of those voicing disagreement.

8. The greater the difference between the opinion of the person and the opinion of the one voicing disagreement, and, hence, the greater the number of elements which are dissonant between the cognitive clusters corresponding to the two opinions, the greater will be the magnitude of dissonance.

One now comes to the point of stating the central hypotheses of the theory, namely:

1. The presence of dissonance gives rise to pressures to reduce that dissonance.

2. The strength of the pressure to reduce dissonance is a function of the magnitude of the existing dissonance.

These hypotheses lead, naturally, to a consideration of the ways in which dissonance may be reduced. There are three major ways in which this may be done.

1. By changing one or more of the elements involved in dissonant relations.

2. By adding new cognitive elements that are consonant with already existing cognition.

3. By decreasing the importance of the elements involved in the dissonant relations.

Applying these considerations to actual situations leads to the following:

1. Postdecision dissonance may be reduced by increasing the attractiveness of the chosen alternative, decreasing the attractiveness of the unchosen alternatives, or both.

2. Postdecision dissonance may be reduced by perceiving some characteristics of the chosen and unchosen alternatives as identical.

3. Postdecision dissonance may be reduced by decreasing the importance of various aspects of the decision.

4. If forced compliance has been elicited, the dissonance may be reduced by changing private opinion to bring it into line with the overt behavior or by magnifying the amount of reward or punishment involved.

5. If forced compliance fails to be elicited, dissonance may be reduced by intensifying the original private opinion or by minimizing the reward or punishment involved.

6. The presence of dissonance leads to seeking new information which will provide cognition consonant with existing cognitive elements and to avoiding those sources of new information which would be likely to increase the existing dissonance.

7. When some of the cognitive elements involved in a dissonance are cognitions about one's own behavior, the disso-

nance can be reduced by changing the behavior, thus directly changing the cognitive elements.

8. Forced or accidental exposure to new information which tends to increase dissonance will frequently result in misinterpretation and misperception of the new information by the person thus exposed in an effort to avoid a dissonance increase.

9. Dissonance introduced by disagreement expressed by other persons may be reduced by changing one's own opinion, by influencing the others to change their opinion, and by rejecting those who disagree.

10. The existence of dissonance will lead to seeking out others who already agree with a cognition that one wants to establish or maintain and will also lead to the initiation of communication and influence processes in an effort to obtain more social support.

11. Influence exerted on a person will be more effective in producing opinion change to the extent that the indicated change of opinion reduces dissonance for that person.

12. In situations where many persons who associate with one another all suffer from the identical dissonance, dissonance reduction by obtaining social support is very easy to accomplish.

To conclude this brief summary of the theory, there are a few things to be stated concerning the effectiveness of efforts directed toward dissonance reduction.

1. The effectiveness of efforts to reduce dissonance will depend upon the resistance to change of the cognitive elements involved in the dissonance and on the availability of information which will provide, or of other persons who will supply, new cognitive elements which will be consonant with existing cognition.

2. The major sources of resistance to change for a cogni-

tive element are the responsiveness of such cognitive elements to "reality" and the extent to which an element exists in consonant relations with many other elements.

3. The maximum dissonance which can exist between two elements is equal to the resistance to change of the less resistant of the two elements. If the dissonance exceeds this magnitude, the less resistant cognitive element will be changed, thus reducing the dissonance.

This brief summary can hardly hope to give an adequate picture of the theory, but perhaps it can help the reader to see more clearly the nature of the theory and where it goes. I will not attempt to provide any summary of the empirical evidence which has been presented.

In the course of thinking about the theory, conducting studies designed to test its implications, and searching the literature for data, numerous ideas have suggested themselves which seem promising but about which there is no evidence. The degree of confirmation of the theory of dissonance in those areas where data have been obtained seems sufficient to encourage me to spell out here those implications from, and ideas about, the theory of dissonance for which no evidence is available. The remainder of this chapter consists, then, of an assortment of suggestions which vary all the way from derivations from the theory to hunches about variables which affect the processes of dissonance reduction.

Some Notions Concerning Personality Differences

There are, certainly, individual differences among people in the degree to which, and in the manner that, they react to the existence of dissonance. For some people dissonance is an extremely painful and intolerable thing, while there are others who seem to be able to tolerate a large amount of dissonance. This variation in "tolerance for dissonance" would seem to be measurable in at least a rough way. Persons with low tolerance for dissonance should show more discomfort in the presence of dissonance and should manifest greater efforts to reduce dissonance than persons who have high tolerance. Because of this variation in efforts to reduce dissonance, it would be plausible to expect that persons with low tolerance would actually have considerably less existing dissonance at any time than comparable persons who have a rather high tolerance for dissonance. One would expect a person with low tolerance for dissonance to see issues more in terms of "black and white" than would a person with high tolerance for dissonance who might be expected to be able to maintain "grays" in his cognition. Thus, for example, let us imagine a person who is a Democrat. If he has a high tolerance for dissonance, it might be possible for him to continue being a Democrat and yet also believe that there were certain issues on which the Democrats are wrong. In essence, he would be maintaining two sets of cognitions which are dissonant with one another since, considering only the fact that he thinks the Democrats are wrong on some issues, and ignoring all other relevant cognition for the moment, the obverse of "being a Democrat" would follow.

A person with a low tolerance for dissonance would, perhaps, be unable to maintain such dissonances and would struggle to eliminate them. Thus, one would expect that if a person with low tolerance for dissonance were a Democrat, he would show tendencies to accept everything the Democrats stood for. For such a person, then, clusters of relevant cognitive elements would be mainly consonant. His opinions on issues might be characterized as extreme or as cast in terms of black and white. It would seem that a measure of "tolerance for dissonance" based upon these considerations would be possible.

At this point many readers will feel like suggesting that perhaps such a test already exists, having recognized a certain similarity between our discussion immediately above and some descriptions of "authoritarian personalities" and some descriptions of people with high "intolerance for ambiguity." My own suspicion would be that existing tests such as the F scale do measure, to some extent, the degree to which people hold extreme opinions, that is, opinions where dissonance has been effectively eliminated. Such tests also measure so many other things, however, that they would not be very satisfactory for this purpose. Tests which simply measure "intolerance of ambiguity" may be closer to the purpose which concerns us here. These are empirical questions. The validation procedure for any test which is to be used as a measure of tolerance for dissonance is clear, however. It should relate to the degree to which subjects show evidence of pressure to reduce dissonance in an experimental situation where dissonance has been introduced under controlled conditions.

Once such a measure of tolerance for dissonance is available, there are a number of interesting conjectures which it would be possible to test empirically. Let us consider persons at one extreme end of the range of tolerance for dissonance, that is, persons for whom dissonance is especially painful. One might expect that in such extreme instances a person would act so as to avoid the occurrence of dissonance. Having learned, during the course of his existence, how unpleasant dissonance is, he may very likely avoid those situations which he has learned lead to dissonance. Thus, for example, he would undoubtedly have experienced the unpleasantness that exists following a decision since there is almost always dissonance. If such a person, for whom dissonance is extremely painful, attempts to avoid the occurrence of dissonance, one would expect to observe that he tries to avoid making decisions or even becomes incapable of making decisions. At this extreme, of course, it becomes possibly a pathological affair. Let us examine further what one would expect of a person who, through fear of dissonance and its unpleasantness, actually prefers to stay in conflict and shows an inability to make decisions.

If such a person is, indeed, reacting in anticipation of dissonance which is for him highly unpleasant, then it is clear that he must have frequently suffered such dissonance in order to learn this anticipatory avoidance reaction. One would, consequently, also expect that he would have developed some mechanisms for reducing dissonance which, while perhaps not very effective (or else why the avoidance of dissonance), would nevertheless be serviceable in the long run. The existence of these mechanisms, together with the strong pressure to reduce dissonance when it existed, would make it highly likely that he would have managed to eliminate any dissonance which may have existed in long-established cognitive clusters. One would expect such a person to have very positive and one-sided opinions about many issues and not to be able, very effectively, to see "both sides of a question." If this is correct, one would then find the almost paradoxical situation where a person who is very "decided" concerning opinions, issues, and values also shows an inability to make decisions.

One would also expect that such a person would react very vigorously to the introduction of dissonance into his cognition. This must follow if, indeed, the inability to make decisions is a reaction to fear of dissonance. There is at least one kind of situation where a person cannot avoid dissonance unless he makes an absolute recluse out of himself.

That is, occasionally people discuss things, have disagreements, and voice their disagreements. Since the knowledge that someone like oneself holds one opinion is dissonant with holding a contrary opinion, a person for whom dissonance is extremely unpleasant would be expected to react very vigorously to the expression of disagreement from others. He might argue vigorously, be dogmatic, be stubborn, and the like. This syndrome of inability to make decisions, of being very "decided" and "one-sided" about issues, and of reacting vigorously in the face of disagreement from others, is one which would be consistent with an interpretation that the person has such low tolerance for dissonance that he has learned to react in anticipation of it.

We have been discussing an extreme instance, of course. There are other, milder ways of reacting in anticipation of dissonance in order to avoid it. There are persons who, in avoiding postdecision dissonance, make decisions without making them. This can be done sometimes by assuming a passive role with respect to the environment so that, at least in some instances, decisions get made because the ground, so to speak, has moved under one's feet. Thus the decision is made but the person is not responsible for it. Avoiding postdecision dissonance can also be accomplished to some extent by psychologically revoking the decision as soon as it is made. Thus, for example, if immediately after having made a decision, irrevocable though it may be in actuality, the person is convinced that it was absolutely the wrong thing to do, he is again preparing himself for the impact of possible dissonance and avoiding this impact. Such avoidance of dissonance should exist only for persons who have very low tolerance for dissonance coupled with relatively inefficient mechanisms for reducing dissonance once it occurs.

This brings us, of course, to the problem of the variability from person to person in the effectiveness of the techniques they use for reducing dissonance and in the preference for one technique or mechanism over another. But I have little to say on this point beyond the acknowledgment that such differences among people certainly exist. Undoubtedly, some people typically attempt to reduce dissonance by focusing on the elements of cognition which are involved in the dissonant relations and attempting to alter or to discard some of them. Other people habitually deal with dissonance by focusing mainly on the cognitive elements involved in consonant relations and attempting to add new elements which are also consonant with others. The extent to which selective forgetting of cognitive elements involved in dissonant relations is an effective means of dissonance reduction has also been insufficiently explored. Other means of reducing dissonance, which are theoretically possible but about which we have little evidence, are, for example, reducing the importance of the whole area of cognitive content in which dissonance exists, compartmentalizing different cognitive clusters so that they, in effect, have nothing to do with one another. I mention these merely to indicate some of the problems involved and the possible scope of inquiry rather than because I have any ideas about how to deal with these aspects of personality in relation to dissonance.

Some Effects of Changes in Status and Role

The problem of drawing implications of a general nature from the theory of cognitive dissonance is, of course, one of independently identifying situations or circumstances which produce dissonance habitually. On a very general level it seems plausible that if a person is subjected to a sudden change in his way of life, some cognitive dissonance will result. Many of the actions he will engage in because of his altered circumstances will very likely be dissonant with some of the opinions or values which he acquired previously. If specific situations could be identified where this would be true, one would be able to predict certain specific ideological changes or opinion changes subsequent to the change in the person's way of life. Such change of opinion would, of course, be one way to reduce the dissonance between existing opinions and knowledge of the actions now engaged in. I will discuss some such situations which can be specifically identified to illustrate the kind of implication to be drawn from a consideration of dissonance and the pressure to reduce it.

It sometimes happens that a person's "role" or "position" in some organization, or in society, changes. Thus, a graduate student passes his examinations, receives his Ph.D., and accepts a position teaching in some college. Suddenly his position in life and the things he must do are considerably changed. He is no longer a student but someone who teaches others; instead of being the recipient of grades, he gives grades to others, and the like. Many of the things he does will introduce dissonance into his cognition. As a student he may, for example, have held certain derogatory opinions about teachers who came to class unprepared and delivered poor lectures. He now may find himself doing this occasionally. As a student he may have acquired certain opinions about the grading system and its value. Now, as a teacher, he may frequently find that he has to give grades without sufficient basis for making differentiations. And many other similar instances may arise. Such dissonance may be reduced by changing his old opinions. While he is associating with other teachers, it is probably not too difficult for him to acquire a set of opinions which are consonant with the things he does. In other words, he accepts the opinions and the values of the position into which he has moved.

Exactly the same kind of analysis may be made for other kinds of sudden change in the job which a person does. A worker in a factory, for example, may be promoted to the job of foreman. Suddenly he finds himself giving orders instead of receiving them, supervising the work of others instead of being supervised, and the like. Again, these new actions will be dissonant, in many instances, with opinions and values which he acquired as a worker and still holds. In the pursuit of dissonance reduction, one would expect this person to quite rapidly accept the opinions and values of other foremen, that is, opinions and values which are consonant with the things he now does. It would also not be surprising to find that such a person starts seeing less of the workers with whom he used to associate since these other workers will not support the changes of opinion which will lead to dissonance reduction. I do not mean to imply that this is a completely sudden change of opinion that occurs or that it is an "all or none" process. Indeed, it may take some time, and some opinions may be very resistant to change so that some dissonance is never eliminated. But the pressure to reduce the dissonance does exist, and a large degree of acceptance of values and opinions appropriate to the new position should be evident.

There are other types of changes, other than changes in "job," that produce the same kinds of dissonance between existing opinions and new actions which a person takes because of the changed situation. Thus, for example, the last decade in the United States has seen a sharp rise in the living standard of many people and the growth of a new "suburbia." If a change over a period of a few years may be called sudden, then these persons changed many aspects of their way of life suddenly. But even if it is to be called a gradual change, the fact remains that the change occurred and produced behavior and actions which, in many instances, were undoubtedly dissonant with existing opinions.

A person who had always lived in the middle of a city, and had acquired certain opinions about how one lives and how one spends one's time, may now find himself with a small lawn that requires attention and mowing. A person who had always paid rent may now find himself paying taxes on the home he purchased and having reactions to taxes which are dissonant with his opinions concerning how high taxes should be. Once more, such dissonance can be reduced through change of opinion, and we would expect such ideological change to occur. It would be reflected to some extent in change of political opinions and to some extent in change of social opinions and values. In short, one would expect to see the acceptance and adoption of the opinions and values of the social class into which these people moved.

The fact that changes in role or in status affect people's opinions and beliefs has, of course, been recognized and commented on by many writers. Emphasis has been placed on two factors—namely, that people who occupy a certain role or position respond to the expectations which others have of that role or position, and that one is influenced by the persons one associates with while occupying a given role. The interpretation I have given in terms of the theory of cognitive dissonance does not discount the effect of factors such as these, but rather casts them in a new light. The influence which others in similar positions exert on persons who move into a new role is undoubtedly important. But if my interpretation is correct, the person who moves into the new role is not, so to speak, a victim of this influence, but rather seeks it out. As we saw in Chapter Nine, in discussing the McGuire study, influence that reduces dissonance is considerably more effective than influence that tends to increase dissonance. Without the availability of others who are willing, and able, to exert influence in the direction which will reduce the dissonance created by the new situation, the ensuing dissonance reduction in the form of opinion change would not be able to occur so easily.

Such factors as the expectations which others have of the role and the requirements of the role are, undoubtedly, important in producing the dissonance in the first place. For example, a worker who accepts a promotion to the job of foreman in a large factory may intend to behave differently from all foremen he has known in his past. In other words, he initially sees himself as behaving in manners consonant with his current opinions. But the expectations of the workers that he finds himself supervising, and their perception of the role of the foreman, may simply not allow this. He may find himself, willy nilly, acting like a foreman.

Certainly, such a change in role is complicated in the sense that many factors are undoubtedly at work affecting the person's behavior and opinions. In the new role, he also has experiences which he never had before. All I wish to point out, however, is that the phenomenon of acceptance of the values associated with a role by a person who moves into that position can be adequately understood in terms of dissonance reduction.

The Scope of the Theory of Dissonance

In the various chapters of this book, I have presented data from a wide range of contexts which are relevant to the theory of dissonance. The material dealt with has ranged all the way from the situation in which an individual finds himself after having made a decision, a purely psychological problem, to a concern with the level of proselyting in certain types of mass movements, a problem which would probably interest sociologists more than psychologists. And indeed, the theory of dissonance does seem to have wide scope. The existence of dissonance is probably so prevalent, and various circumstances which can give rise to dissonance probably occur so frequently, that evidence of dissonance and manifestations of the pressure to reduce it are likely to be found in almost any context.

Indeed, there are some obvious ramifications of the theory of dissonance which I have almost totally ignored. For example, any time a dissonance exists between one set of cognitions which correspond to, say, information or opinions, and another set of cognitions which correspond to behavior in which the person is engaging, it is clear that this dissonance can be reduced by changing the behavior. Actually, cognitions that represent knowledge of a person's own actions are, in a sense, the easiest kinds of cognitive elements to change since this can be accomplished by merely changing the behavior involved. This may be contrasted with the great difficulty of changing cognitive elements that correspond to knowledge about the environment that has impinged on the person directly through his senses. Consequently, it is clear that one would expect appropriate modification of behavior to be a frequent reaction to the existence of dissonance.

But precisely because the theory has such wide scope, it is important to attempt to delimit precisely where it is relevant and where it is not. There are many factors affecting people's behavior, attitudes, and opinions about which the theory of dissonance has nothing to say. For example, we have said little or nothing about motivation throughout the course of this book. Dissonance itself can, of course, be considered as a motivating factor, but there are many other motives which affect human beings and we have skirted the question of any relationship between these other motivations and the pressure to reduce dissonance. There are, however, in some circumstances, clear relationships. There are instances where motives define whether a relation between two cognitive elements is dissonant or consonant. For example, consider the experiment on voluntary seeking of information in a gambling situation which was described in Chapter Seven. There I assumed, plausibly, that cognition experientially acquired by someone who had been losing fairly steadily was dissonant with the cognition that he continued to play on the same side he originally chose. But stating that the relation between these two sets of cognitions was dissonant depends on the assumption that the person is motivated to win. If, by some chance, a subject in this experiment wanted to lose, these two cognitive clusters would exist, for him, in a consonant relationship.

Other motives which may operate also will enter the picture insofar as they make certain cognitive elements resistant to change, thus perhaps hindering the reduction of dissonance. A consideration of such other motivations would also undoubtedly be necessary in order to predict the occurrence of dissonance. But what I want to stress here is that I have not dealt with problems of motivation, and that these problems would, by and large, be distinct from the problems with which the theory of dissonance does deal.

If one starts using the concept of dissonance loosely, however, this distinction is easily lost sight of. For example, does cognitive dissonance exist any time a person is in a frustrating situation, that is, any time progress toward some objective which he is motivated to achieve is blocked? The answer to this is No, but it is worth while detailing the answer since I think it will help clarify the limitations of the scope of the theory of dissonance. If a person is driving a car on a lonely road at night, has a flat tire, and discovers he does not have an automobile jack with him, we would certainly describe him as being in a frustrating situation. But let us consider his cognition to see if any dissonant relations exist. He knows he has a flat tire, he knows he has no jack, he knows it is night time on a lonely road, he knows that he is supposed to be in such and such a place at such and such a time. But none of these cognitions are dissonant with one another. None of them, considered alone, would lead to the obverse of one of the others.

Such a frustrating situation .could also involve cognitive dissonance. If the person in the above situation proceeded to use his wrench to take off all the bolts on the wheel on which the tire was flat, his cognition about that action would be dissonant with knowing he cannot change the tire because he has no jack. He might attempt to reduce such dissonance by convincing himself that even though it is late at night on a lonely road, surely another car will come along and stop to help him. But it is clear that his reactions to this possible dissonance are quite different from his reactions (which he will undoubtedly have) to the frustration.

It would be unfortunate indeed if the concept of dissonance were used so loosely as to have it encompass everything, thus depriving it of meaning entirely. Of course, the possibility of such loose use exists only because of the occasional vagueness in the definition of dissonance and, especially, vagueness in how to denote, a priori, whether or not the relation between two cognitive elements is dissonant or not. The vagueness in the conceptual definition of dissonance—namely, two elements are dissonant if considering them alone, the obverse of one follows from the other—lies in the words "follows from" and in the phrase "considering them alone." One element may follow from another because of logic, because of cultural mores, because of things one has experienced and learned, and perhaps in other senses too. Thus, the specification of the phrase "follows from" involves specification of the operations by means of which one can say that for a given person, element A follows from element B. The specification of the meaning of the phrase "considering them alone" also boils down to a specification of the procedures by means of which one determines whether or not dissonance exists. Thus, this degree of vagueness is almost inherent in any theoretical statement which is new in the sense that little empirical work relevant to the theory has as yet been done. Thus, for example, I do not believe there is any vagueness in the a priori determination of dissonance which exists as a result of having made a decision. This has been clarified empirically. Additional empirical work in other contexts will further clarify the procedures for determining the existence of dissonance.

But perhaps the best way of avoiding loose usage of the concept of dissonance is to emphasize its clarity rather than its vagueness. Dissonance is not anything which exists all by itself. It is a characterization of a relationship between cognitive elements. Thus, determining whether or not dissonance exists should take the form of first specifying the cognitive elements, or clusters, which are under consideration and then examining whether, considering either one alone, the obverse of the other follows. If it seems plausible to assert that the relation is dissonant, it is usually also helpful to specify on what grounds—logical, experiential, cultural, or otherwise—the "follows from" holds in that instance. It is also clearly necessary to be able to specify what specific changes in cognition, or what new cognitive elements, would reduce the magnitude of the dissonance thus determined. If treated as precisely and specifically as possible, I believe the theory of cognitive dissonance will prove a useful explanatory and predictive device.

References

1. Adams, D. K. Conflict and integration. *J. Personality*, 1954, **22**, 548–56.
2. Back, K. The exertion of influence through social communication. *J. Abnormal and Social Psychology*, 1951, **46**, 9–24.
3. Baxter, D. Interpersonal contact and exposure to mass media during a presidential campaign. Unpublished doctor's dissertation, Columbia University, 1951.
4. Bennett, E. B. Discussion, decision, commitment, and consensus in "group decision." *Human Relations*, 1955, **8**, 251–73.
5. Bettelheim, B. Individual and mass behavior in extreme situations. *J. Abnormal and Social Psychology*, 1943, **38**, 417–52.
6. Blau, P. Orientation of college students toward international relations. *American J. Sociology*, 1953, **59**, 205–14.
7. Brehm, J. Post-decision changes in the desirability of alternatives. *J. Abnormal and Social Psychology*, 1956, **52**, 384–89.
8. Brodbeck, M. The role of small groups in mediating the effects of propaganda. *J. Abnormal and Social Psychology*, 1956, **52**, 166–70.

9. Burdick, H. The compliant behavior of deviates under conditions of threat. Unpublished doctor's dissertation, University of Minnesota, 1955.

10. Coch, L., & French, J. R. P. Overcoming resistance to change. *Human Relations,* 1948, **1**, 512–32.

11. Cooper, E., & Jahoda, M. The evasion of propaganda: How prejudiced people respond to anti-prejudice propaganda. *J. Psychology,* 1947, **23**, 15–25.

12. Deutsch, M., & Collins, M. M. *Interracial housing: A psychological evaluation of a social experiment.* Minneapolis: Univ. of Minnesota Press, 1951.

13. Ehrlich, D., Guttman, I., Schönbach, P., & Mills, J. Postdecision exposure to relevant information. *J. Abnormal and Social Psychology,* 1957, **54**, 98–102.

14. Ewing, T. A study of certain factors involved in changes of opinion. *J. Social Psychology,* 1942, **16**, 63–88.

15. Festinger, L. Informal social communication. *Psychological Review,* 1950, **57**, 271–82.

16. Festinger, L. An analysis of compliant behavior. In M. Sherif & M. Wilson (eds.), *Group behavior at the crossroads.* New York: Harper, 1953.

17. Festinger, L. A theory of social comparison processes. *Human Relations,* 1954, **7**, 117–40.

18. Festinger, L., Gerard, H. B., Hymovitch, B., Kelley, H. H., & Raven, B. The influence process in the presence of extreme deviates. *Human Relations,* 1952, **5**, 327–46.

19. Festinger, L., Riecken, H., & Schachter, S. *When prophecy fails.* Minneapolis: Univ. of Minnesota Press, 1956.

20. Festinger, L., & Thibaut, J. Interpersonal communication in small groups. *J. Abnormal and Social Psychology,* 1951, **46**, 92–100.

21. Filer, R. Frustration, satisfaction, and other factors affecting the attractiveness of goal objects. *J. Abnormal and Social Psychology,* 1952, **47**, 203–12.

22. Freud, S. *Collected papers*, Vol. III. London: Hogarth Press, 1946.

23. Gerard, H. B. The effect of different dimensions of disagreement on the communication process in small groups. *Human Relations*, 1953, **6**, 249–72.

24. Hastorf, A., & Cantril, H. They saw a game: A case study. *J. Abnormal and Social Psychology*, 1954, **49**, 129–34.

25. Heider, F. The psychology of interpersonal relations. Unpublished manuscript.

26. Hochbaum, G. Self-confidence and reactions to group pressures. *American Sociological Review*, 1954, **19**, 678–87.

27. Hovland, C., & Sears, R. R. Experiments on motor conflict. I. Types of conflict and modes of resolution. *J. Experimental Psychology*, 1938, **23**, 477–93.

28. Irwin, F., & Gebhard, M. Studies of object preferences: The effect of ownership and other social influences. *J. Experimental Psychology*, 1943, **33**, 64–72.

29. Janis, I., & King, B. The influence of role-playing on opinion change. *J. Abnormal and Social Psychology*, 1954, **49**, 211–18.

30. Kelman, H. Attitude change as a function of response restriction. *Human Relations*, 1953, **6**, 185–214.

31. King, B., & Janis, I. Comparison of the effectiveness of improvised versus non-improvised role-playing in producing opinion changes. *Human Relations*, 1956, **9**, 177–86.

32. Klapper, J. *Effects of the mass media*. New York: Bureau of Applied Social Research, Columbia University, August, 1949. (A report to the director of the Public Library Inquiry.)

33. Lazarsfeld, P. Effects of radio on public opinion. In D. Waples (ed.), *Print, radio, and film in a democracy*. Chicago: Univ. of Chicago Press, 1942.

34. Lewin, K. *A dynamic theory of personality*. New York: McGraw-Hill, 1935.

35. Lewin, K. *Field theory in social science*. New York: Harper, 1951.

36. Lewin, K. Group decision and social change. In G. Swanson, T. Newcomb, & E. Hartley (eds.), *Readings in social psychology*. New York: Henry Holt, 1952.

37. Lipset, S. M., Lazarsfeld, P., Barton, A., & Linz, J. The psychology of voting: An analysis of political behavior. In G. Lindzey (ed.), *Handbook of social psychology*, Vol. II. Cambridge, Mass.: Addison-Wesley, 1954.

38. Martin, A. H. An experimental study of the factors and types of voluntary choice. *Archives of Psychology*, 1922, No. 51.

39. McBride, D. The effects of public and private changes of opinion on intragroup communication. Unpublished doctor's dissertation, University of Minnesota, 1954.

40. Murray, H. A. The effect of fear upon estimates of the maliciousness of other personalities. *J. Social Psychology*, 1933, 4, 310–29.

41. Myrdal, G. *An American dilemma*. New York: Harper, 1944.

42. Nichol, F. D. *The midnight cry: A defense of William Miller and the Millerites*. Washington, D.C.: Review and Herald Publishing Co., 1945.

43. Osgood, C. E., & Tannenbaum, P. The principle of congruity and the prediction of attitude change. *Psychological Review*, 1955, 62, 42–55.

44. Prasad, J. A comparative study of rumours and reports in earthquakes. *British J. Psychology*, 1950, 41, 129–44.

45. Sady, R. R. The function of rumors in relocation centers. Unpublished doctor's dissertation, University of Chicago, 1948.

46. Schachter, S. Deviation, rejection, and communication. *J. Abnormal and Social Psychology*, 1951, 46, 190–208.

47. Schachter, S., & Burdick, H. A field experiment on rumor transmission and distortion. *J. Abnormal and Social Psychology*, 1955, 50, 363–71.

48. Sears, C. E. *Days of delusion: A strange bit of history*. Boston: Houghton Mifflin, 1924.

49. Sinha, D. Behaviour in a catastrophic situation: A psychological study of reports and rumours. *British J. Psychology,* 1952, **43,** 200–209.

50. Smock, C. D. The influence of stress on the perception of incongruity. *J. Abnormal and Social Psychology,* 1955, **50,** 354–62.

51. Spiro, M. Ghosts: An anthropological inquiry into learning and perception. *J. Abnormal and Social Psychology,* 1953, **48,** 376–82.

52. Wallen, R. Ego-involvement as a determinant of selective forgetting. *J. Abnormal and Social Psychology,* 1942, **37,** 20–39.

Newspapers and Pamphlets

53. The American public discuss cancer and the American Cancer Society campaign: A national survey. Ann Arbor: Survey Research Center, University of Michigan, December, 1948.

54. *Minneapolis Sunday Tribune,* March 21, 1954.

55. *Nippon Times,* December 2, 1945.

56. A personal message: A test of its effectiveness and distribution. Washington, D.C.: Surveys Division, Bureau of Special Services, Office of War Information, July, 1943.

57. The security campaign in Jacksonville, Florida. Special Memorandum No. 98. Washington, D.C.: Surveys Division, Bureau of Special Services, Office of War Information, January, 1944.

Index

Hastorf, A., 150, 283
Heider, F., 7, 68, 283
Hochbaum, G., 186, 283
Hovland, C. I., 35, 283
Hymovitch, B., 223, 282

Ifaluk, 22
Influence processes
  and attraction to group, 184–85
  conditions for effective, 190–92
  initiation of, 189–90, 217 ff.
  lack of resistance to, 126
  and opinion change, 100
  reduction of dissonance by,
    204 ff.
  resistance to, 216–17
  theory of, 177 ff.
  voluntary exposure to, 120–21
Information
  accidental exposure to, 132
  avoidance of sources of, 53
  dissonance created by, 173–74
  ineffectiveness of, 136
  invalidation of, 153–56
  involuntary exposure to, 131 ff.,
    149 ff.
  irrelevant exposure to, 132
  reactions to, 134–36
Information seeking
  and absence of dissonance,
    163, 171
  and expectation, 129–31
  and future action, 124–26,
    139–44
  nonselective, 125–26, 127
  patterns of, 162 ff.
  to reduce dissonance, 127–28,
    144 ff., 163, 171
  selective, 22, 30

Interpretation, ambiguity of,
  139–40, 141, 147, 154
Irwin, F. W., 56, 69–70, 283

Jahoda, M., 134–35, 282
Janis, I., 104, 106, 108–9, 111,
  283
Justification, 73

Kelley, H. H., 223, 282
Kelman, H., 112, 114, 119, 283
King, B., 104–5, 108–9, 111, 283
Klapper, J., 138, 283

Lazarsfeld, P., 145, 283, 284
Lewin, K., 33, 35, 78, 283, 284
Linz, J., 284
Lipset, S. M., 205, 284

Martin, A. H., 71, 73, 284
McBride, D., 88, 99, 101, 284
McGuire, W. J., 211, 274
Mass phenomena, dramatic na-
  ture of, 233
Mass proselyting
  analysis of, 200–202, 246 ff.
  conditions for increase of,
    247–48
  after disproof of belief, 250–51,
    258–59
Measurement, of private opinion,
  86–87, 100
Millerite movement, 248–51
Mills, J., 50, 56, 282
Minneapolis Sunday Tribune,
  285
Minnesota Poll, 153
Misperception, of information,
  135–36, 149–53, 174–75

Murray, H. A., 235, 236, 284
Myrdal, G., 7, 284

Nichol, F. D., 250–51, 284
Nippon Times, 285

Office of War Information, 140, 285
Opinion change
  and attraction to group, 180–81, 184–85
  through creating false expectation, 158–62
  difficulty in making, 158
  after disproof, 257–58
  in face-to-face discussion, 230–31
  following behavior change, 121–22
  after forced compliance, 104 ff.
  after improvised speech, 109–12
  lack of, 205–6
  and magnitude of dissonance, 112 ff.
  after noncompliance, 117–19
  in others, 182
  after persuasive communication, 106–9, 159–60
  to reduce dissonance, 82–83, 94–96, 102–4, 182, 204–9
  and social contact, 208–9
  in strongly resistant areas, 120–22
  after writing essay, 117 ff.
Osgood, C. E., 8, 284
Ownership, effect of, 68–70

Personality differences, 31, 266–71

Persuasive communication; *see also* Communication
  effectiveness of, 213–17
  opinion change after, 106–9, 159–60
  reactions to, 226–28, 231–32
Prasad, J., 236–39, 241, 284
Propaganda, trustworthiness of, 160–61
Punishment, excessive, 90–93

Rationalization, 73
Raven, B., 223, 282
Reality
  denial of, 198–200, 243–46
  responsiveness of cognition to, 10–11, 19–21, 24–27
Reward, excessive, 90–93
Riecken, H., 252, 282
Role, change of, 271–75
Rumors
  arising from dissonance, 196–98
  conditions for spread of, 196–97
  content of, 236–43
  fear-justifying, 237–38, 239

Sady, R. R., 241, 244, 284
Schachter, S., 185–87, 242, 252, 282, 284
Schönbach, P., 50, 162, 282
Sears, C. E., 250–51, 284
Sears, R. R., 35, 283
Selective forgetting, 53–54, 156–58
Sinha, D., 239–41, 285
Smock, C. D., 39, 285
Social reality, 27

Social support
  conditions for obtaining,
    192–93, 194, 195
  toward dissonance reduction,
    188 ff.
  readily obtainable, 244 ff.
  seeking of, 21, 217–18
Spiro, M., 22, 285

Survey Research Center, 147,
  285

Tannenbaum, P., 8, 284
Thibaut, J., 188, 282

Wallen, R., 156, 285

24397